D1215323

JLA

KID AMAZO!

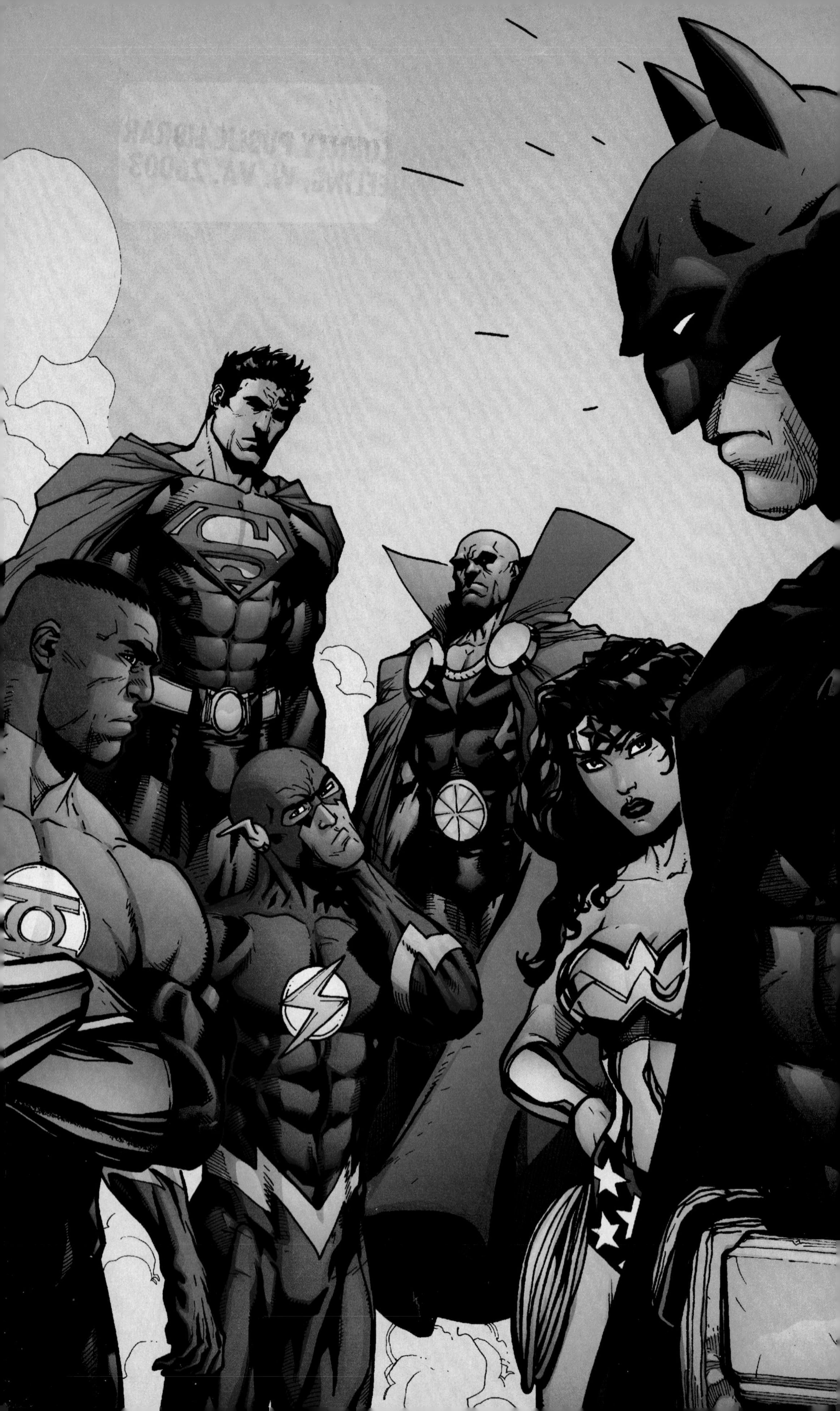

Written by
PETER MILLIGAN

Art by
CARLOS D'ANDA

I.L.L.
Colorist

Jared K. Fletcher
Letterer

Dan DiDio Senior VP-Executive Editor

Mike Carlin Editor-original series

Tom Palmer, Jr. Associate Editor-original series

Bob Harras Editor-collected edition

Robbin Brosterman Senior Art Director

Paul Levitz President & Publisher

Georg Brewer VP-Design & DC Direct Creative

Richard Bruning Senior VP-Creative Director

Patrick Caldon Executive VP-Finance & Operations

Chris Caramalis VP-Finance

John Cunningham VP-Marketing

Terri Cunningham VP-Managing Editor

Alison Gill VP-Manufacturing

David Hyde VP-Publicity

Hank Kanalz VP-General Manager, WildStorm

Jim Lee Editorial Director-WildStorm

Paula Lowitt Senior VP-Business & Legal Affairs

MaryEllen McLaughlin VP-Advertising & Custom Publishing

John Nee Senior VP-Business Development

Gregory Noveck Senior VP-Creative Affairs

Sue Pohja VP-Book Trade Sales

Steve Rotterdam Senior VP-Sales & Marketing

Cheryl Rubin Senior VP-Brand Management

Jeff Trojan VP-Business Development, DC Direct

Bob Wayne VP-Sales

Cover by: Sami Basri

JLA: KID AMAZO

DC Comics, 1700 Broadway, New York, NY 10019
A Warner Bros. Entertainment Company
Printed in Canada. First Printing.
ISBN: 978-1-4012-1630-6

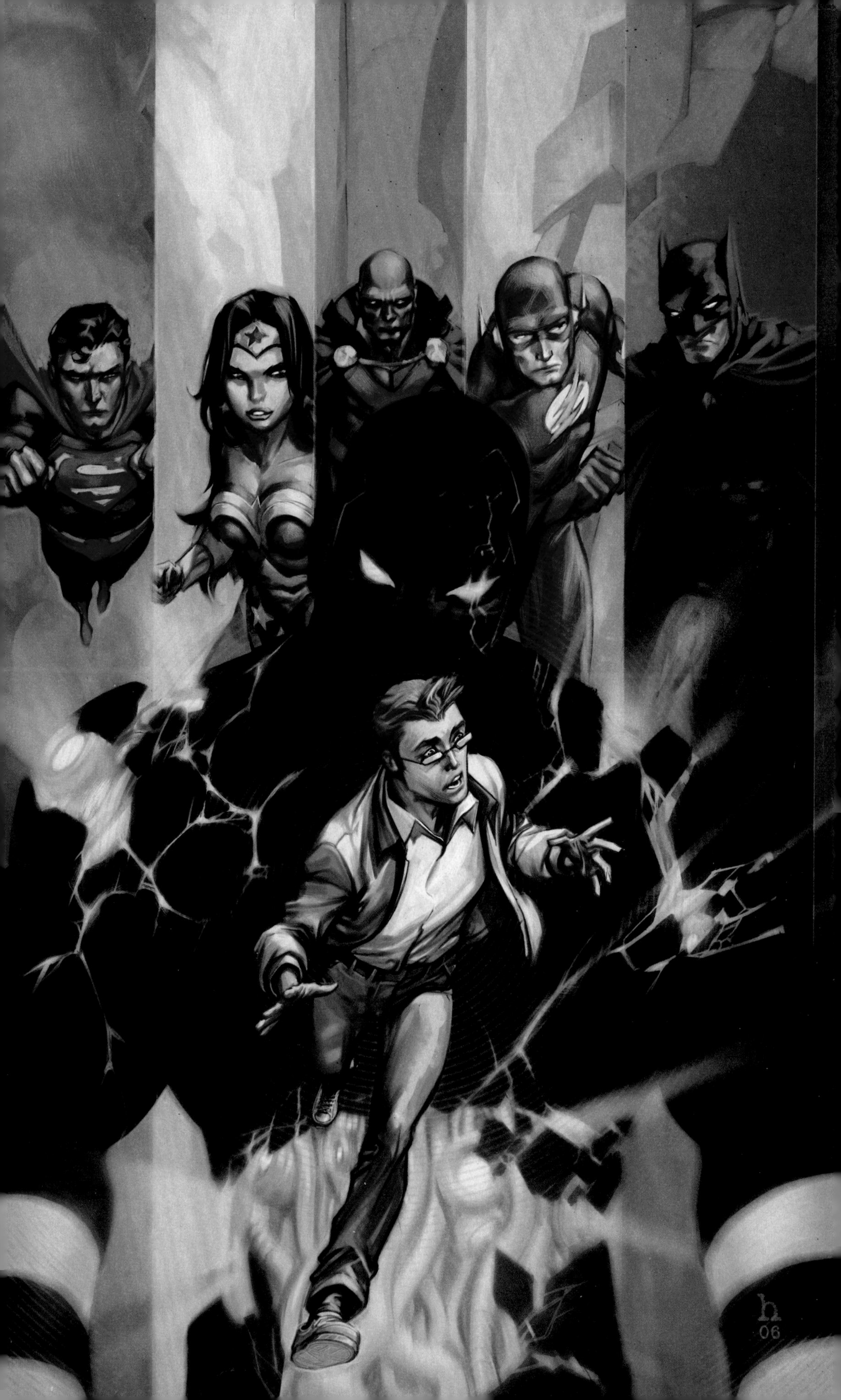
h
06

Chapter One
INTO THE ABYSS!

COVER ART BY HOWARD PORTER

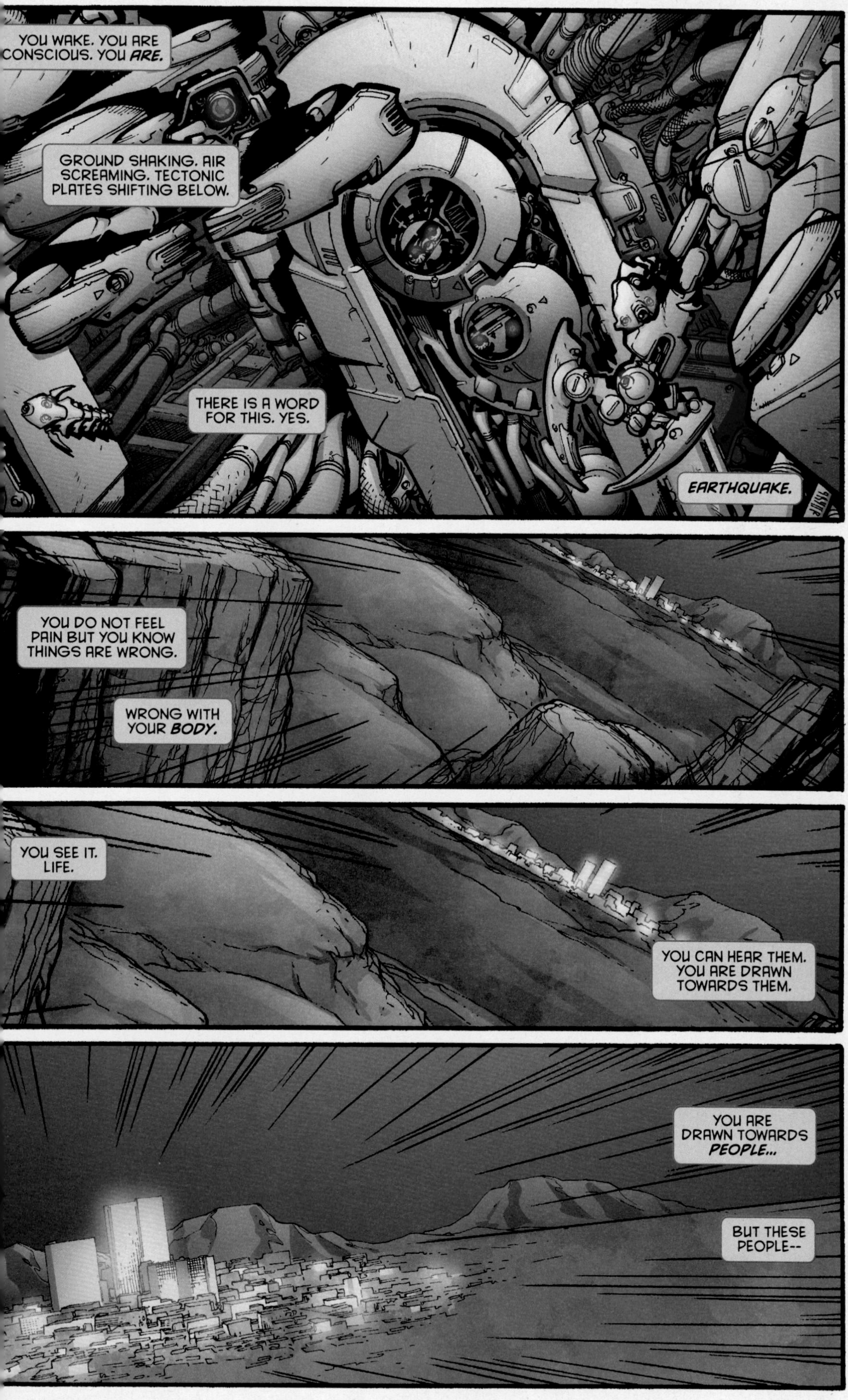
YOU WAKE. YOU ARE CONSCIOUS. YOU *ARE.*
GROUND SHAKING. AIR SCREAMING. TECTONIC PLATES SHIFTING BELOW.
THERE IS A WORD FOR THIS. YES.
EARTHQUAKE.
YOU DO NOT FEEL PAIN BUT YOU KNOW THINGS ARE WRONG.
WRONG WITH YOUR *BODY.*
YOU SEE IT. LIFE.
YOU CAN HEAR THEM. YOU ARE DRAWN TOWARDS THEM.
YOU ARE DRAWN TOWARDS *PEOPLE...*
BUT THESE PEOPLE--

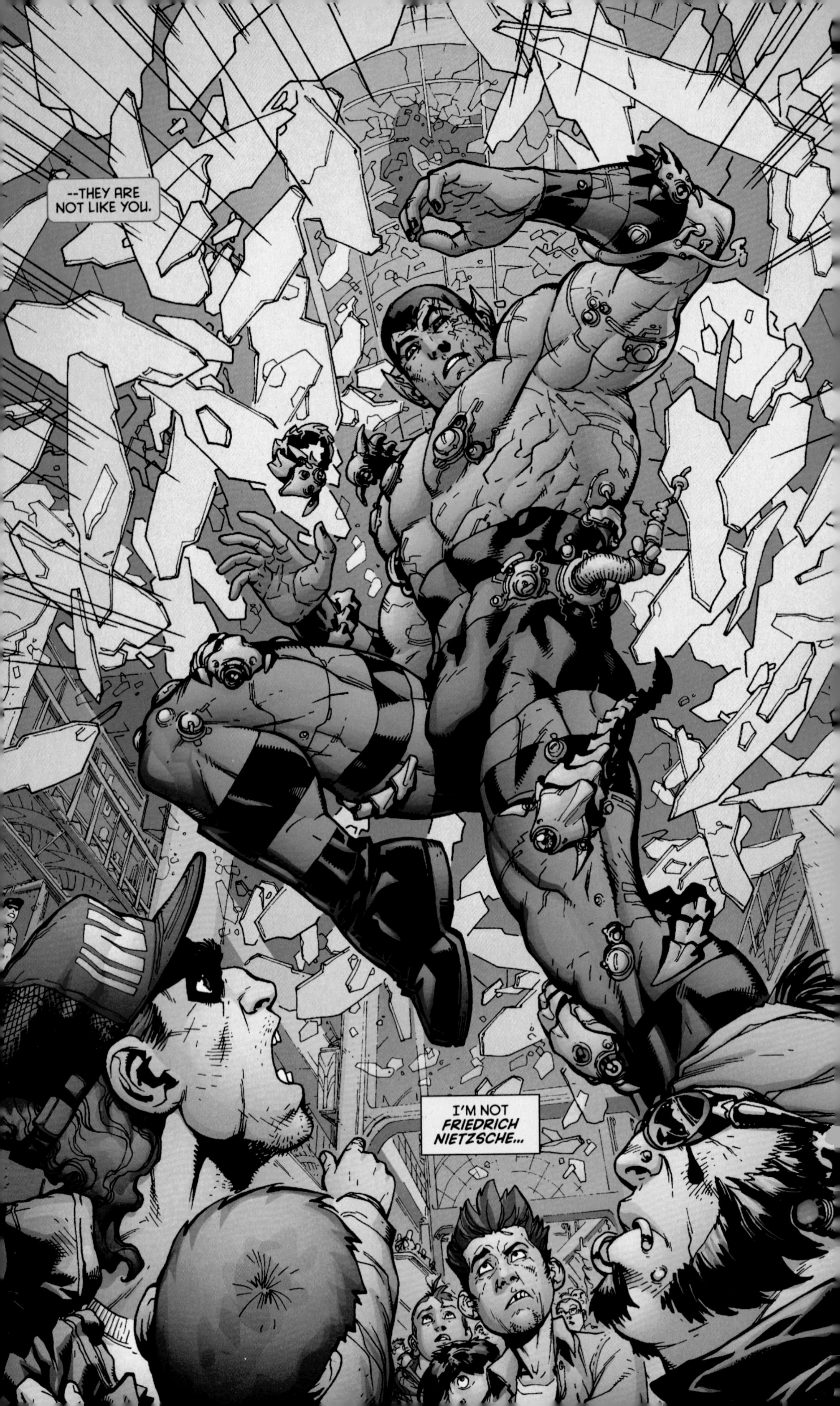
--THEY ARE NOT LIKE YOU.
I'M NOT *FRIEDRICH NIETZSCHE*...

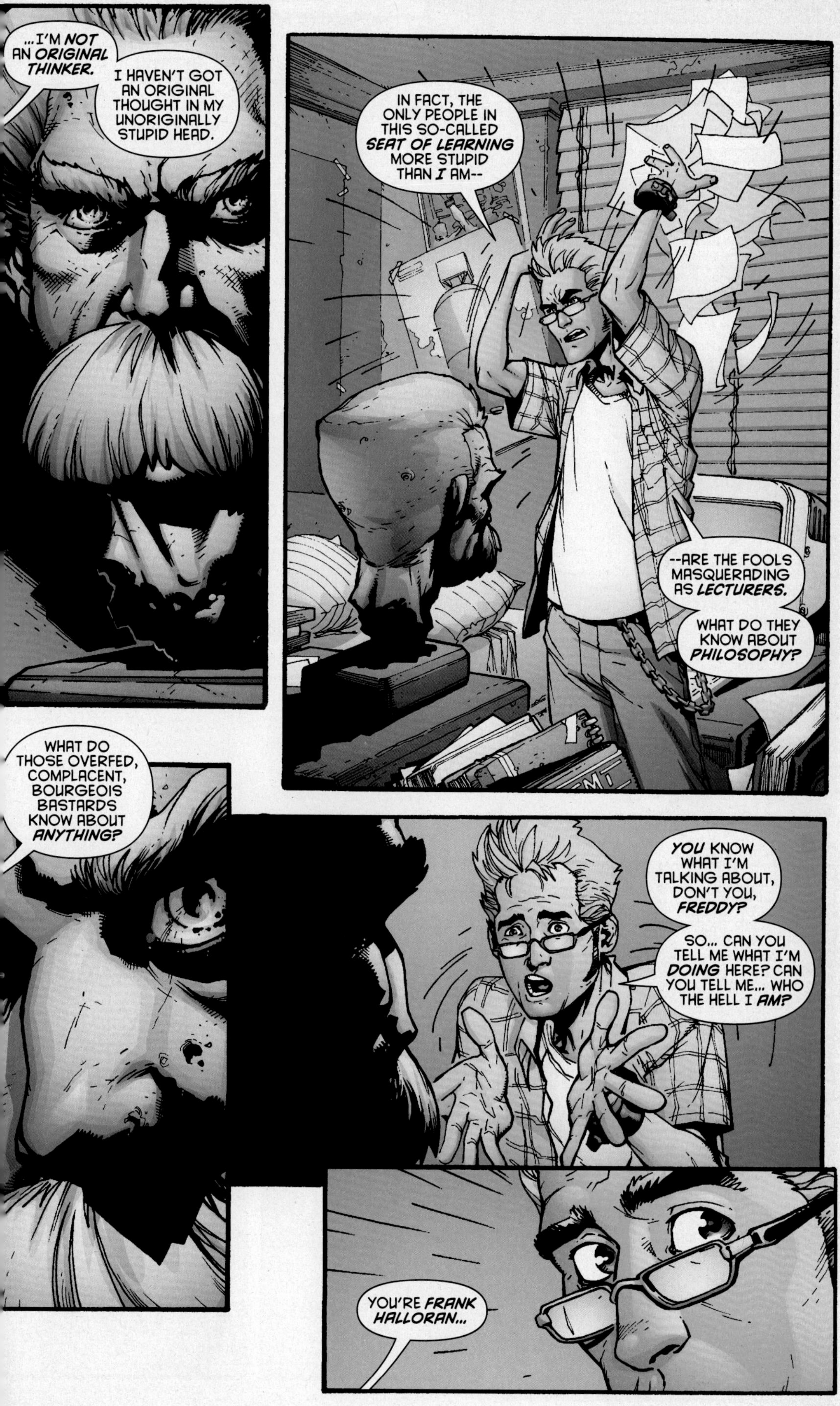
...I'M NOT AN ORIGINAL THINKER.
I HAVEN'T GOT AN ORIGINAL THOUGHT IN MY UNORIGINALLY STUPID HEAD.
IN FACT, THE ONLY PEOPLE IN THIS SO-CALLED SEAT OF LEARNING MORE STUPID THAN I AM--
--ARE THE FOOLS MASQUERADING AS LECTURERS.
WHAT DO THEY KNOW ABOUT PHILOSOPHY?
WHAT DO THOSE OVERFED, COMPLACENT, BOURGEOIS BASTARDS KNOW ABOUT ANYTHING?
YOU KNOW WHAT I'M TALKING ABOUT, DON'T YOU, FREDDY?
SO... CAN YOU TELL ME WHAT I'M DOING HERE? CAN YOU TELL ME... WHO THE HELL I AM?
YOU'RE FRANK HALLORAN...

...YOU'VE GOT AN IRISH TEMPER, A LOVELY SMILE, AND A GIRLFRIEND WHO'S CRAZY ABOUT HIM.

SARA? WHAT ARE YOU DOING HERE?

I HEARD YOU HAD ANOTHER FIGHT WITH PROFESSOR GREEN.

THOUGHT YOU MIGHT NEED CHEERING UP.

WHAT I NEED IS TO GET AWAY FROM BERKELEY.

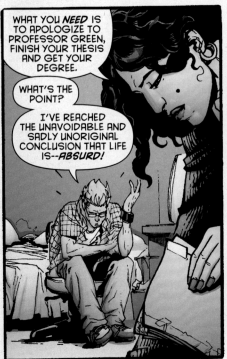

WHAT YOU NEED IS TO APOLOGIZE TO PROFESSOR GREEN, FINISH YOUR THESIS AND GET YOUR DEGREE.

WHAT'S THE POINT?

I'VE REACHED THE UNAVOIDABLE AND SADLY UNORIGINAL CONCLUSION THAT LIFE IS--ABSURD!

ABSURD?

I GUESS IN THAT CASE... YOU WON'T WANT ME TO STAY OVER TONIGHT?

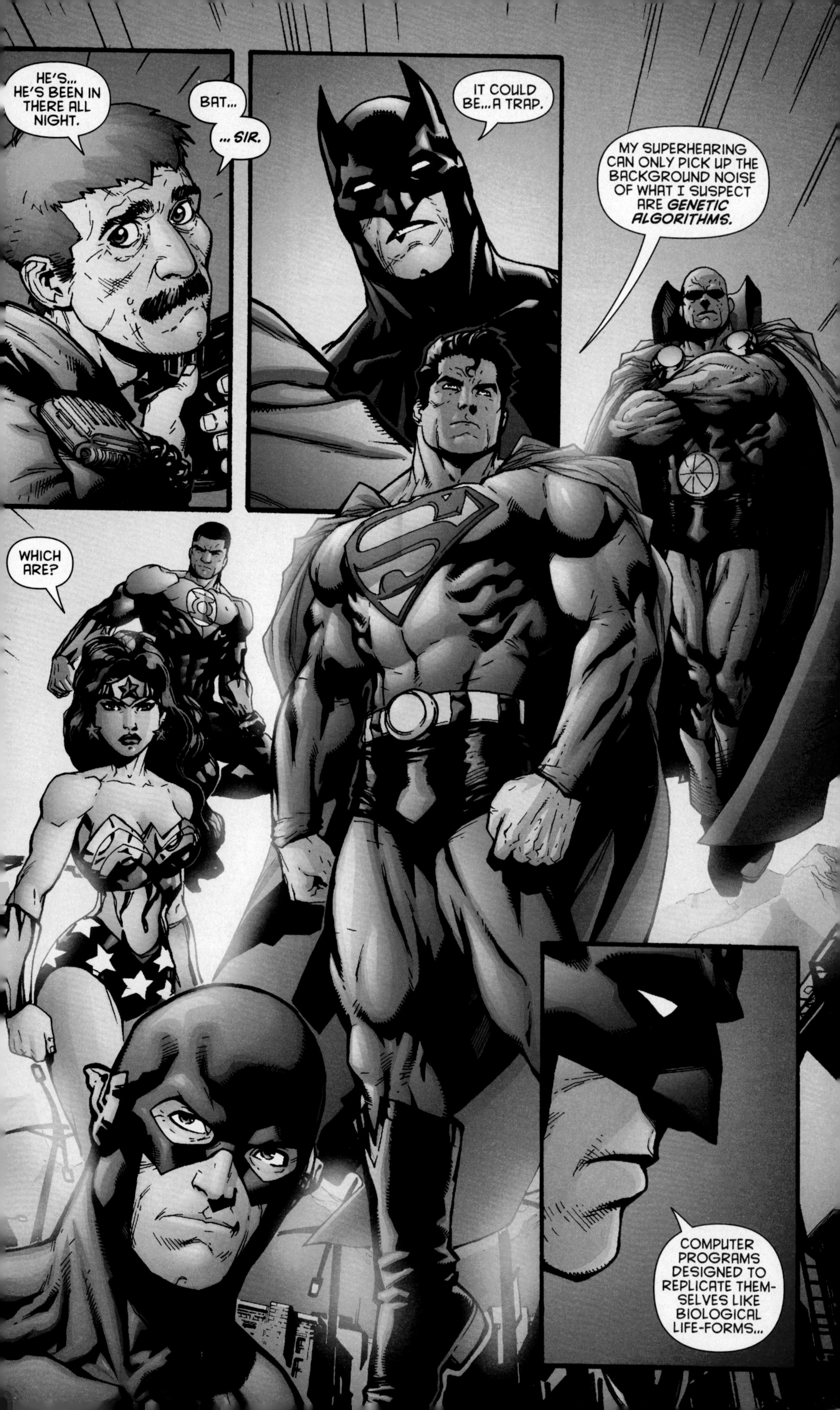
HE'S... HE'S BEEN IN THERE ALL NIGHT.
BAT...
...SIR.
IT COULD BE...A TRAP.
MY SUPERHEARING CAN ONLY PICK UP THE BACKGROUND NOISE OF WHAT I SUSPECT ARE GENETIC ALGORITHMS.
WHICH ARE?
COMPUTER PROGRAMS DESIGNED TO REPLICATE THEM-SELVES LIKE BIOLOGICAL LIFE-FORMS...

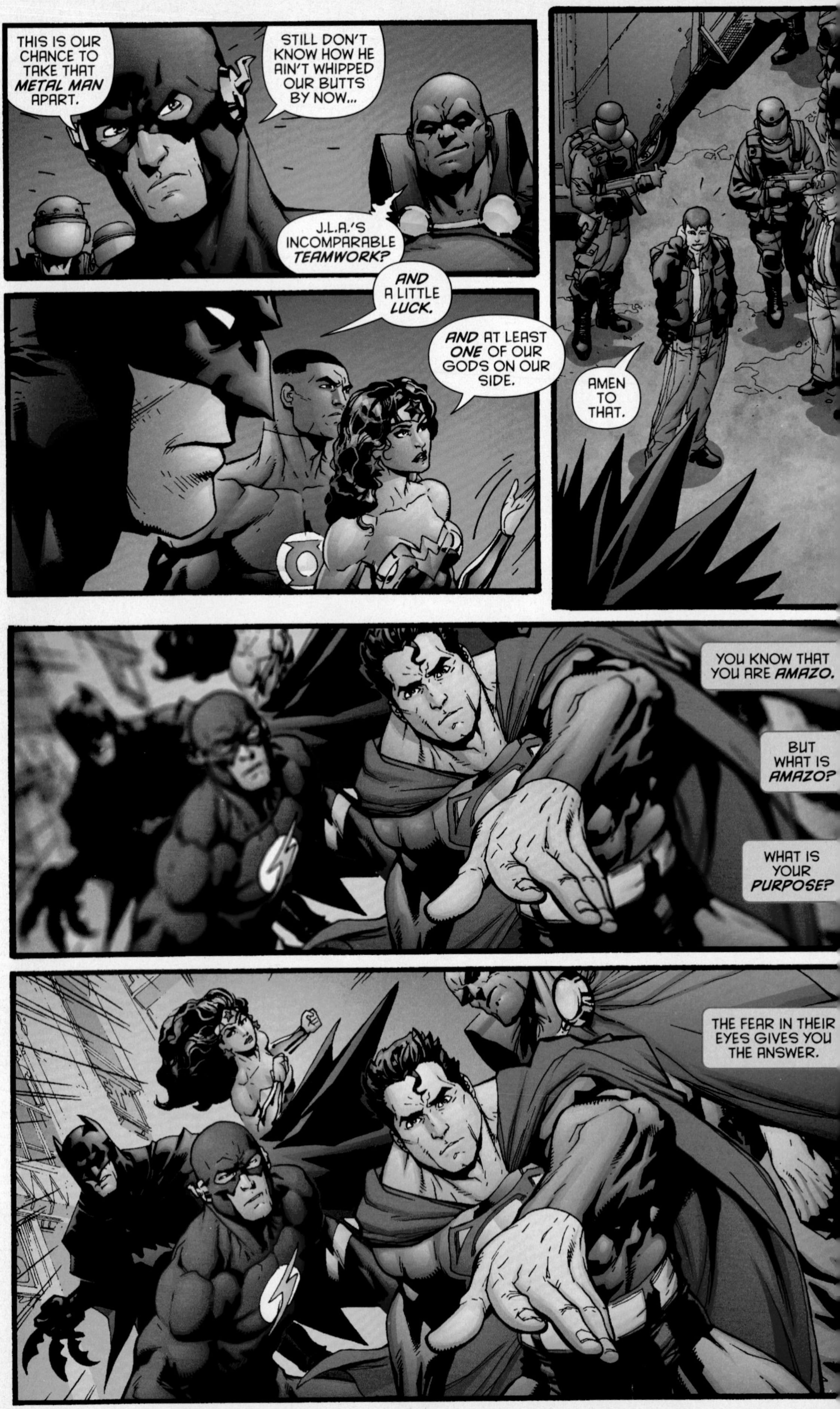
THIS IS OUR CHANCE TO TAKE THAT METAL MAN APART.
STILL DON'T KNOW HOW HE AIN'T WHIPPED OUR BUTTS BY NOW...
J.L.A.'S INCOMPARABLE TEAMWORK?
AND A LITTLE LUCK.
AND AT LEAST ONE OF OUR GODS ON OUR SIDE.
AMEN TO THAT.
YOU KNOW THAT YOU ARE AMAZO.
BUT WHAT IS AMAZO?
WHAT IS YOUR PURPOSE?
THE FEAR IN THEIR EYES GIVES YOU THE ANSWER.

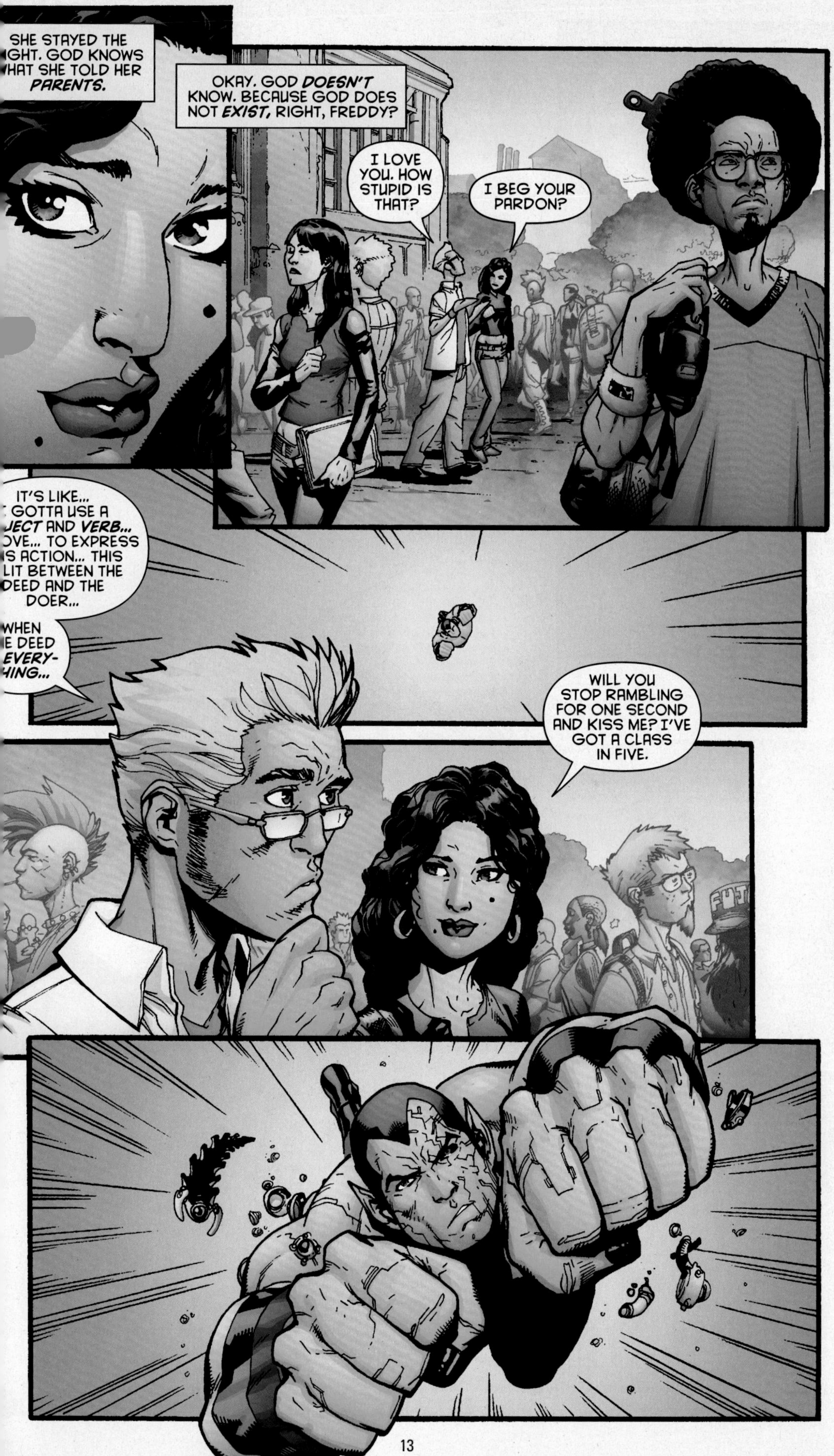
SHE STAYED THE
GHT. GOD KNOWS
HAT SHE TOLD HER
PARENTS.
OKAY. GOD DOESN'T KNOW. BECAUSE GOD DOES NOT EXIST, RIGHT, FREDDY?
I LOVE YOU. HOW STUPID IS THAT?
I BEG YOUR PARDON?
IT'S LIKE...
GOTTA USE A
JECT AND VERB...
OVE... TO EXPRESS
S ACTION... THIS
LIT BETWEEN THE
DEED AND THE
DOER...
WHEN
E DEED
EVERY-
HING...
WILL YOU STOP RAMBLING FOR ONE SECOND AND KISS ME? I'VE GOT A CLASS IN FIVE.

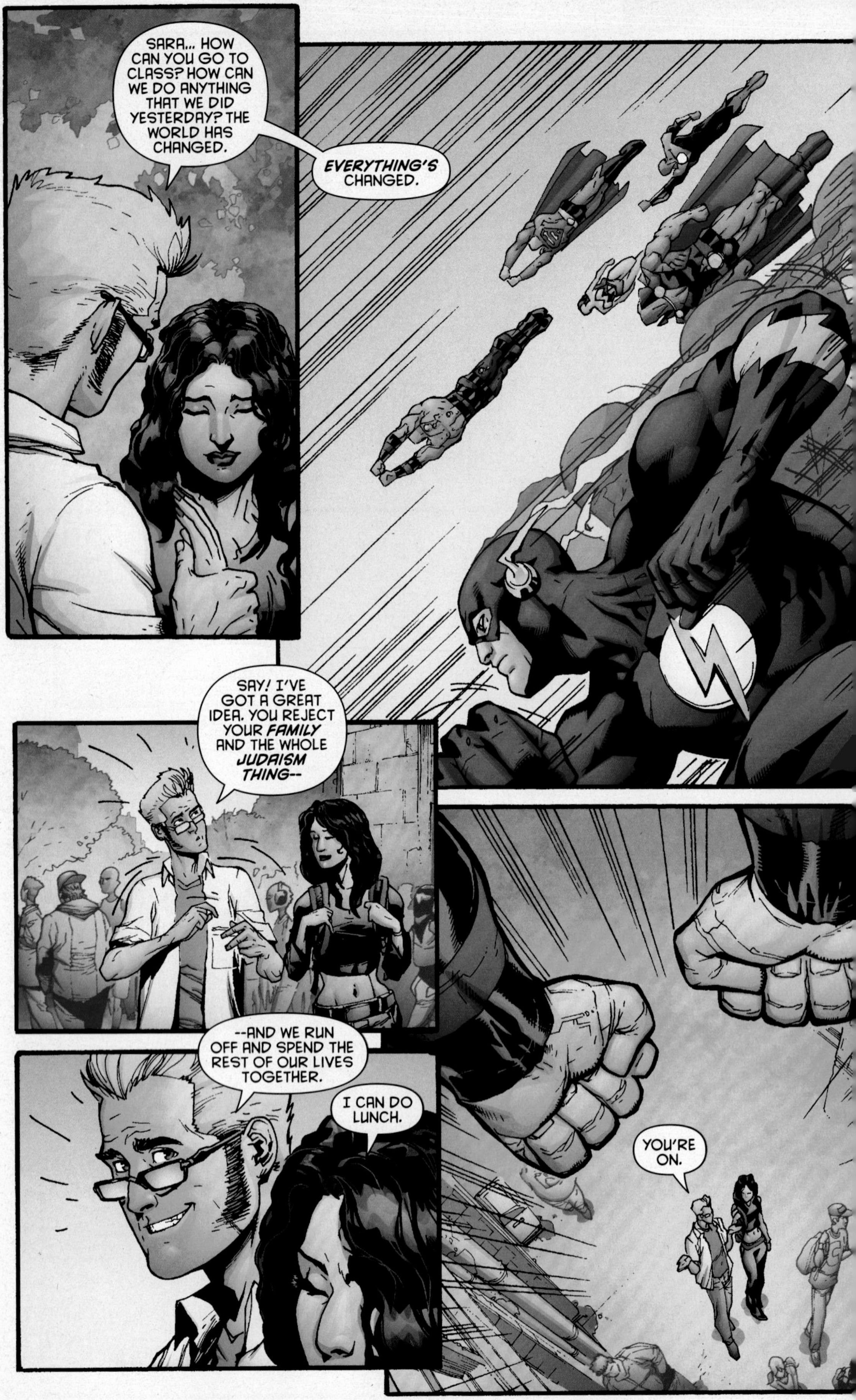
SARA... HOW CAN YOU GO TO CLASS? HOW CAN WE DO ANYTHING THAT WE DID YESTERDAY? THE WORLD HAS CHANGED.
EVERYTHING'S CHANGED.
SAY! I'VE GOT A GREAT IDEA. YOU REJECT YOUR FAMILY AND THE WHOLE JUDAISM THING--
--AND WE RUN OFF AND SPEND THE REST OF OUR LIVES TOGETHER.
I CAN DO LUNCH.
YOU'RE ON.

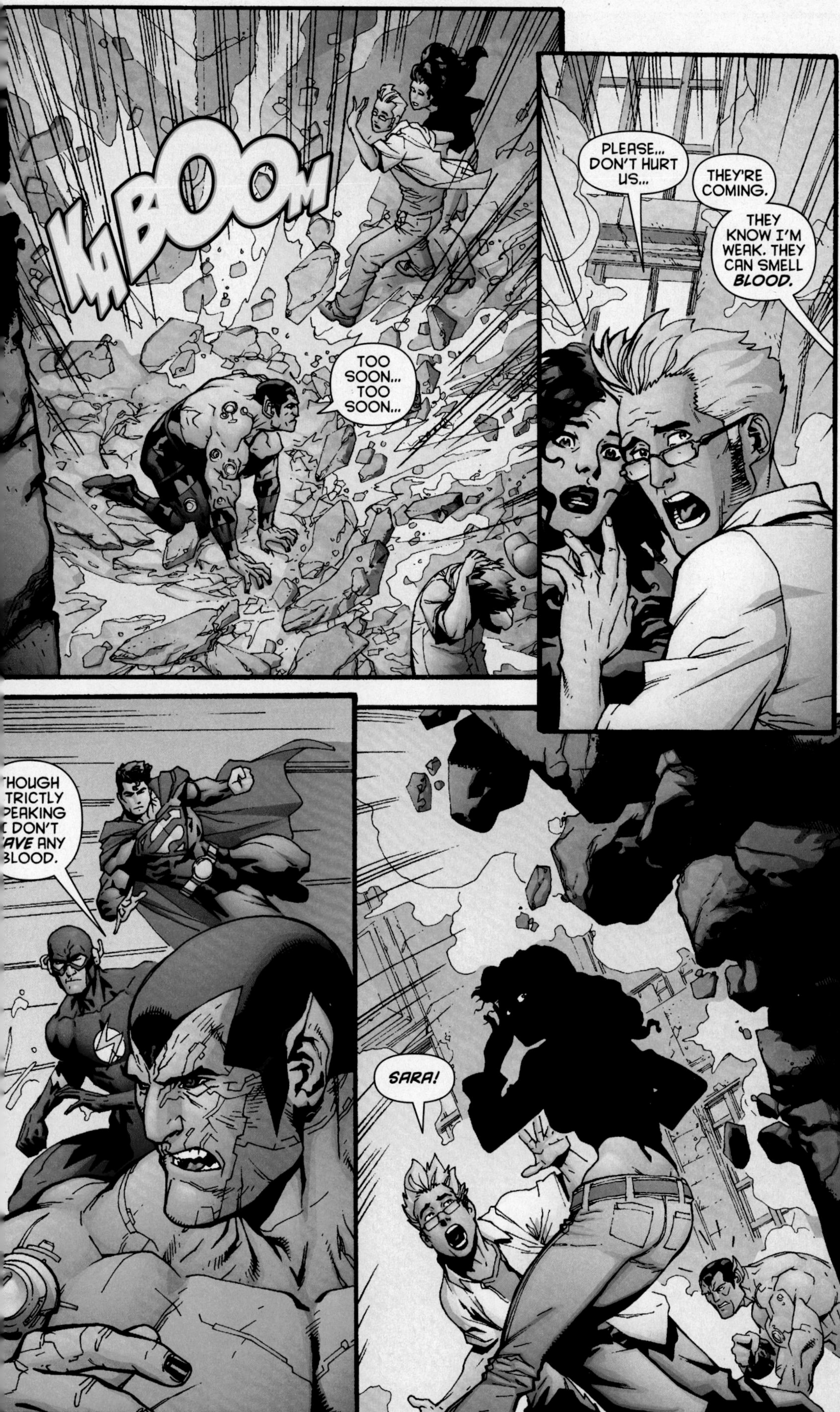
KABOOM
TOO SOON... TOO SOON...
PLEASE... DON'T HURT US...
THEY'RE COMING.
THEY KNOW I'M WEAK. THEY CAN SMELL *BLOOD.*
THOUGH TRICTLY PEAKING DON'T AVE ANY BLOOD.
SARA!

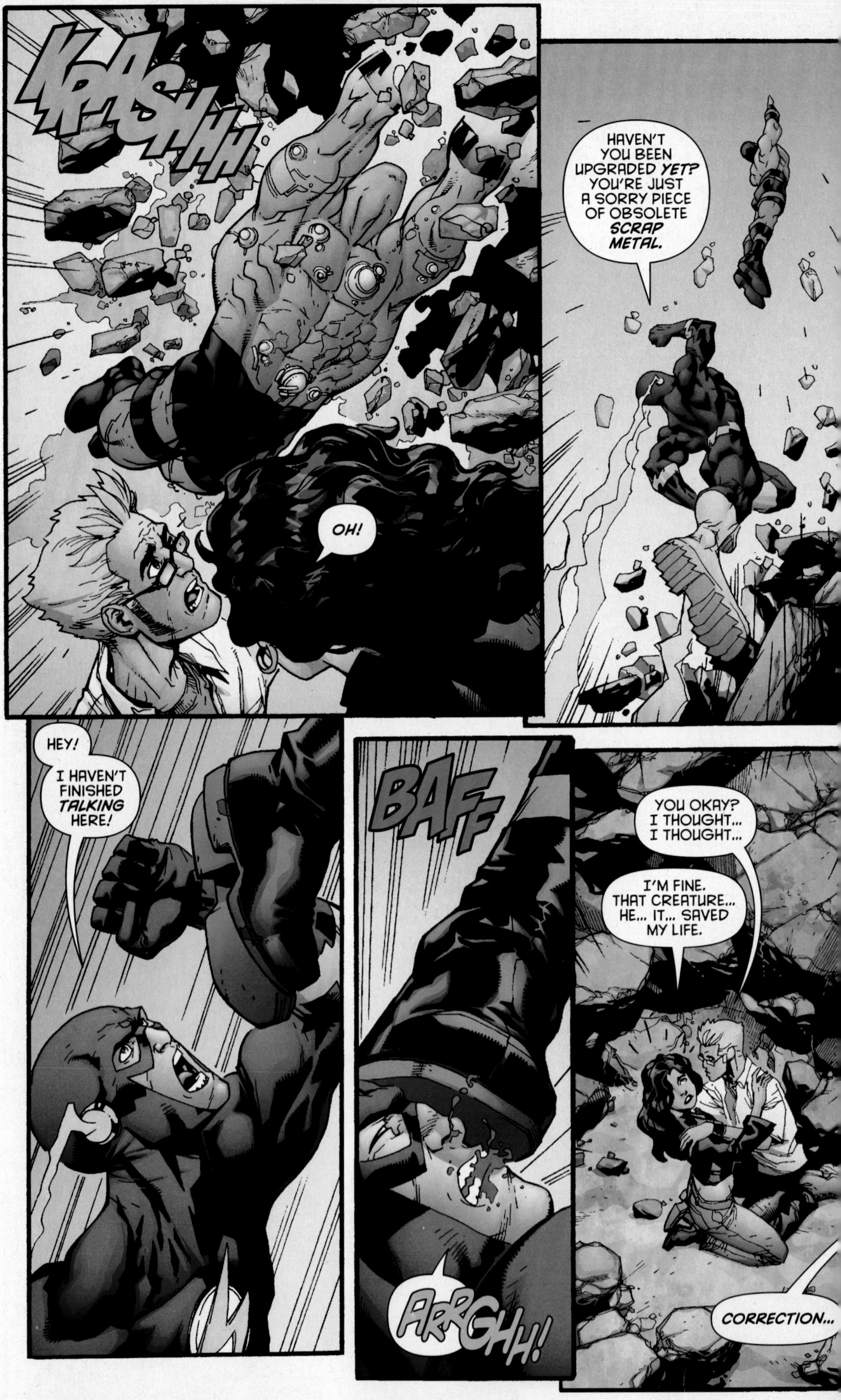
KRASH
KRASHHH
HAVEN'T YOU BEEN UPGRADED *YET?* YOU'RE JUST A SORRY PIECE OF OBSOLETE *SCRAP METAL.*
OH!
HEY! I HAVEN'T FINISHED *TALKING* HERE!
BAFF
ARRGHH!
YOU OKAY? I THOUGHT... I THOUGHT...
I'M FINE. THAT CREATURE... HE... IT... SAVED MY LIFE.
CORRECTION...

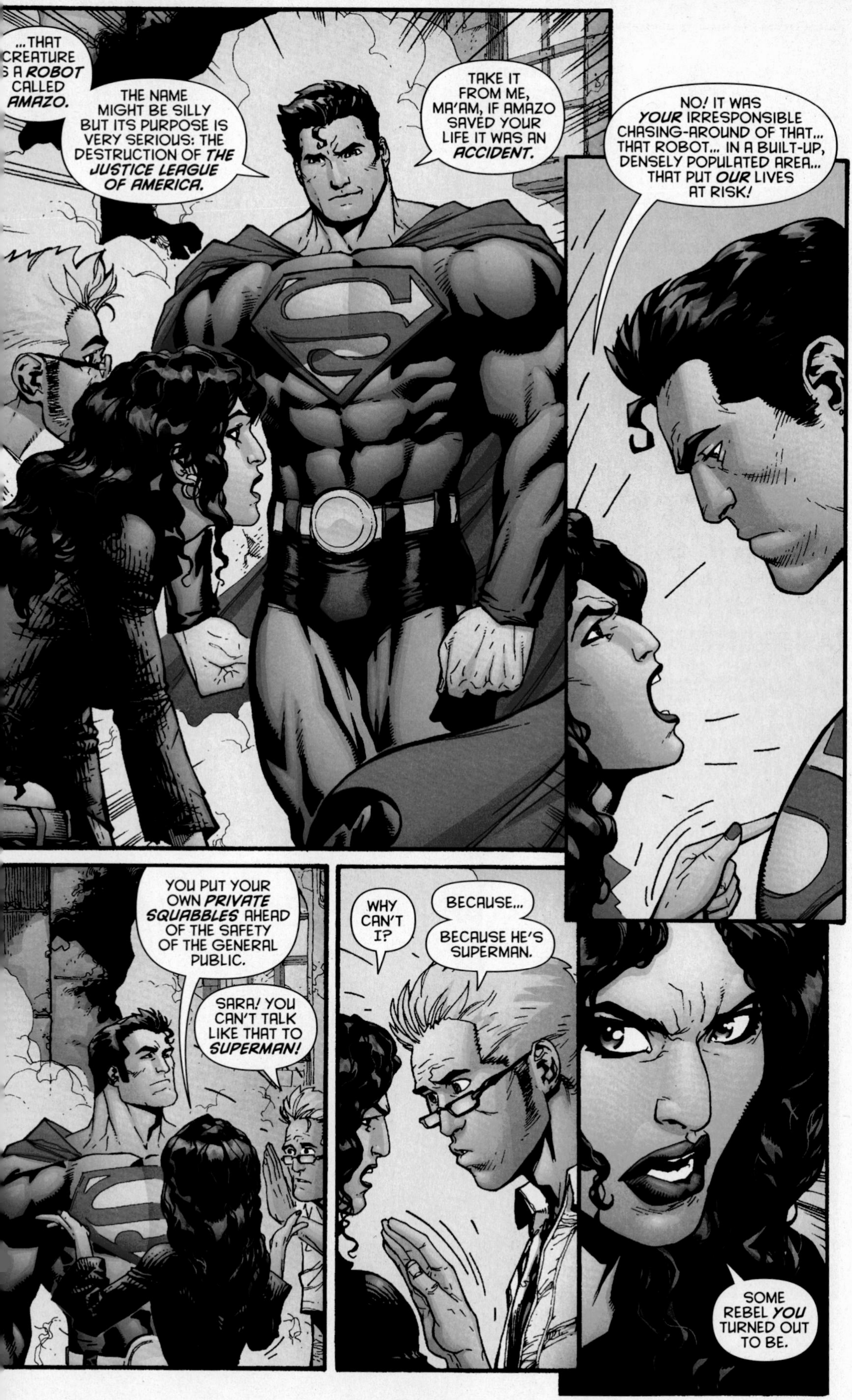
...THAT CREATURE S A ROBOT CALLED AMAZO.
THE NAME MIGHT BE SILLY BUT ITS PURPOSE IS VERY SERIOUS: THE DESTRUCTION OF THE JUSTICE LEAGUE OF AMERICA.
TAKE IT FROM ME, MA'AM, IF AMAZO SAVED YOUR LIFE IT WAS AN ACCIDENT.
NO! IT WAS YOUR IRRESPONSIBLE CHASING-AROUND OF THAT... THAT ROBOT... IN A BUILT-UP, DENSELY POPULATED AREA... THAT PUT OUR LIVES AT RISK!
YOU PUT YOUR OWN PRIVATE SQUABBLES AHEAD OF THE SAFETY OF THE GENERAL PUBLIC.
SARA! YOU CAN'T TALK LIKE THAT TO SUPERMAN!
WHY CAN'T I?
BECAUSE...
BECAUSE HE'S SUPERMAN.
SOME REBEL YOU TURNED OUT TO BE.

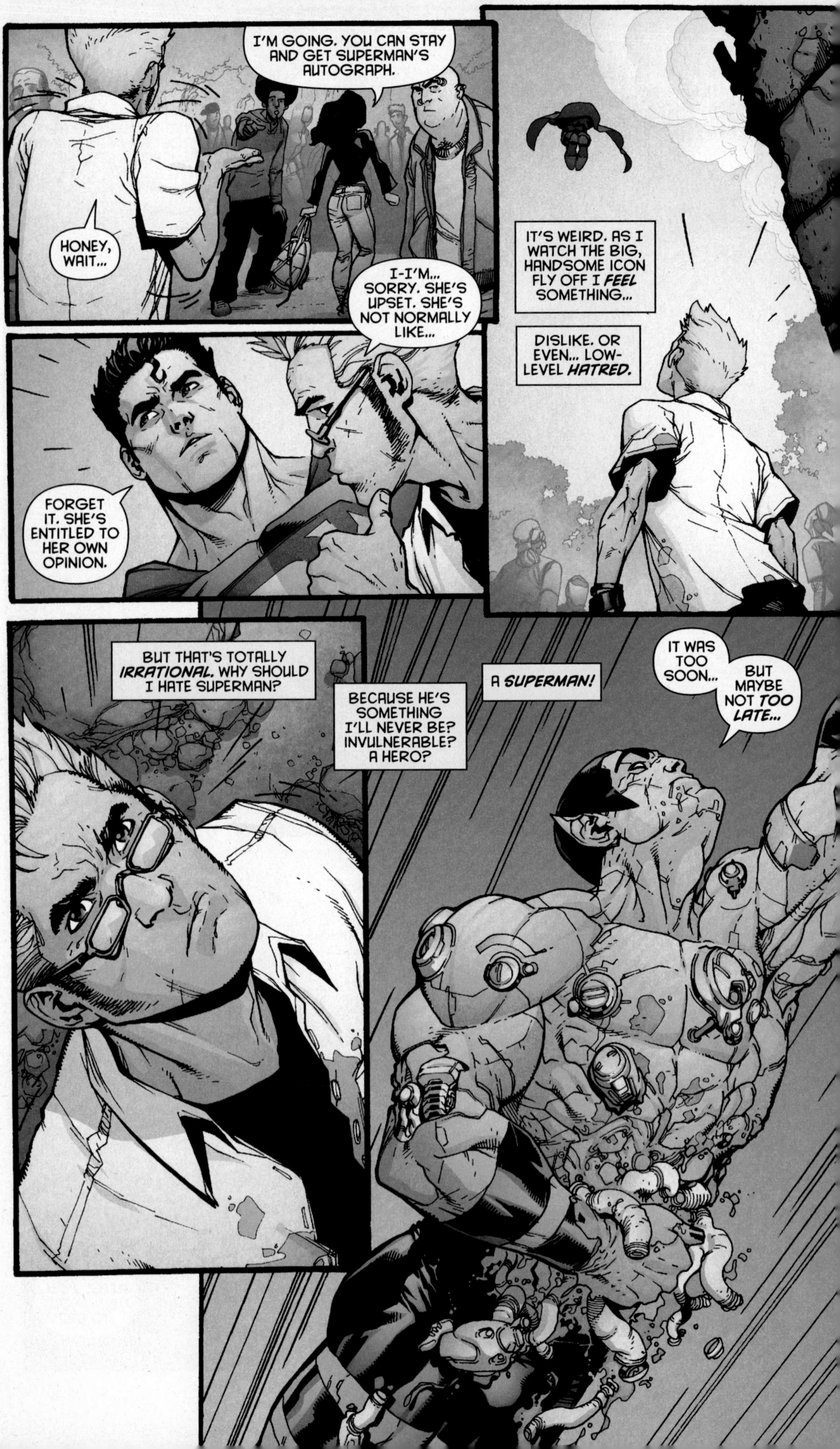

I'M GOING. YOU CAN STAY AND GET SUPERMAN'S AUTOGRAPH.
HONEY, WAIT...
I-I'M... SORRY. SHE'S UPSET. SHE'S NOT NORMALLY LIKE...
FORGET IT. SHE'S ENTITLED TO HER OWN OPINION.
IT'S WEIRD. AS I WATCH THE BIG, HANDSOME ICON FLY OFF I *FEEL* SOMETHING...
DISLIKE. OR EVEN... LOW-LEVEL *HATRED.*
BUT THAT'S TOTALLY *IRRATIONAL.* WHY SHOULD I HATE SUPERMAN?
BECAUSE HE'S SOMETHING I'LL NEVER BE? INVULNERABLE? A HERO?
A *SUPERMAN!*
IT WAS TOO SOON...
BUT MAYBE NOT *TOO LATE...*

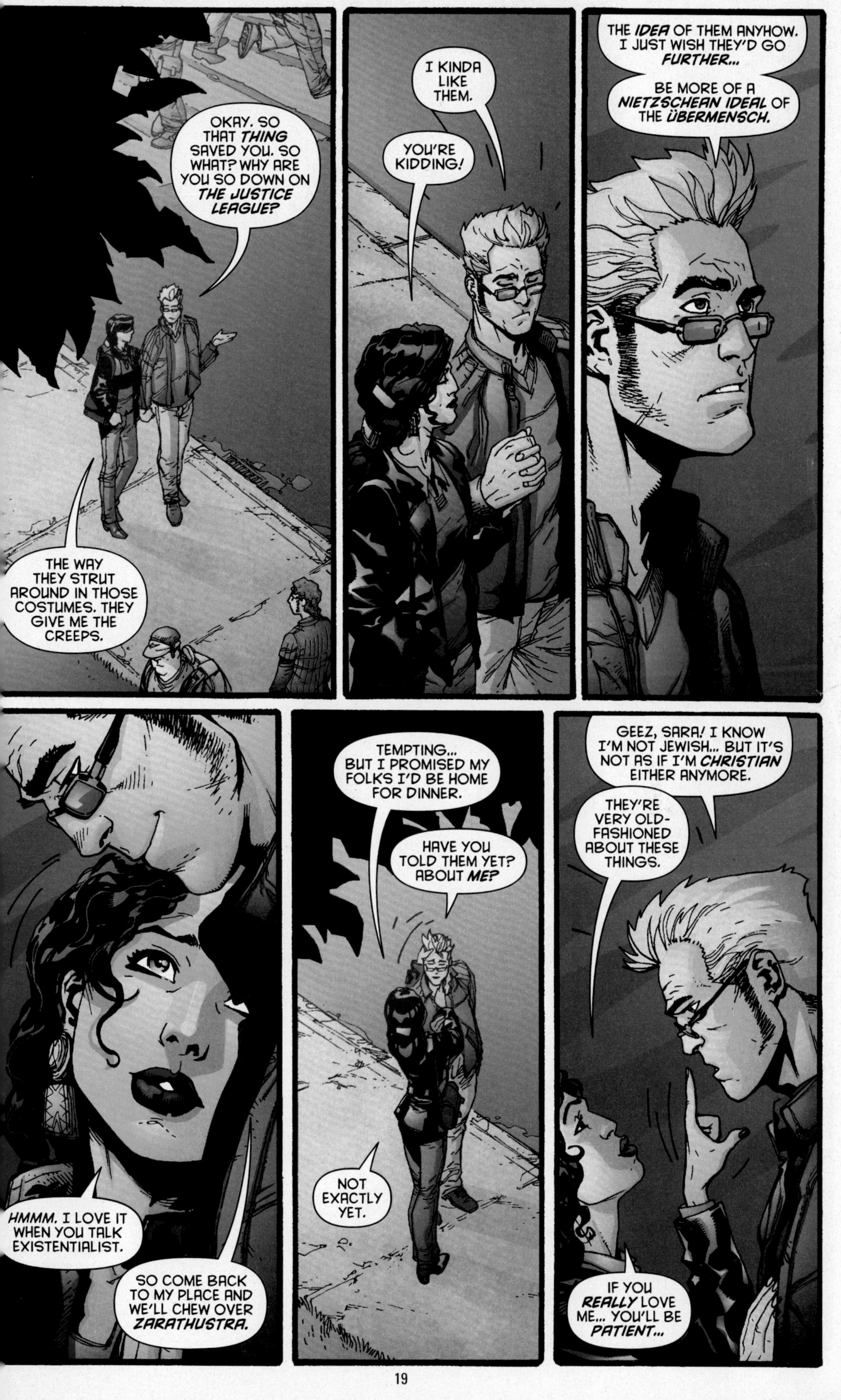
OKAY. SO THAT THING SAVED YOU. SO WHAT? WHY ARE YOU SO DOWN ON THE JUSTICE LEAGUE?
THE WAY THEY STRUT AROUND IN THOSE COSTUMES. THEY GIVE ME THE CREEPS.
I KINDA LIKE THEM.
YOU'RE KIDDING!
THE IDEA OF THEM ANYHOW. I JUST WISH THEY'D GO FURTHER...
BE MORE OF A NIETZSCHEAN IDEAL OF THE ÜBERMENSCH.
HMMM. I LOVE IT WHEN YOU TALK EXISTENTIALIST.
SO COME BACK TO MY PLACE AND WE'LL CHEW OVER ZARATHUSTRA.
TEMPTING... BUT I PROMISED MY FOLKS I'D BE HOME FOR DINNER.
HAVE YOU TOLD THEM YET? ABOUT ME?
NOT EXACTLY YET.
GEEZ, SARA! I KNOW I'M NOT JEWISH... BUT IT'S NOT AS IF I'M CHRISTIAN EITHER ANYMORE.
THEY'RE VERY OLD-FASHIONED ABOUT THESE THINGS.
IF YOU REALLY LOVE ME... YOU'LL BE PATIENT...

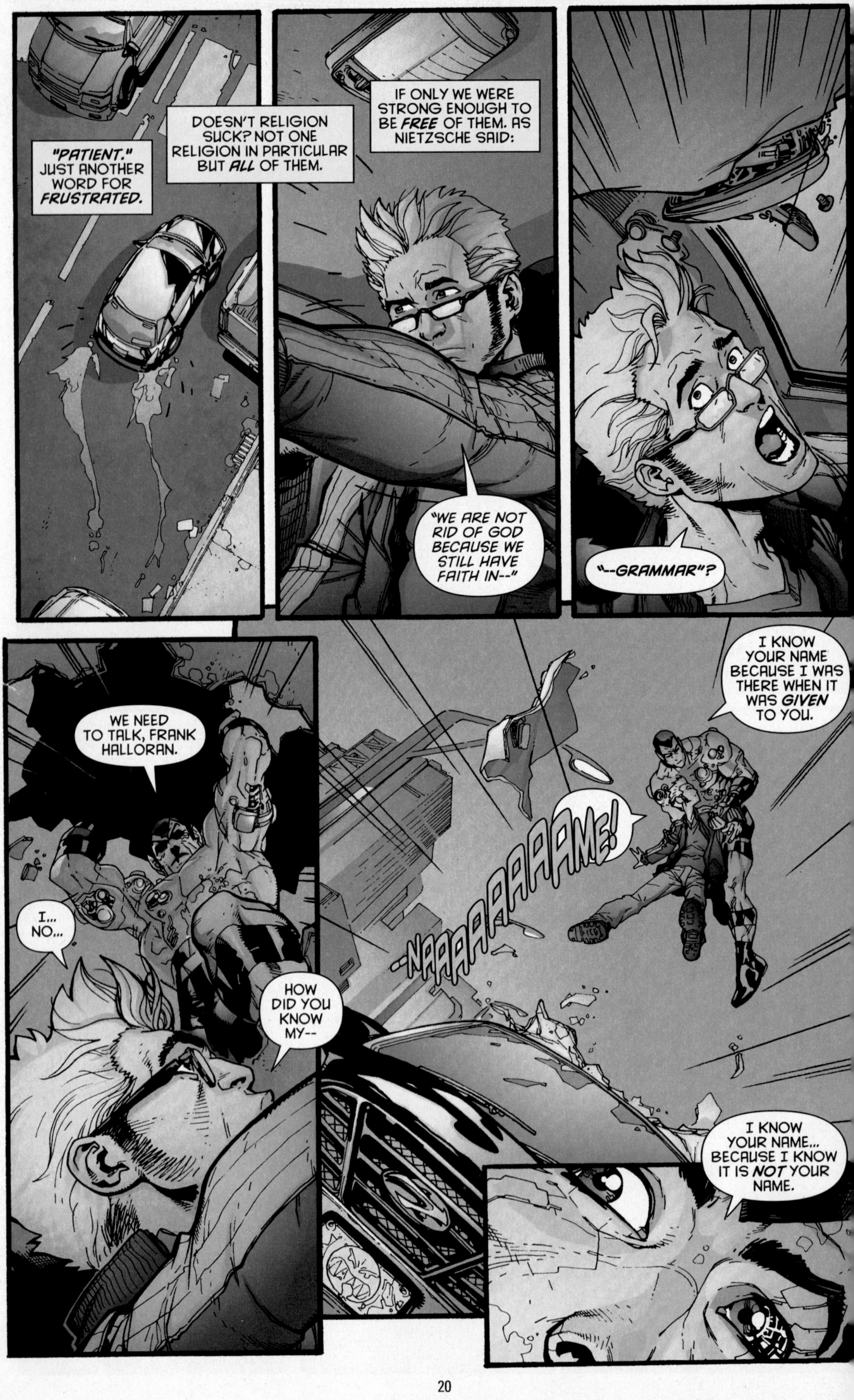
"PATIENT." JUST ANOTHER WORD FOR FRUSTRATED.
DOESN'T RELIGION SUCK? NOT ONE RELIGION IN PARTICULAR BUT ALL OF THEM.
IF ONLY WE WERE STRONG ENOUGH TO BE FREE OF THEM. AS NIETZSCHE SAID:
"WE ARE NOT RID OF GOD BECAUSE WE STILL HAVE FAITH IN--"
"--GRAMMAR"?
WE NEED TO TALK, FRANK HALLORAN.
I... NO...
HOW DID YOU KNOW MY--
-NAAAAAAAAAAAME!
I KNOW YOUR NAME BECAUSE I WAS THERE WHEN IT WAS GIVEN TO YOU.
I KNOW YOUR NAME... BECAUSE I KNOW IT IS NOT YOUR NAME.

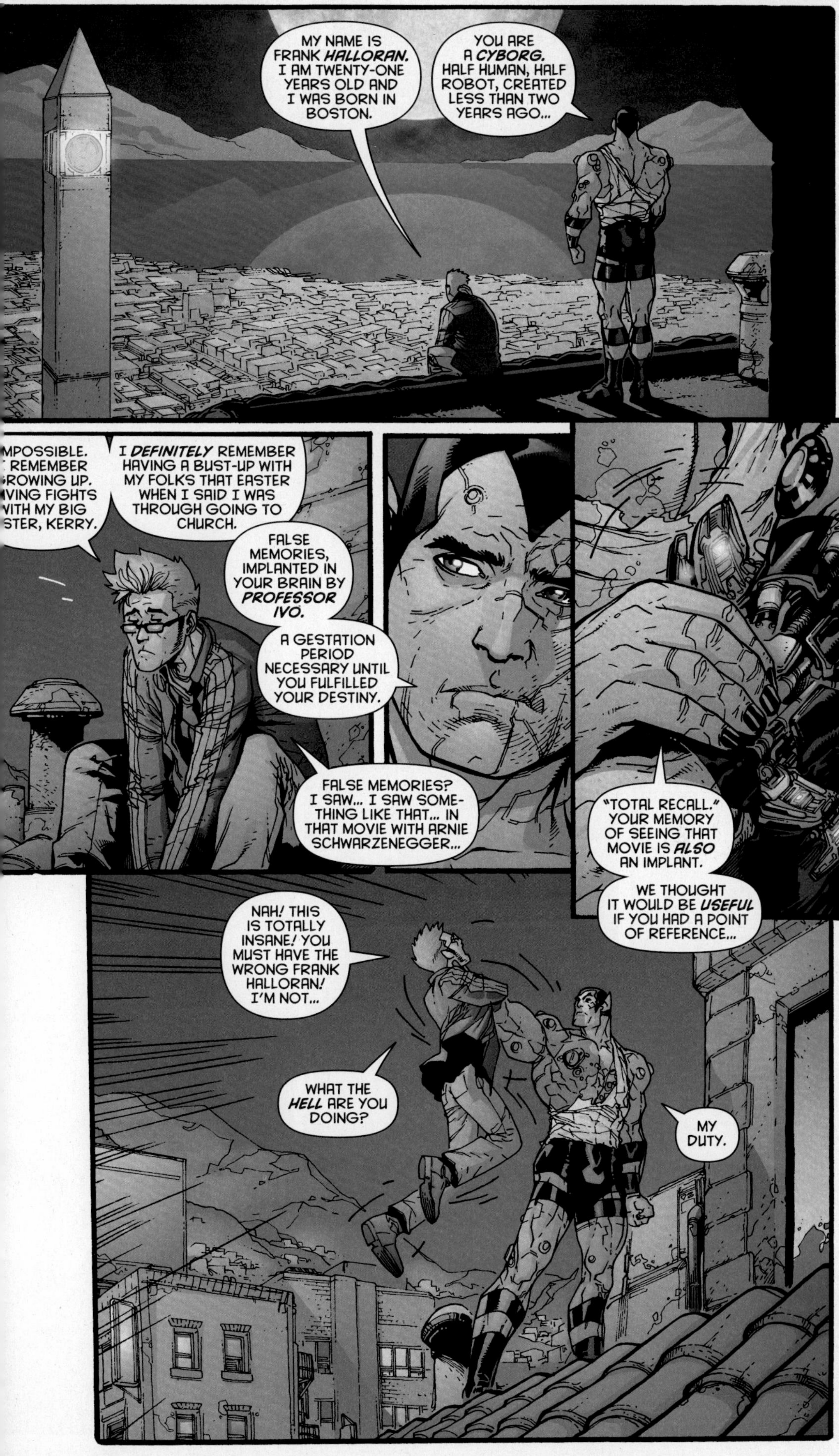

MY NAME IS FRANK HALLORAN. I AM TWENTY-ONE YEARS OLD AND I WAS BORN IN BOSTON.
YOU ARE A CYBORG. HALF HUMAN, HALF ROBOT, CREATED LESS THAN TWO YEARS AGO...
MPOSSIBLE. REMEMBER GROWING UP. VING FIGHTS WITH MY BIG STER, KERRY.
I DEFINITELY REMEMBER HAVING A BUST-UP WITH MY FOLKS THAT EASTER WHEN I SAID I WAS THROUGH GOING TO CHURCH.
FALSE MEMORIES, IMPLANTED IN YOUR BRAIN BY PROFESSOR IVO.
A GESTATION PERIOD NECESSARY UNTIL YOU FULFILLED YOUR DESTINY.
FALSE MEMORIES? I SAW... I SAW SOME-THING LIKE THAT... IN THAT MOVIE WITH ARNIE SCHWARZENEGGER...
"TOTAL RECALL." YOUR MEMORY OF SEEING THAT MOVIE IS ALSO AN IMPLANT.
WE THOUGHT IT WOULD BE USEFUL IF YOU HAD A POINT OF REFERENCE...
NAH! THIS IS TOTALLY INSANE! YOU MUST HAVE THE WRONG FRANK HALLORAN! I'M NOT...
WHAT THE HELL ARE YOU DOING?
MY DUTY.

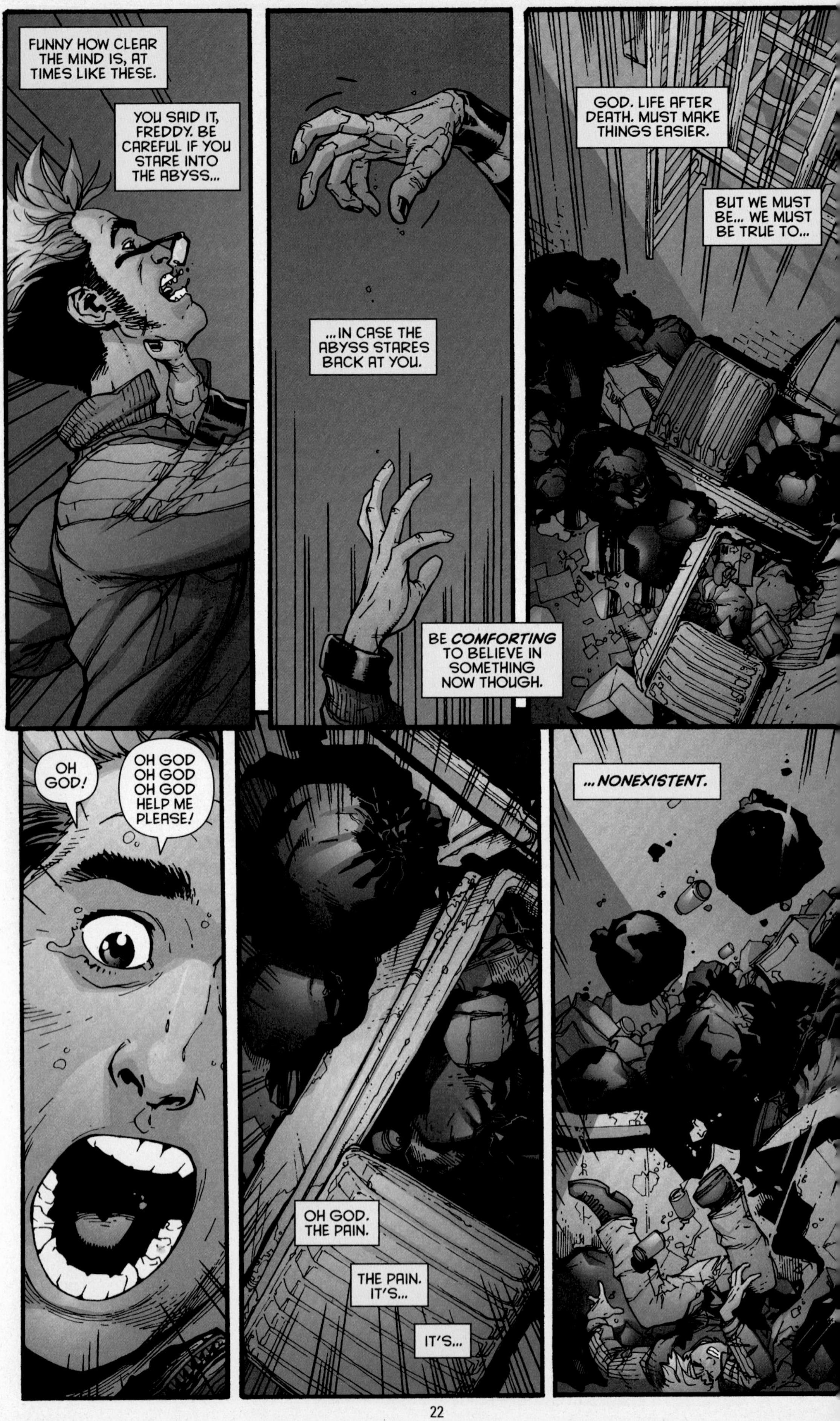
FUNNY HOW CLEAR THE MIND IS, AT TIMES LIKE THESE.
YOU SAID IT, FREDDY. BE CAREFUL IF YOU STARE INTO THE ABYSS...
...IN CASE THE ABYSS STARES BACK AT YOU.
BE *COMFORTING* TO BELIEVE IN SOMETHING NOW THOUGH.
GOD. LIFE AFTER DEATH. MUST MAKE THINGS EASIER.
BUT WE MUST BE... WE MUST BE TRUE TO...
OH GOD!
OH GOD OH GOD OH GOD HELP ME PLEASE!
OH GOD. THE PAIN.
THE PAIN. IT'S...
IT'S...
...NONEXISTENT.

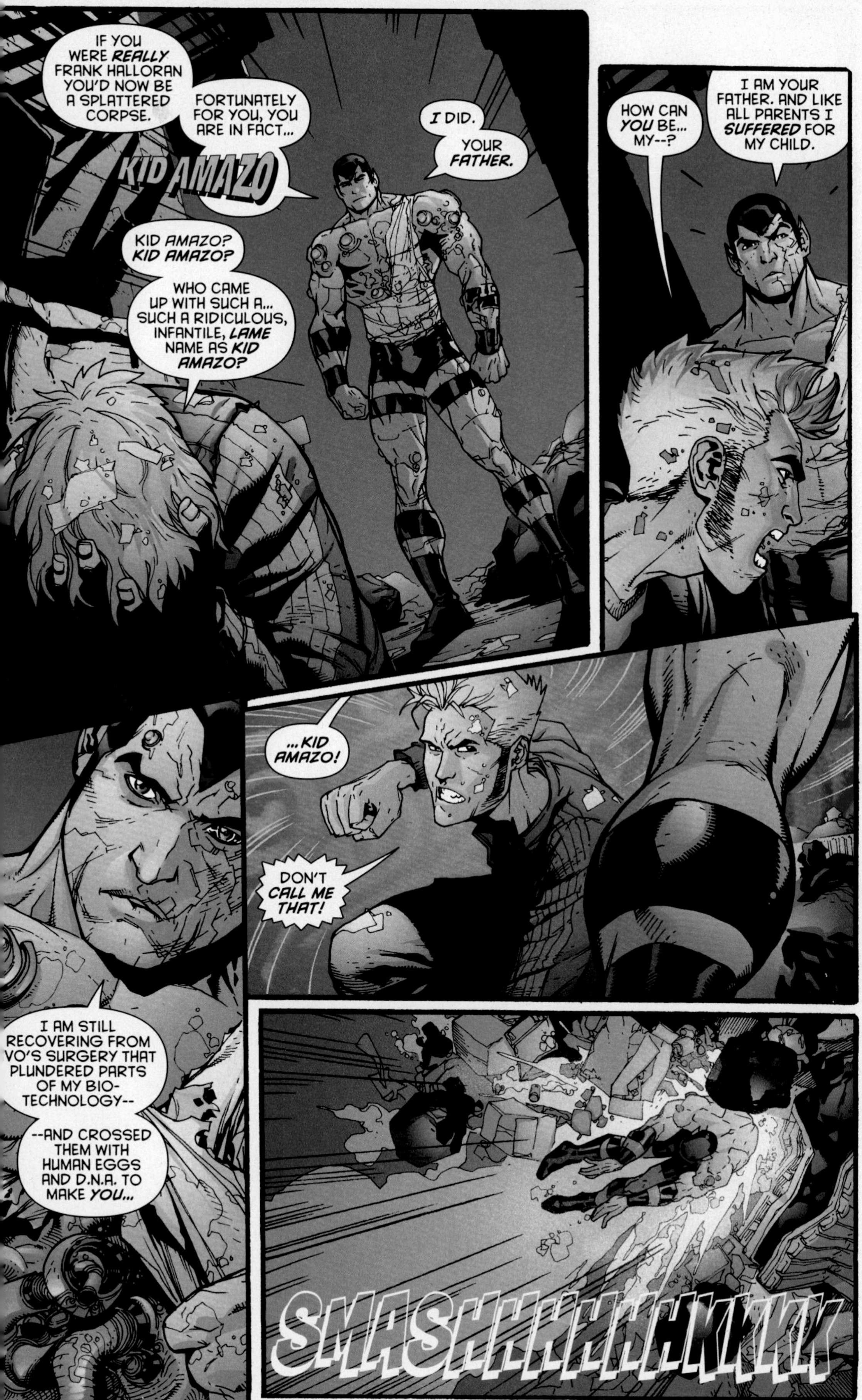
IF YOU WERE REALLY FRANK HALLORAN YOU'D NOW BE A SPLATTERED CORPSE.
FORTUNATELY FOR YOU, YOU ARE IN FACT...
KID AMAZO
KID AMAZO? KID AMAZO?
WHO CAME UP WITH SUCH A... SUCH A RIDICULOUS, INFANTILE, LAME NAME AS KID AMAZO?
I DID.
YOUR FATHER.
HOW CAN YOU BE... MY--?
I AM YOUR FATHER. AND LIKE ALL PARENTS I SUFFERED FOR MY CHILD.
I AM STILL RECOVERING FROM VO'S SURGERY THAT PLUNDERED PARTS OF MY BIO-TECHNOLOGY--
--AND CROSSED THEM WITH HUMAN EGGS AND D.N.A. TO MAKE YOU...
...KID AMAZO!
DON'T CALL ME THAT!
SMASHHHHHKKKK

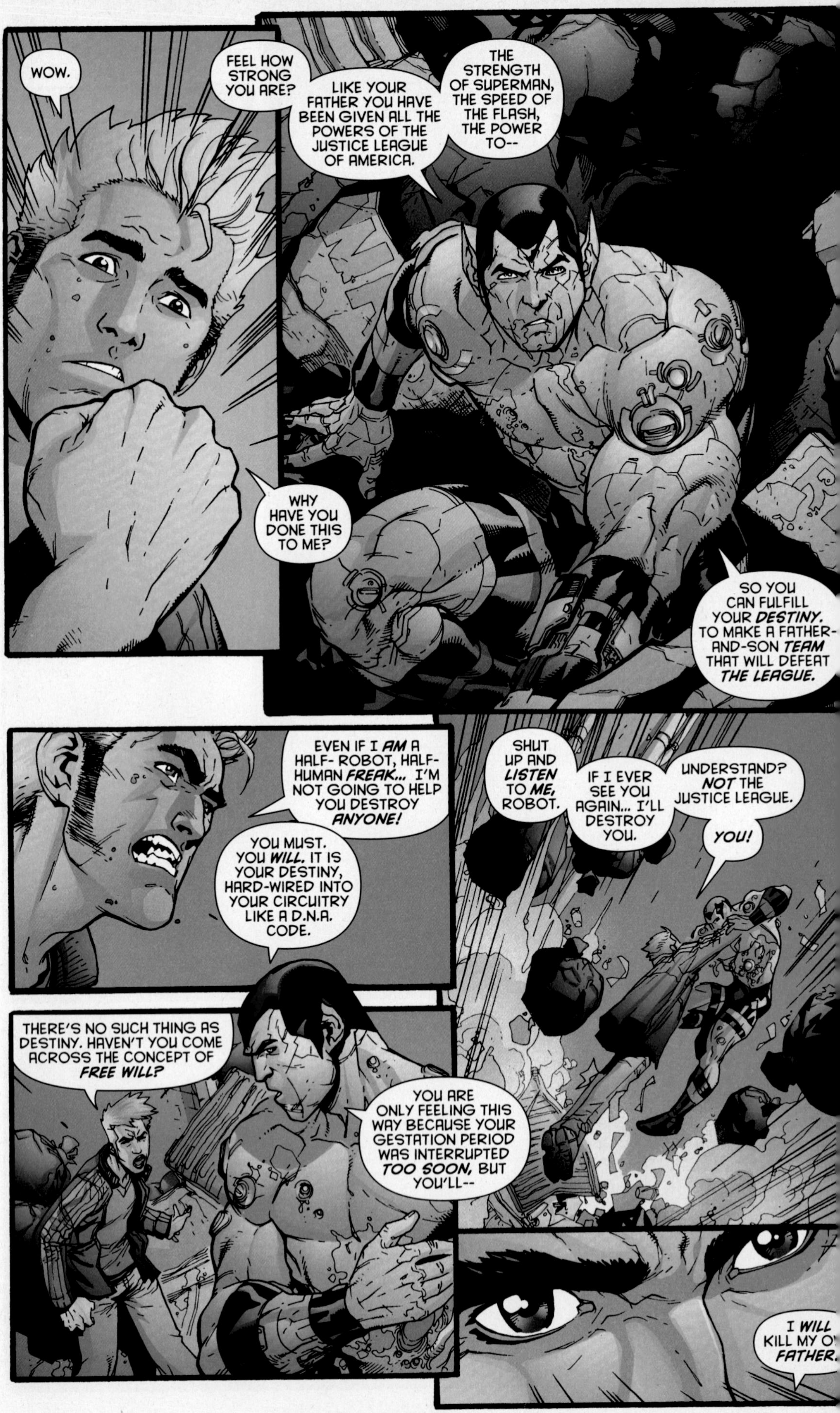
WOW.
FEEL HOW STRONG YOU ARE?
LIKE YOUR FATHER YOU HAVE BEEN GIVEN ALL THE POWERS OF THE JUSTICE LEAGUE OF AMERICA.
THE STRENGTH OF SUPERMAN, THE SPEED OF THE FLASH, THE POWER TO--
WHY HAVE YOU DONE THIS TO ME?
SO YOU CAN FULFILL YOUR *DESTINY.* TO MAKE A FATHER-AND-SON *TEAM* THAT WILL DEFEAT *THE LEAGUE.*
EVEN IF I *AM* A HALF- ROBOT, HALF-HUMAN *FREAK...* I'M NOT GOING TO HELP YOU DESTROY *ANYONE!*
YOU MUST. YOU *WILL.* IT IS YOUR DESTINY, HARD-WIRED INTO YOUR CIRCUITRY LIKE A D.N.A. CODE.
THERE'S NO SUCH THING AS DESTINY. HAVEN'T YOU COME ACROSS THE CONCEPT OF *FREE WILL?*
YOU ARE ONLY FEELING THIS WAY BECAUSE YOUR GESTATION PERIOD WAS INTERRUPTED *TOO SOON,* BUT YOU'LL--
SHUT UP AND *LISTEN* TO *ME,* ROBOT.
IF I EVER SEE YOU AGAIN... I'LL DESTROY YOU.
UNDERSTAND? *NOT* THE JUSTICE LEAGUE.
YOU!
I *WILL* KILL MY O
FATHER.

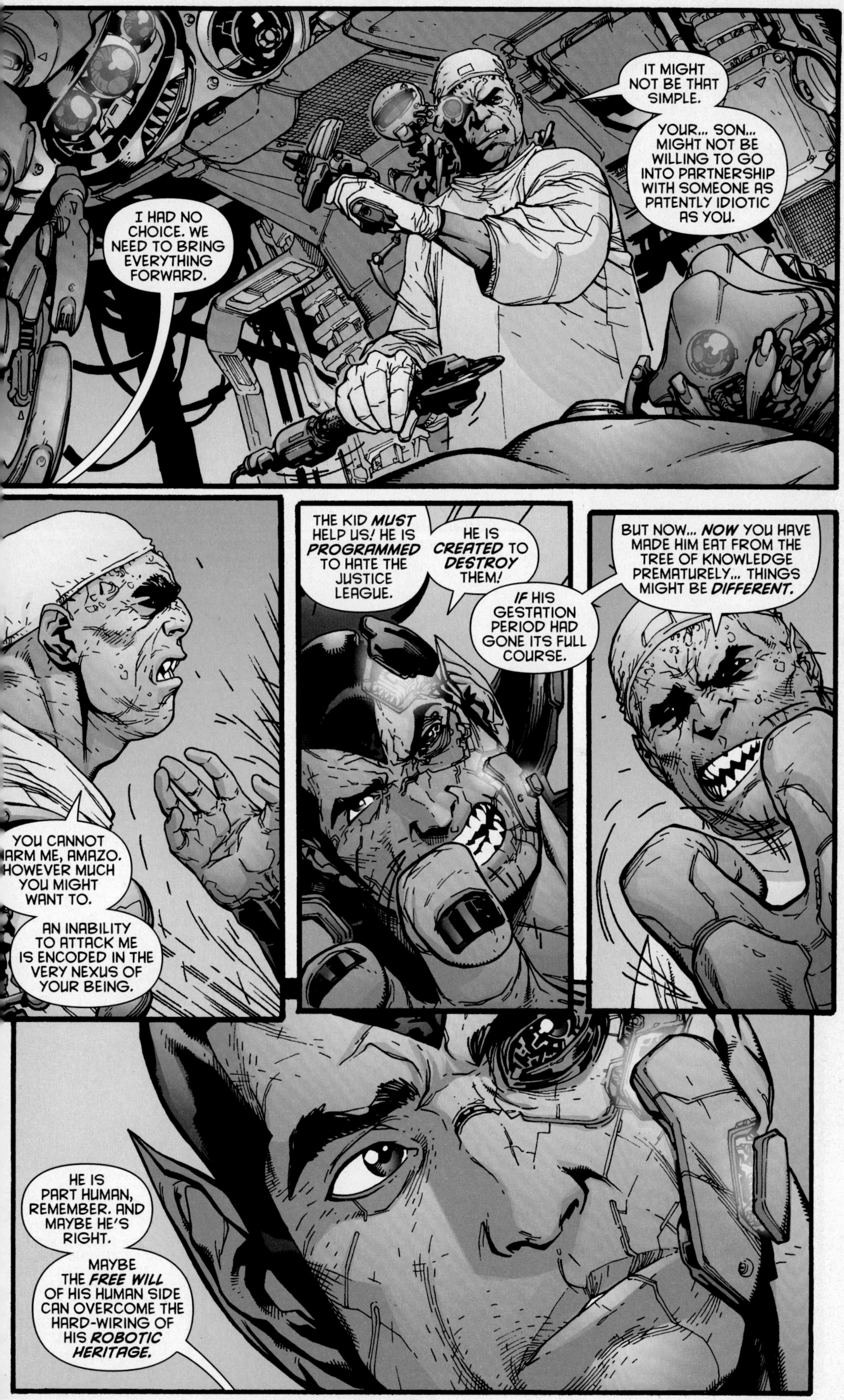

I HAD NO CHOICE. WE NEED TO BRING EVERYTHING FORWARD.
IT MIGHT NOT BE THAT SIMPLE.
YOUR... SON... MIGHT NOT BE WILLING TO GO INTO PARTNERSHIP WITH SOMEONE AS PATENTLY IDIOTIC AS YOU.
YOU CANNOT HARM ME, AMAZO. HOWEVER MUCH YOU MIGHT WANT TO.
AN INABILITY TO ATTACK ME IS ENCODED IN THE VERY NEXUS OF YOUR BEING.
THE KID MUST HELP US! HE IS PROGRAMMED TO HATE THE JUSTICE LEAGUE.
HE IS CREATED TO DESTROY THEM!
IF HIS GESTATION PERIOD HAD GONE ITS FULL COURSE.
BUT NOW... NOW YOU HAVE MADE HIM EAT FROM THE TREE OF KNOWLEDGE PREMATURELY... THINGS MIGHT BE DIFFERENT.
HE IS PART HUMAN, REMEMBER. AND MAYBE HE'S RIGHT.
MAYBE THE FREE WILL OF HIS HUMAN SIDE CAN OVERCOME THE HARD-WIRING OF HIS ROBOTIC HERITAGE.

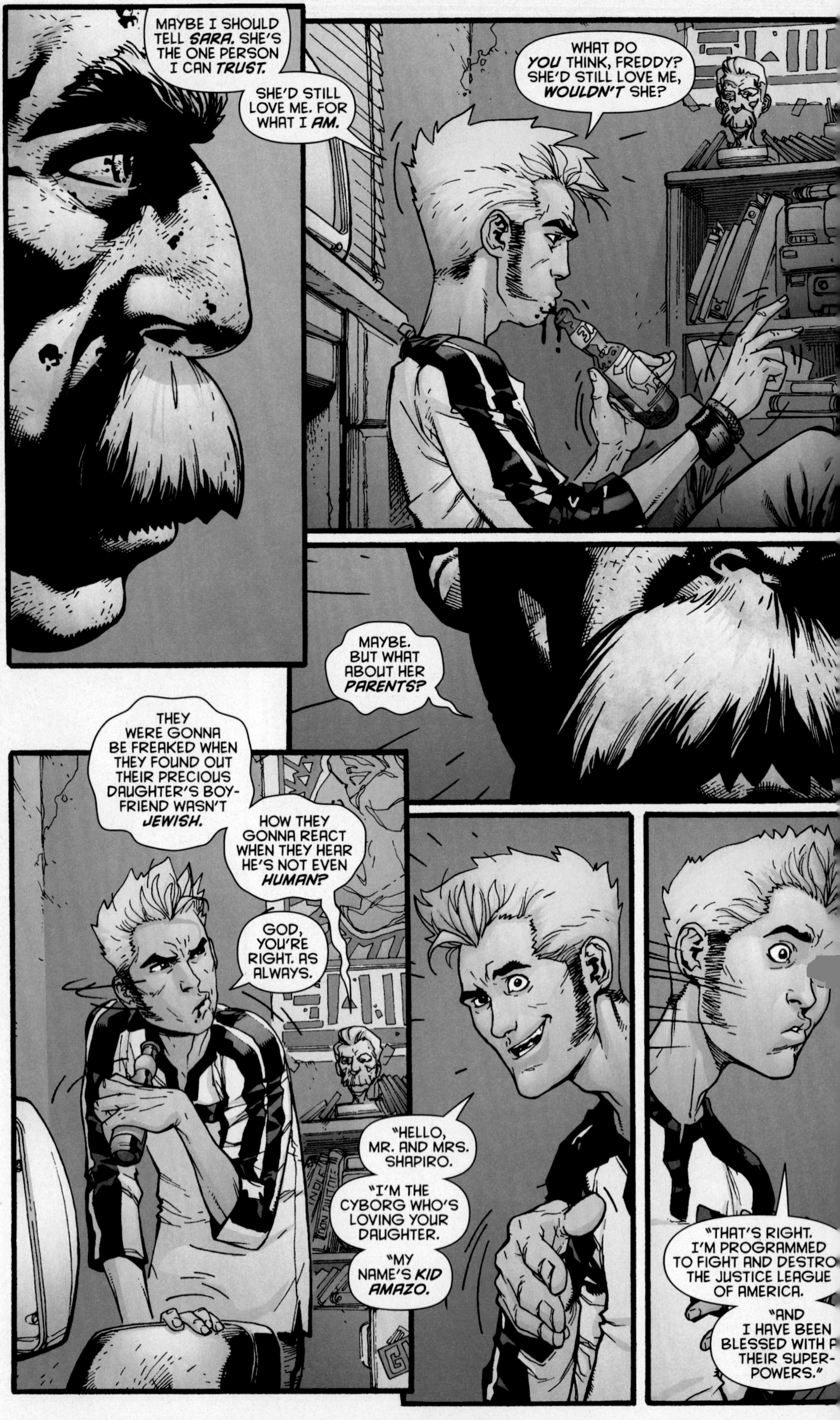
MAYBE I SHOULD TELL *SARA.* SHE'S THE ONE PERSON I CAN *TRUST.*
SHE'D STILL LOVE ME. FOR WHAT I *AM.*
WHAT DO *YOU* THINK, FREDDY? SHE'D STILL LOVE ME, *WOULDN'T* SHE?
MAYBE. BUT WHAT ABOUT HER *PARENTS?*
THEY WERE GONNA BE FREAKED WHEN THEY FOUND OUT THEIR PRECIOUS DAUGHTER'S BOY-FRIEND WASN'T *JEWISH.*
HOW THEY GONNA REACT WHEN THEY HEAR HE'S NOT EVEN *HUMAN?*
GOD, YOU'RE RIGHT. AS ALWAYS.
"HELLO, MR. AND MRS. SHAPIRO.
"I'M THE CYBORG WHO'S LOVING YOUR DAUGHTER.
"MY NAME'S *KID AMAZO.*
"THAT'S RIGHT. I'M PROGRAMMED TO FIGHT AND DESTRO THE JUSTICE LEAGUE OF AMERICA.
"AND I HAVE BEEN BLESSED WITH THEIR SUPER-POWERS."

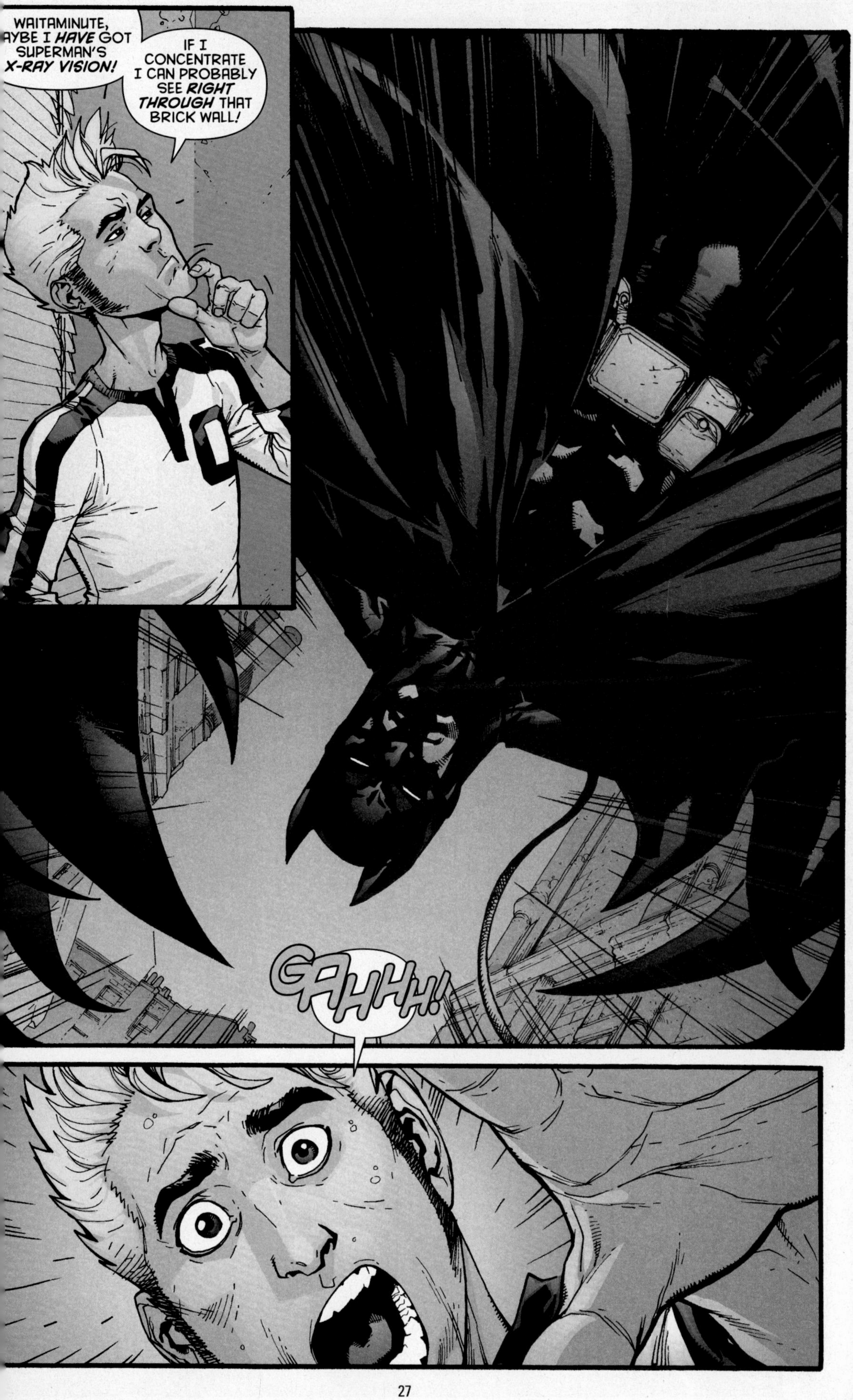
WAITAMINUTE, AYBE I HAVE GOT SUPERMAN'S X-RAY VISION!
IF I CONCENTRATE I CAN PROBABLY SEE RIGHT THROUGH THAT BRICK WALL!
GAHHH!

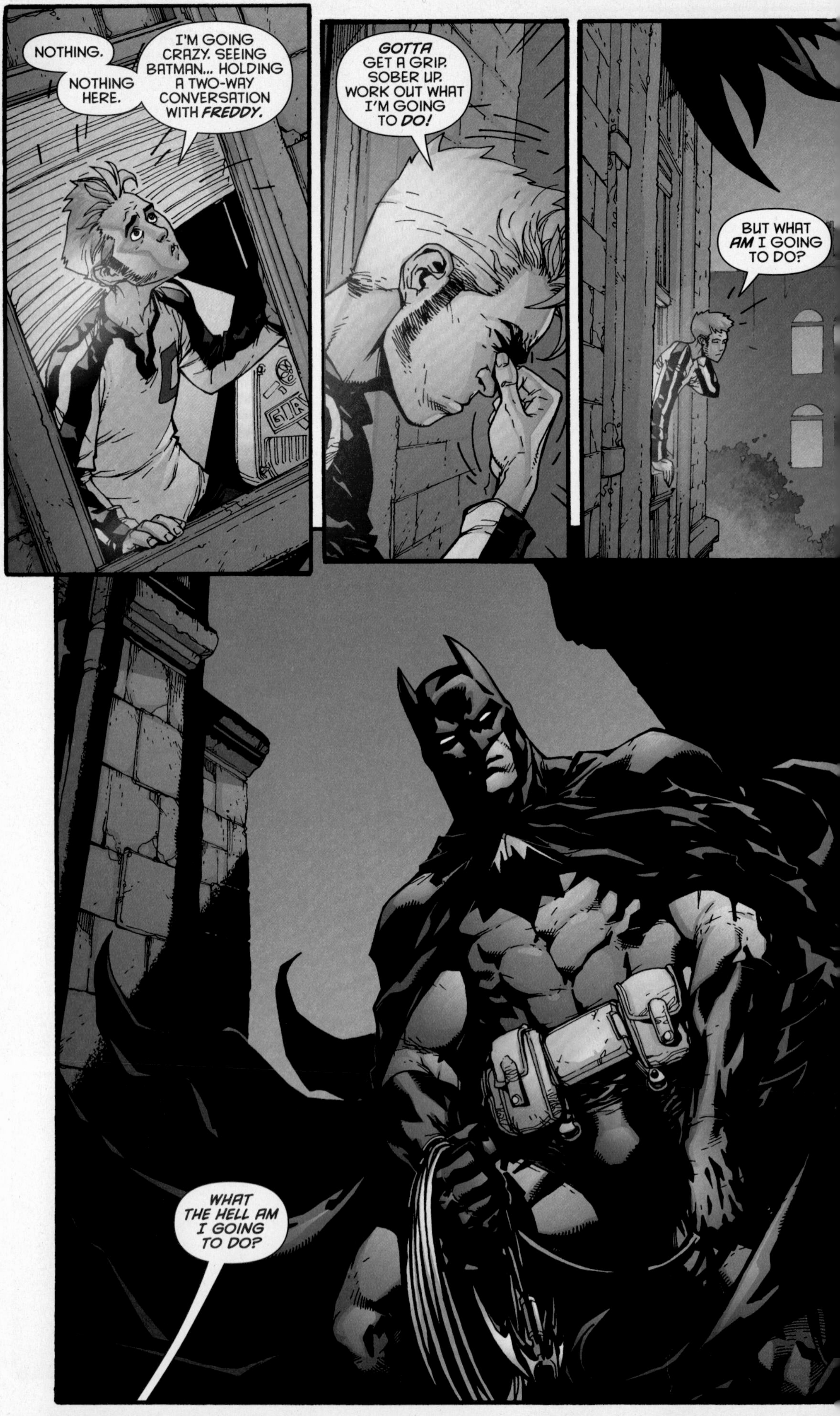

NOTHING.
NOTHING HERE.
I'M GOING CRAZY. SEEING BATMAN... HOLDING A TWO-WAY CONVERSATION WITH FREDDY.
GOTTA GET A GRIP. SOBER UP. WORK OUT WHAT I'M GOING TO DO!
BUT WHAT AM I GOING TO DO?
WHAT THE HELL AM I GOING TO DO?

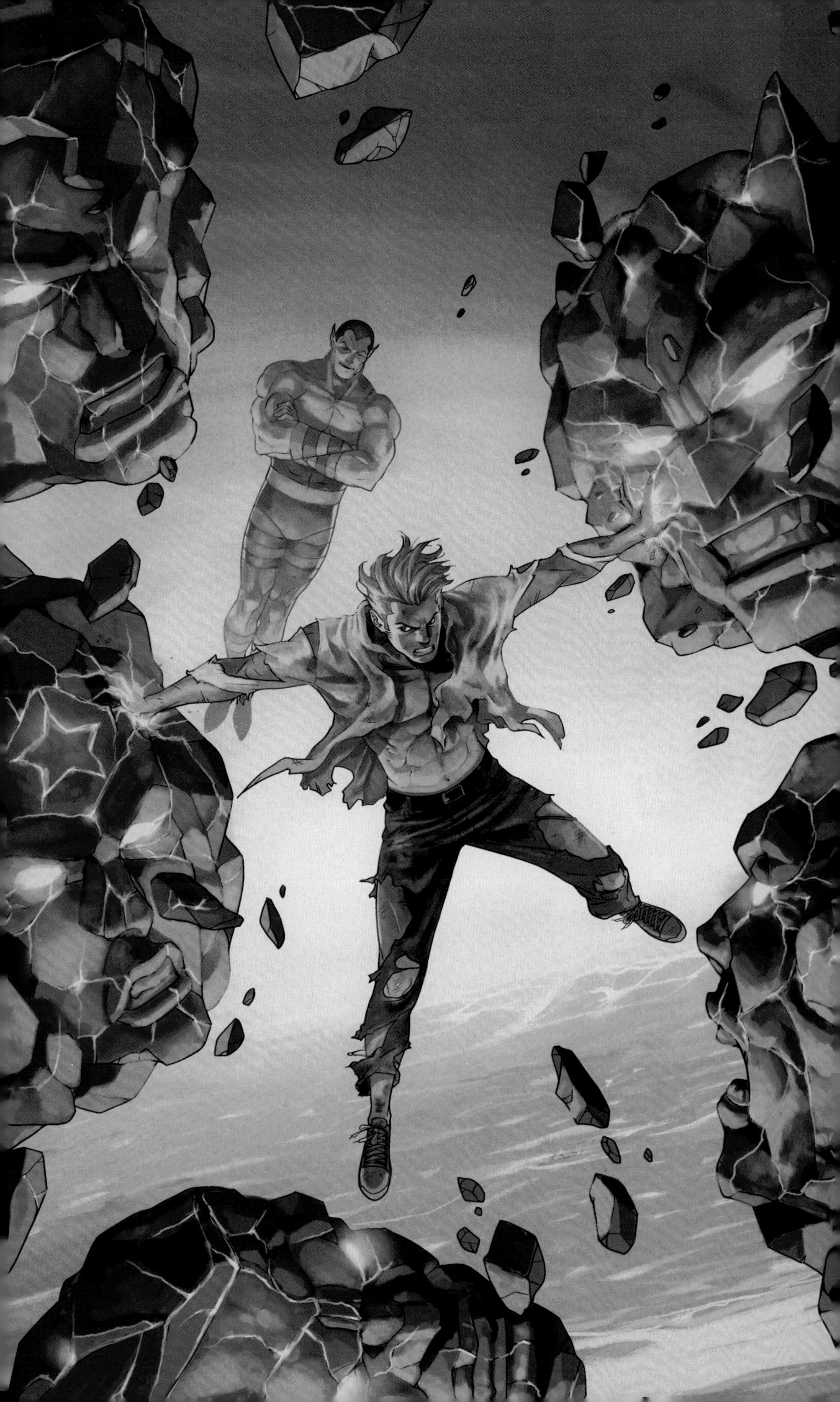

Chapter Two
MAN & SUPERMAN!

COVER ART BY SAMI BASRI

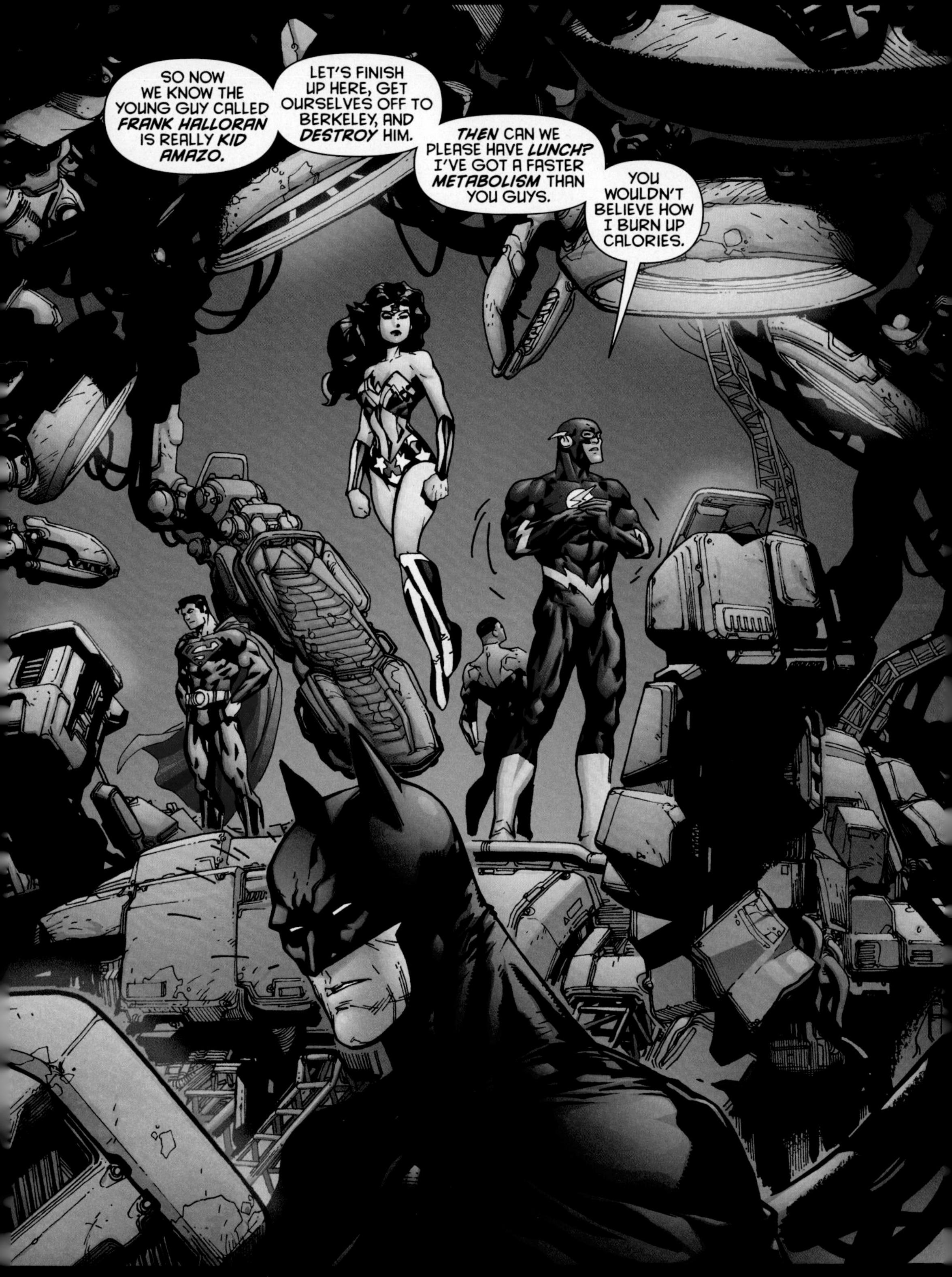

SO NOW WE KNOW THE YOUNG GUY CALLED FRANK HALLORAN IS REALLY KID AMAZO.
LET'S FINISH UP HERE, GET OURSELVES OFF TO BERKELEY, AND DESTROY HIM.
THEN CAN WE PLEASE HAVE LUNCH? I'VE GOT A FASTER METABOLISM THAN YOU GUYS.
YOU WOULDN'T BELIEVE HOW I BURN UP CALORIES.

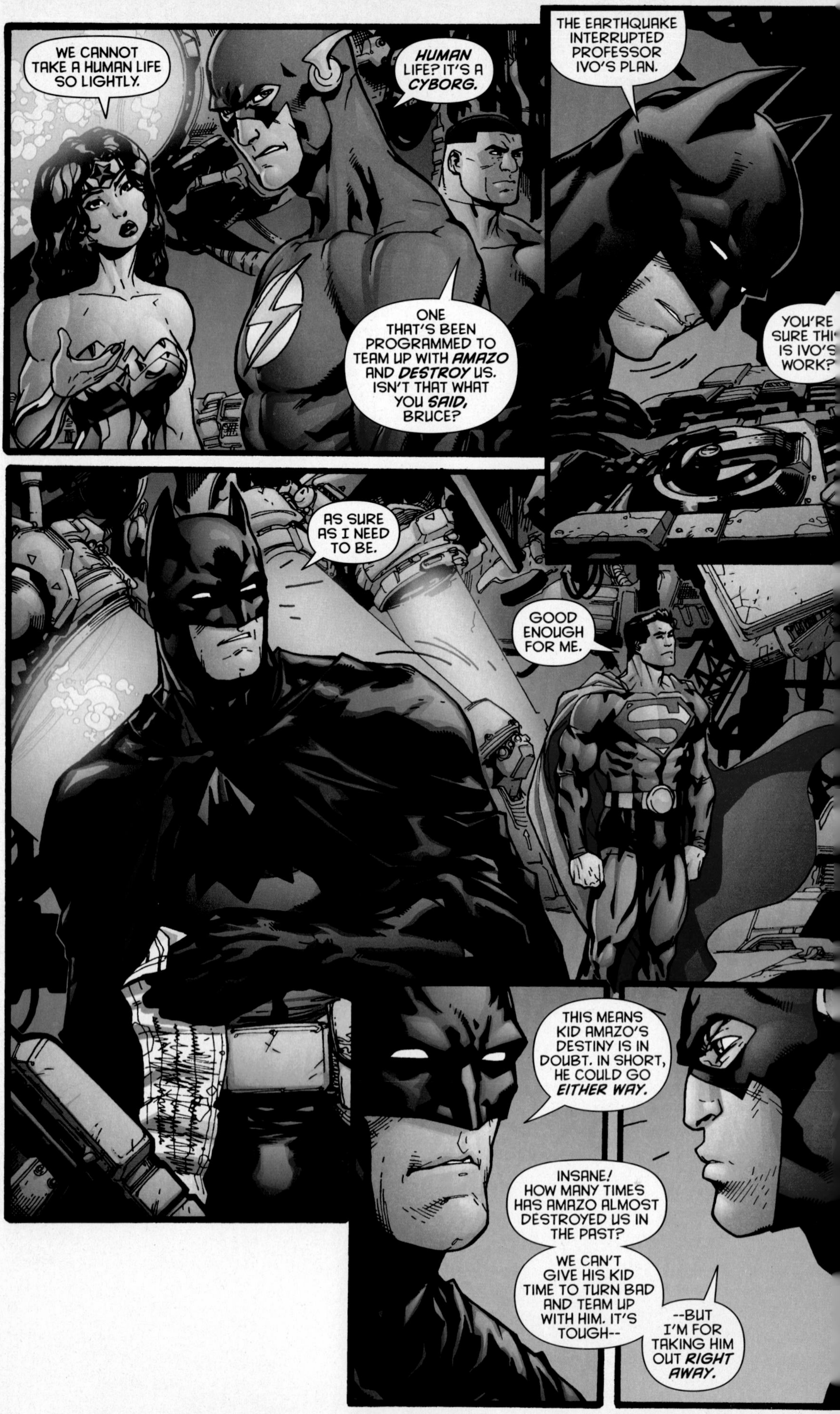
WE CANNOT TAKE A HUMAN LIFE SO LIGHTLY.
HUMAN LIFE? IT'S A CYBORG.
ONE THAT'S BEEN PROGRAMMED TO TEAM UP WITH AMAZO AND DESTROY US. ISN'T THAT WHAT YOU SAID, BRUCE?
THE EARTHQUAKE INTERRUPTED PROFESSOR IVO'S PLAN.
YOU'RE SURE THI IS IVO'S WORK?
AS SURE AS I NEED TO BE.
GOOD ENOUGH FOR ME.
THIS MEANS KID AMAZO'S DESTINY IS IN DOUBT. IN SHORT, HE COULD GO EITHER WAY.
INSANE! HOW MANY TIMES HAS AMAZO ALMOST DESTROYED US IN THE PAST?
WE CAN'T GIVE HIS KID TIME TO TURN BAD AND TEAM UP WITH HIM. IT'S TOUGH--
--BUT I'M FOR TAKING HIM OUT RIGHT AWAY.

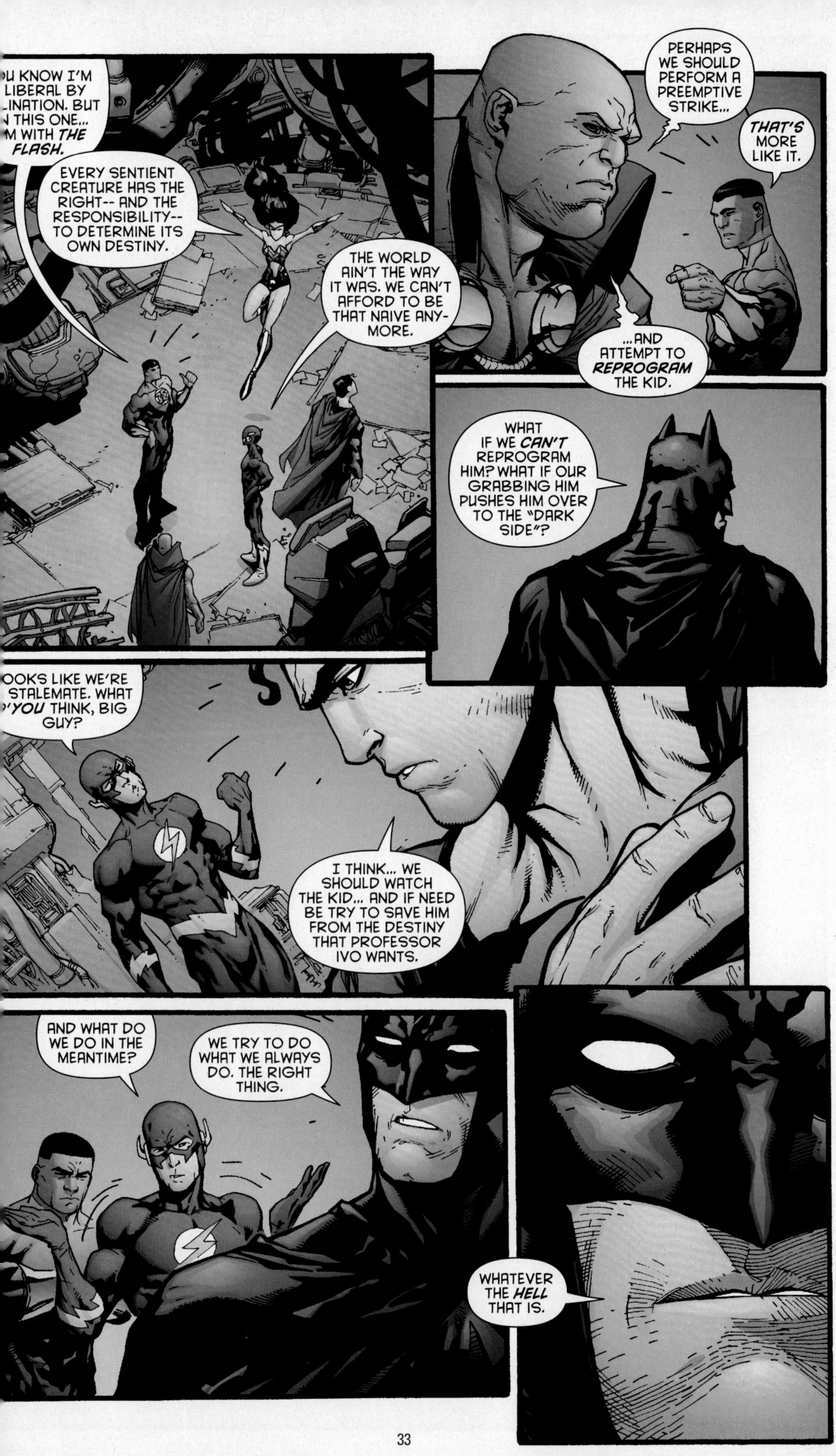

OU KNOW I'M LIBERAL BY LINATION. BUT N THIS ONE... M WITH THE FLASH.
EVERY SENTIENT CREATURE HAS THE RIGHT-- AND THE RESPONSIBILITY-- TO DETERMINE ITS OWN DESTINY.
THE WORLD AIN'T THE WAY IT WAS. WE CAN'T AFFORD TO BE THAT NAIVE ANY-MORE.
PERHAPS WE SHOULD PERFORM A PREEMPTIVE STRIKE...
THAT'S MORE LIKE IT.
...AND ATTEMPT TO REPROGRAM THE KID.
WHAT IF WE CAN'T REPROGRAM HIM? WHAT IF OUR GRABBING HIM PUSHES HIM OVER TO THE "DARK SIDE"?
OOKS LIKE WE'RE STALEMATE. WHAT 'YOU THINK, BIG GUY?
I THINK... WE SHOULD WATCH THE KID... AND IF NEED BE TRY TO SAVE HIM FROM THE DESTINY THAT PROFESSOR IVO WANTS.
AND WHAT DO WE DO IN THE MEANTIME?
WE TRY TO DO WHAT WE ALWAYS DO. THE RIGHT THING.
WHATEVER THE HELL THAT IS.

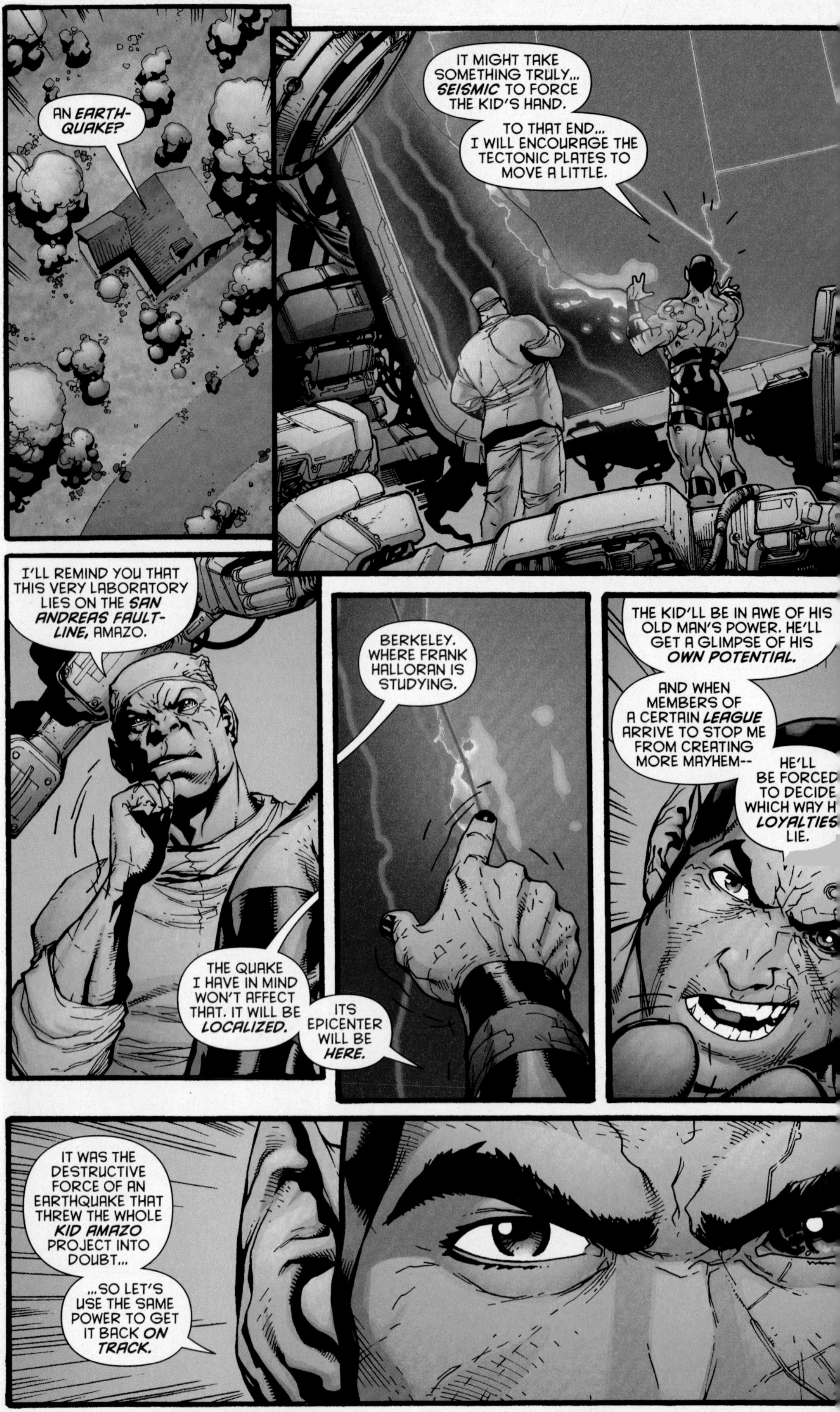
AN EARTH-QUAKE?
IT MIGHT TAKE SOMETHING TRULY... SEISMIC TO FORCE THE KID'S HAND.
TO THAT END... I WILL ENCOURAGE THE TECTONIC PLATES TO MOVE A LITTLE.
I'LL REMIND YOU THAT THIS VERY LABORATORY LIES ON THE SAN ANDREAS FAULT-LINE, AMAZO.
BERKELEY. WHERE FRANK HALLORAN IS STUDYING.
THE QUAKE I HAVE IN MIND WON'T AFFECT THAT. IT WILL BE LOCALIZED.
ITS EPICENTER WILL BE HERE.
THE KID'LL BE IN AWE OF HIS OLD MAN'S POWER. HE'LL GET A GLIMPSE OF HIS OWN POTENTIAL.
AND WHEN MEMBERS OF A CERTAIN LEAGUE ARRIVE TO STOP ME FROM CREATING MORE MAYHEM--
HE'LL BE FORCED TO DECIDE WHICH WAY H LOYALTIES LIE.
IT WAS THE DESTRUCTIVE FORCE OF AN EARTHQUAKE THAT THREW THE WHOLE KID AMAZO PROJECT INTO DOUBT...
...SO LET'S USE THE SAME POWER TO GET IT BACK ON TRACK.

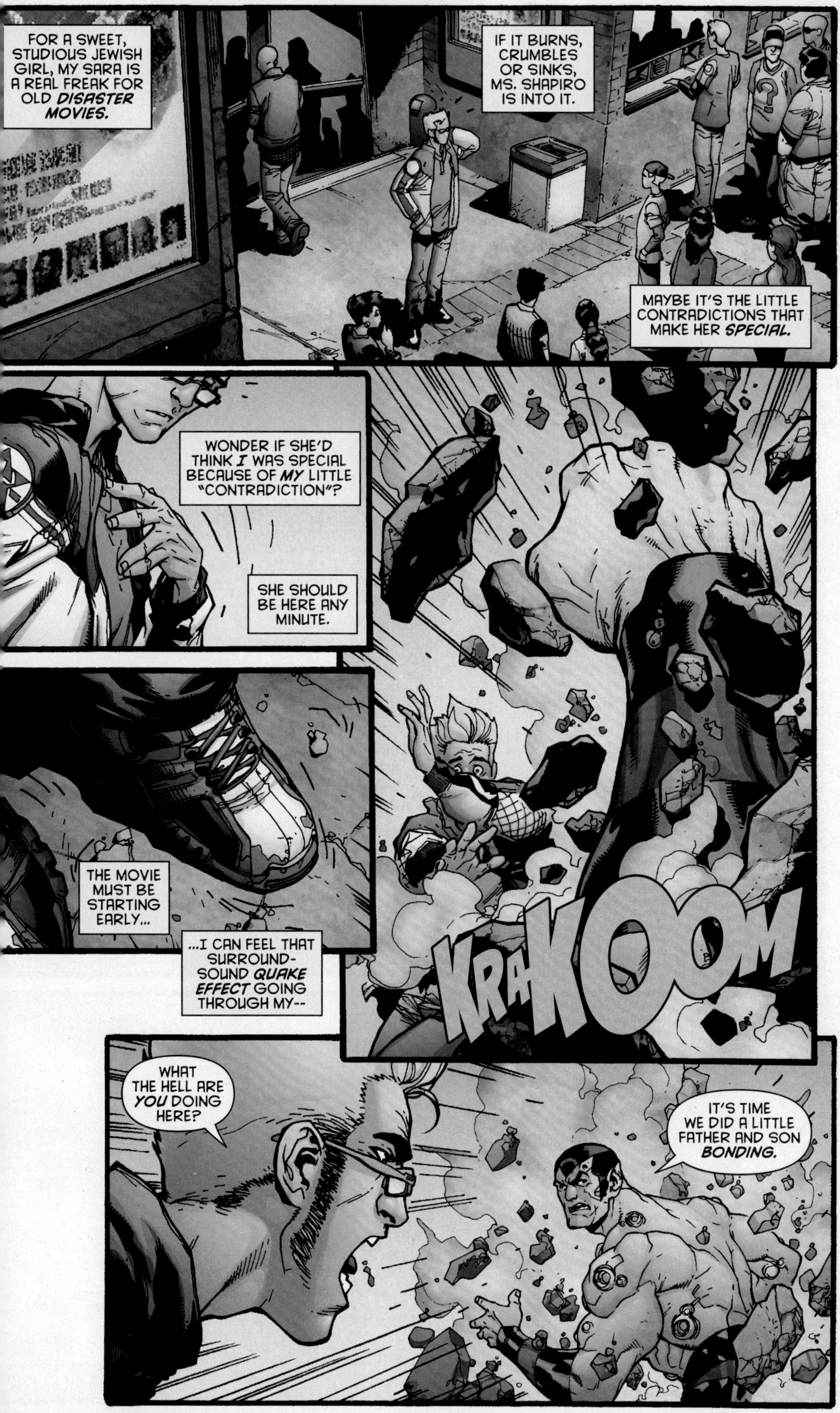
FOR A SWEET, STUDIOUS JEWISH GIRL, MY SARA IS A REAL FREAK FOR OLD *DISASTER MOVIES.*
IF IT BURNS, CRUMBLES OR SINKS, MS. SHAPIRO IS INTO IT.
MAYBE IT'S THE LITTLE CONTRADICTIONS THAT MAKE HER *SPECIAL.*
WONDER IF SHE'D THINK *I* WAS SPECIAL BECAUSE OF *MY* LITTLE "CONTRADICTION"?
SHE SHOULD BE HERE ANY MINUTE.
THE MOVIE MUST BE STARTING EARLY...
...I CAN FEEL THAT SURROUND-SOUND *QUAKE EFFECT* GOING THROUGH MY--
KRAKOOM
WHAT THE HELL ARE *YOU* DOING HERE?
IT'S TIME WE DID A LITTLE FATHER AND SON *BONDING.*

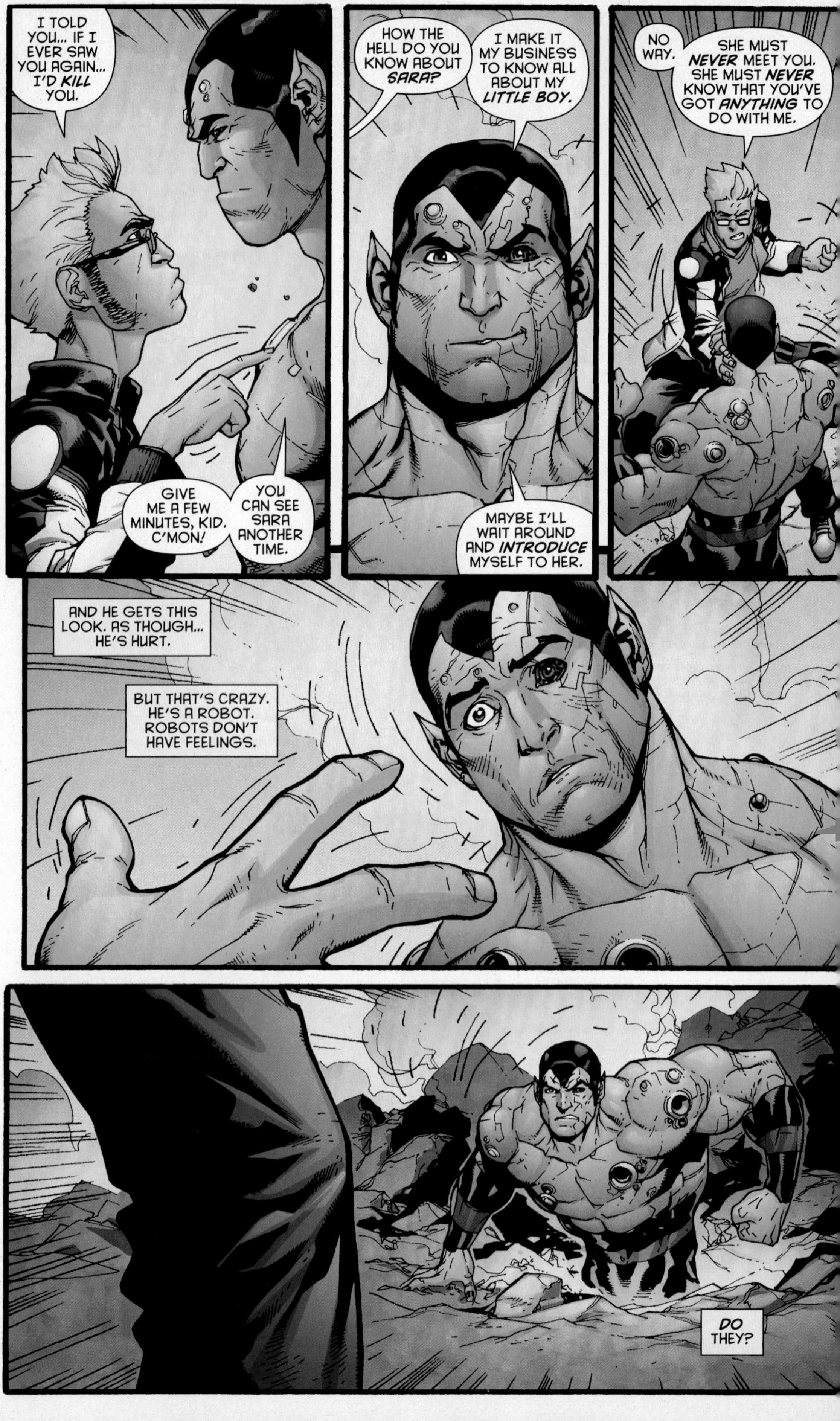

I TOLD YOU... IF I EVER SAW YOU AGAIN... I'D **KILL** YOU.
GIVE ME A FEW MINUTES, KID. C'MON!
YOU CAN SEE SARA ANOTHER TIME.
HOW THE HELL DO YOU KNOW ABOUT **SARA?**
I MAKE IT MY BUSINESS TO KNOW ALL ABOUT MY **LITTLE BOY.**
MAYBE I'LL WAIT AROUND AND **INTRODUCE** MYSELF TO HER.
NO WAY.
SHE MUST **NEVER** MEET YOU. SHE MUST **NEVER** KNOW THAT YOU'VE GOT **ANYTHING** TO DO WITH ME.
AND HE GETS THIS LOOK. AS THOUGH... HE'S HURT.
BUT THAT'S CRAZY. HE'S A ROBOT. ROBOTS DON'T HAVE FEELINGS.
DO THEY?

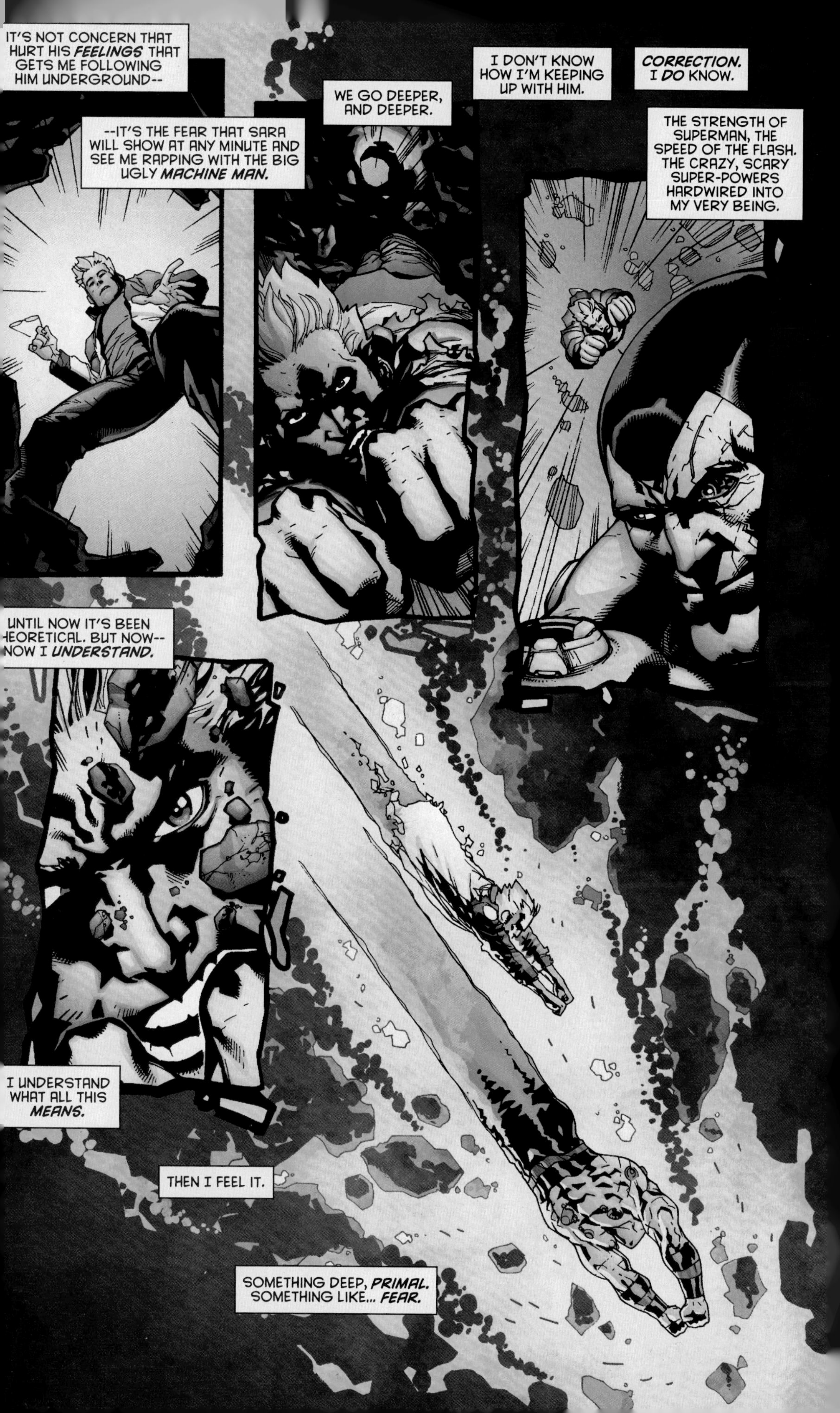
IT'S NOT CONCERN THAT HURT HIS FEELINGS THAT GETS ME FOLLOWING HIM UNDERGROUND--
--IT'S THE FEAR THAT SARA WILL SHOW AT ANY MINUTE AND SEE ME RAPPING WITH THE BIG UGLY MACHINE MAN.
WE GO DEEPER, AND DEEPER.
I DON'T KNOW HOW I'M KEEPING UP WITH HIM.
CORRECTION. I DO KNOW.
THE STRENGTH OF SUPERMAN, THE SPEED OF THE FLASH. THE CRAZY, SCARY SUPER-POWERS HARDWIRED INTO MY VERY BEING.
UNTIL NOW IT'S BEEN HEORETICAL. BUT NOW-- NOW I UNDERSTAND.
I UNDERSTAND WHAT ALL THIS MEANS.
THEN I FEEL IT.
SOMETHING DEEP, PRIMAL. SOMETHING LIKE... FEAR.

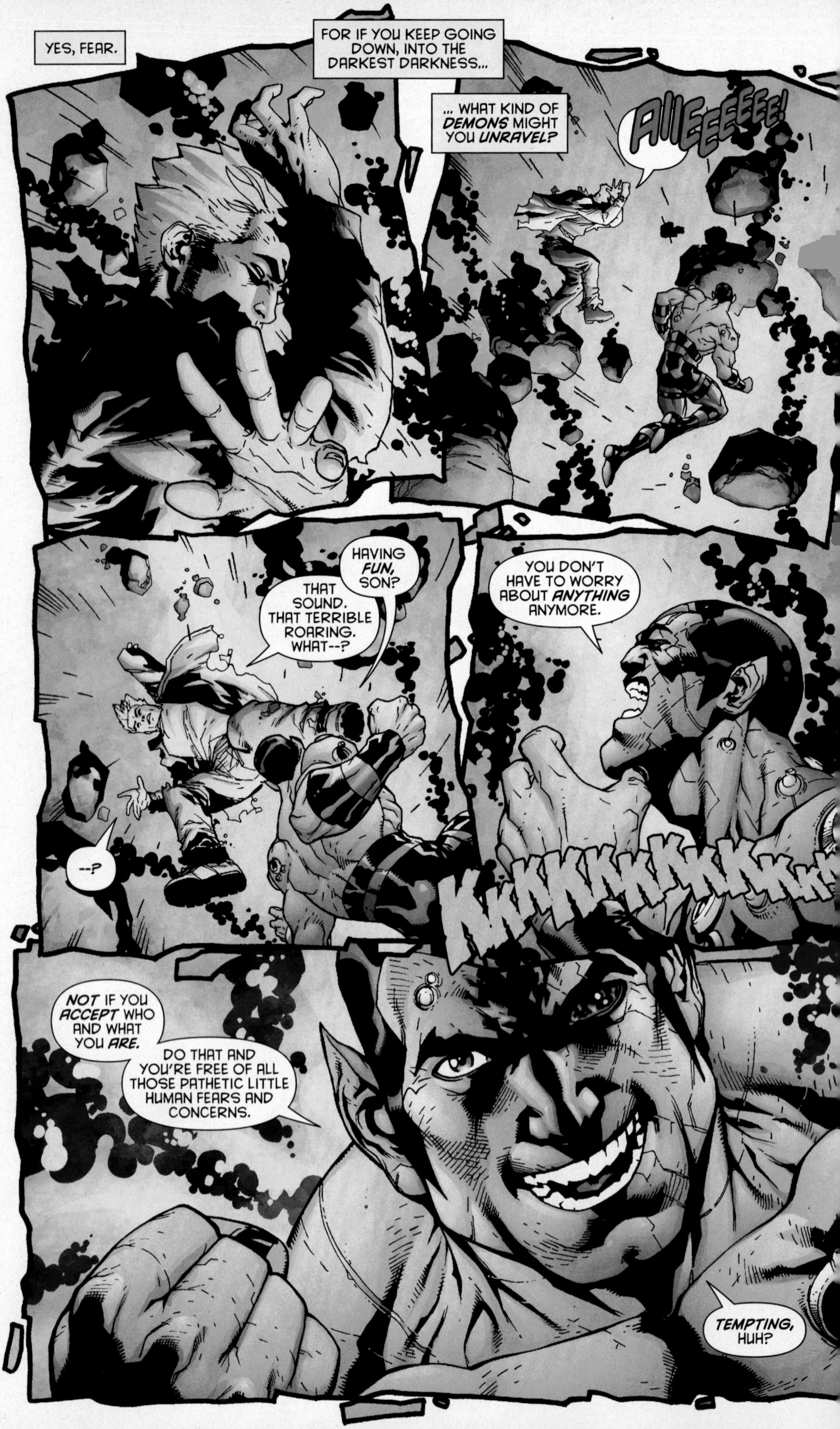
YES, FEAR.
FOR IF YOU KEEP GOING DOWN, INTO THE DARKEST DARKNESS...
... WHAT KIND OF DEMONS MIGHT YOU UNRAVEL?
AIIEEEEEE!
HAVING FUN, SON?
THAT SOUND. THAT TERRIBLE ROARING. WHAT--?
--?
YOU DON'T HAVE TO WORRY ABOUT ANYTHING ANYMORE.
KKKKKKKKKKKK
NOT IF YOU ACCEPT WHO AND WHAT YOU ARE.
DO THAT AND YOU'RE FREE OF ALL THOSE PATHETIC LITTLE HUMAN FEARS AND CONCERNS.
TEMPTING, HUH?

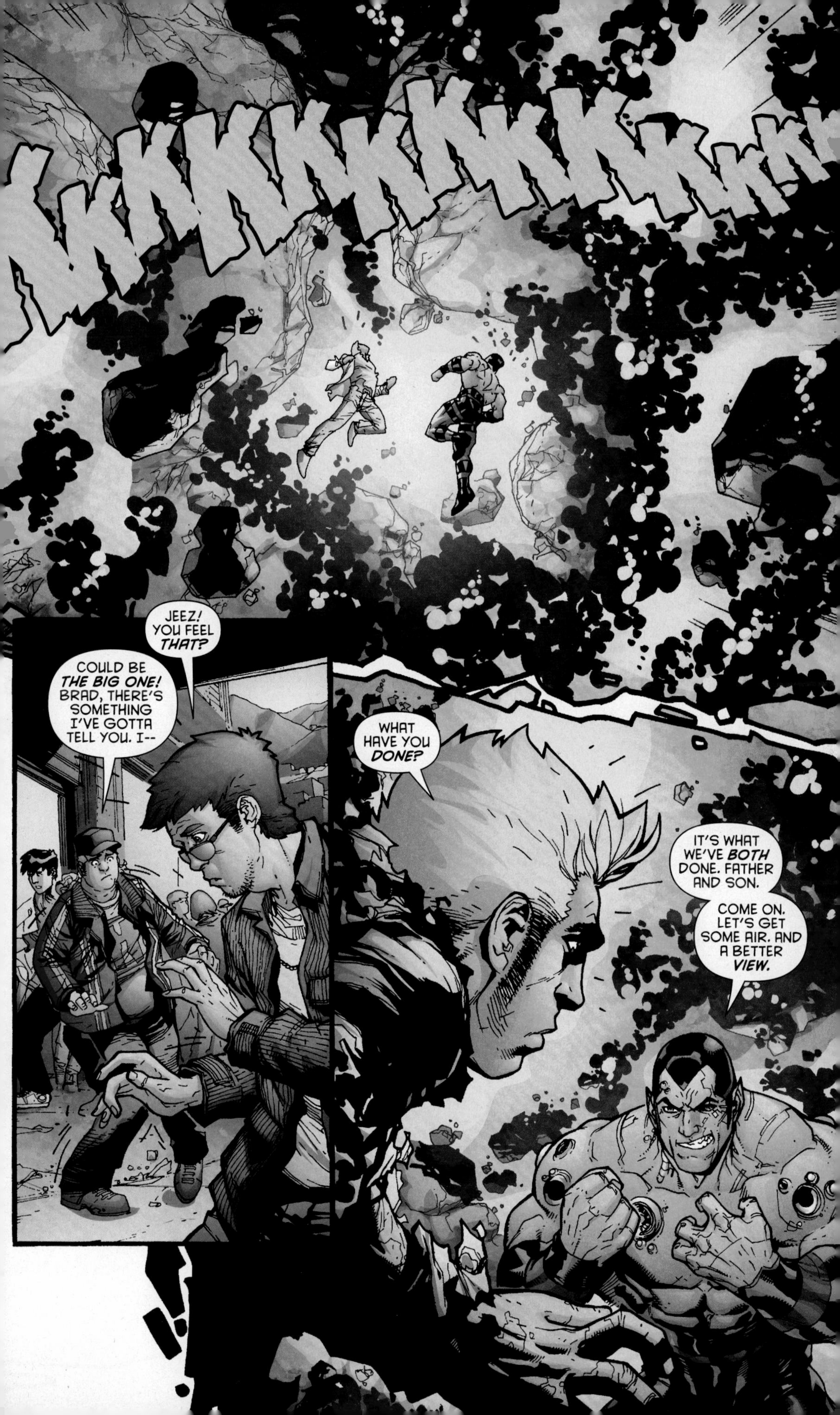
KKKKKKKKKKKKKK
JEEZ! YOU FEEL *THAT?*
COULD BE *THE BIG ONE!* BRAD, THERE'S SOMETHING I'VE GOTTA TELL YOU. I--
WHAT HAVE YOU *DONE?*
IT'S WHAT WE'VE *BOTH* DONE. FATHER AND SON.
COME ON. LET'S GET SOME AIR. AND A BETTER *VIEW.*
!!

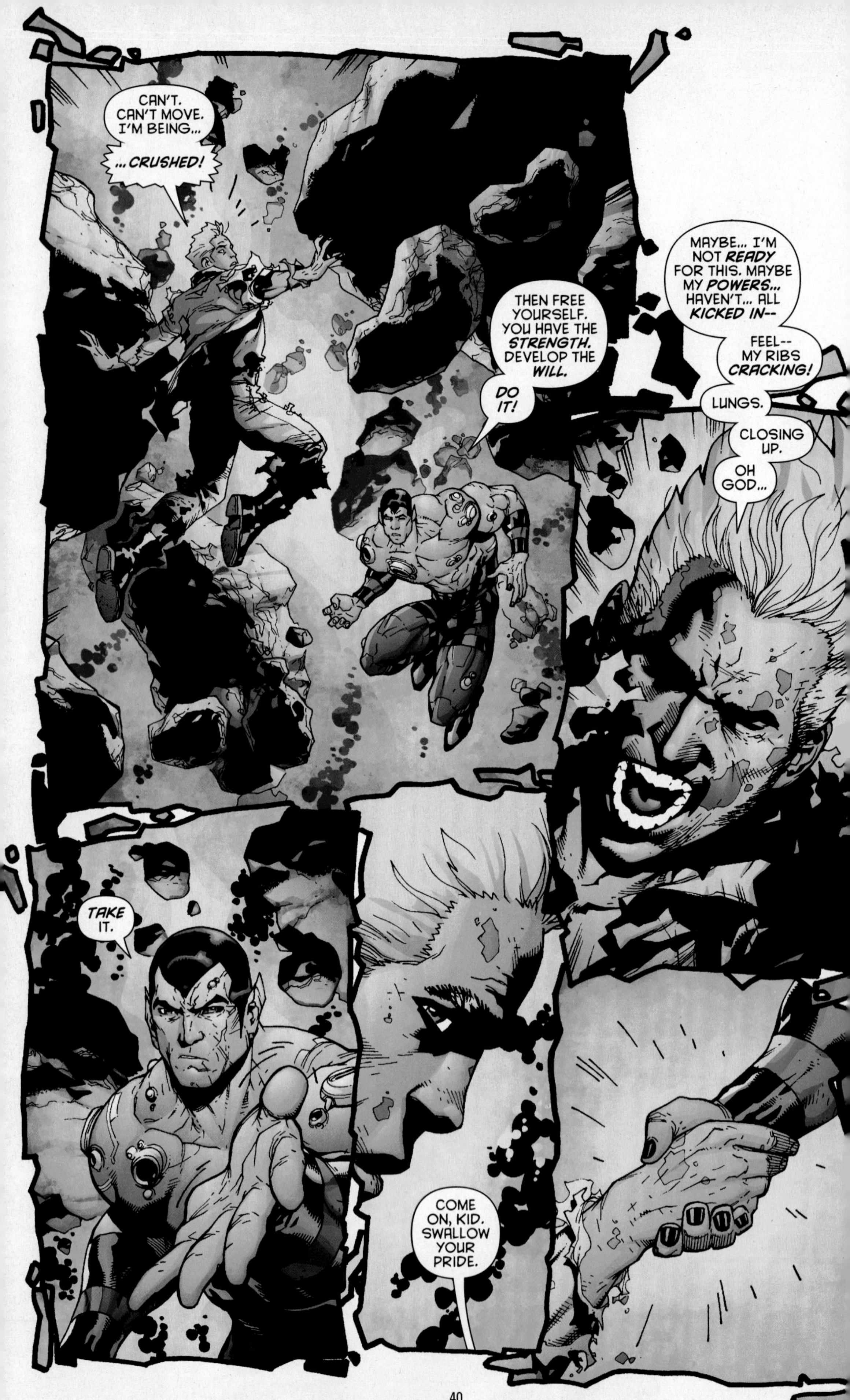
CAN'T. CAN'T MOVE. I'M BEING...
...CRUSHED!
THEN FREE YOURSELF. YOU HAVE THE STRENGTH. DEVELOP THE WILL.
DO IT!
MAYBE... I'M NOT READY FOR THIS. MAYBE MY POWERS... HAVEN'T... ALL KICKED IN--
FEEL-- MY RIBS CRACKING!
LUNGS.
CLOSING UP.
OH GOD...
TAKE IT.
COME ON, KID. SWALLOW YOUR PRIDE.

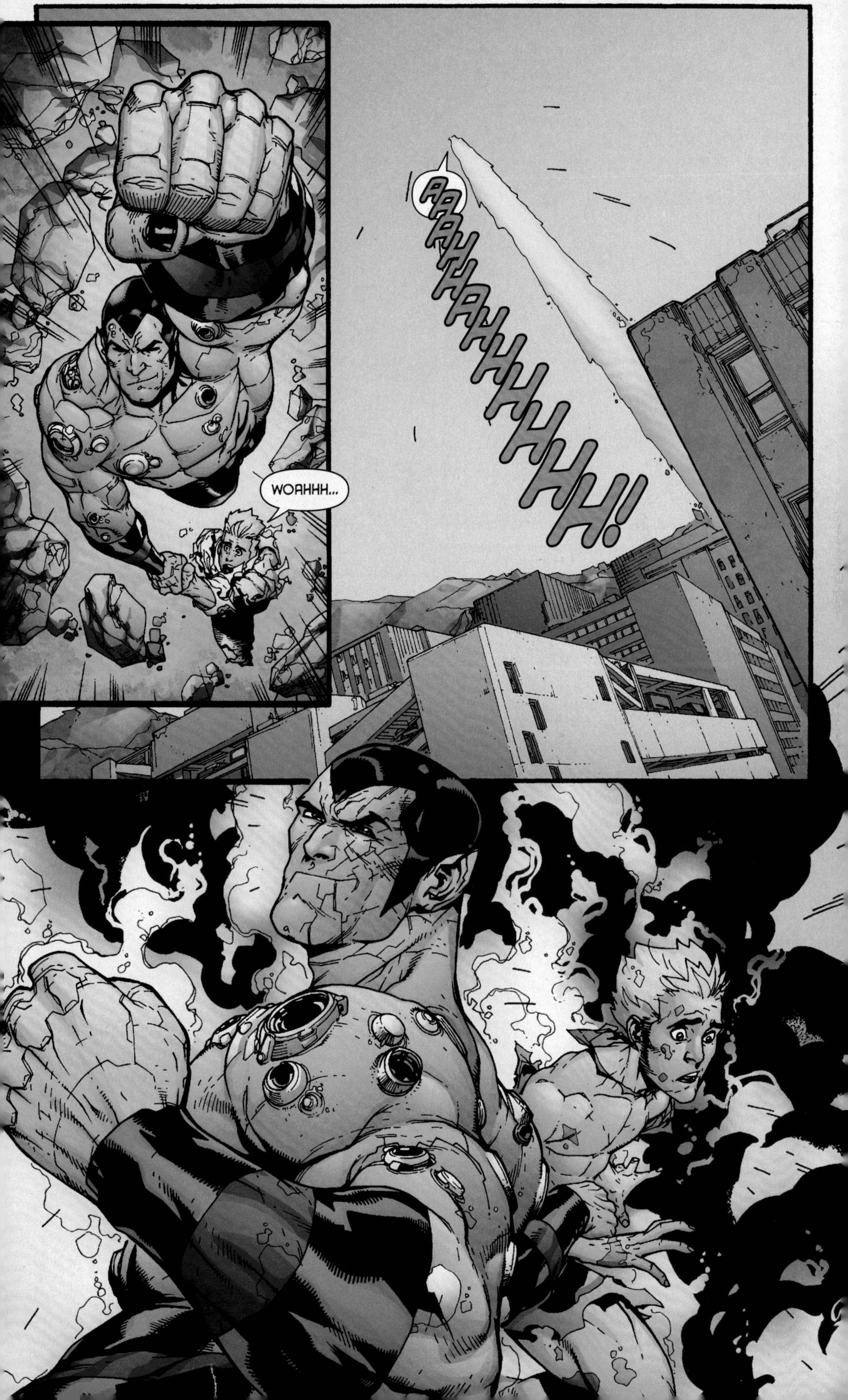
AAAHAHHHHHH!
WOAHHH...

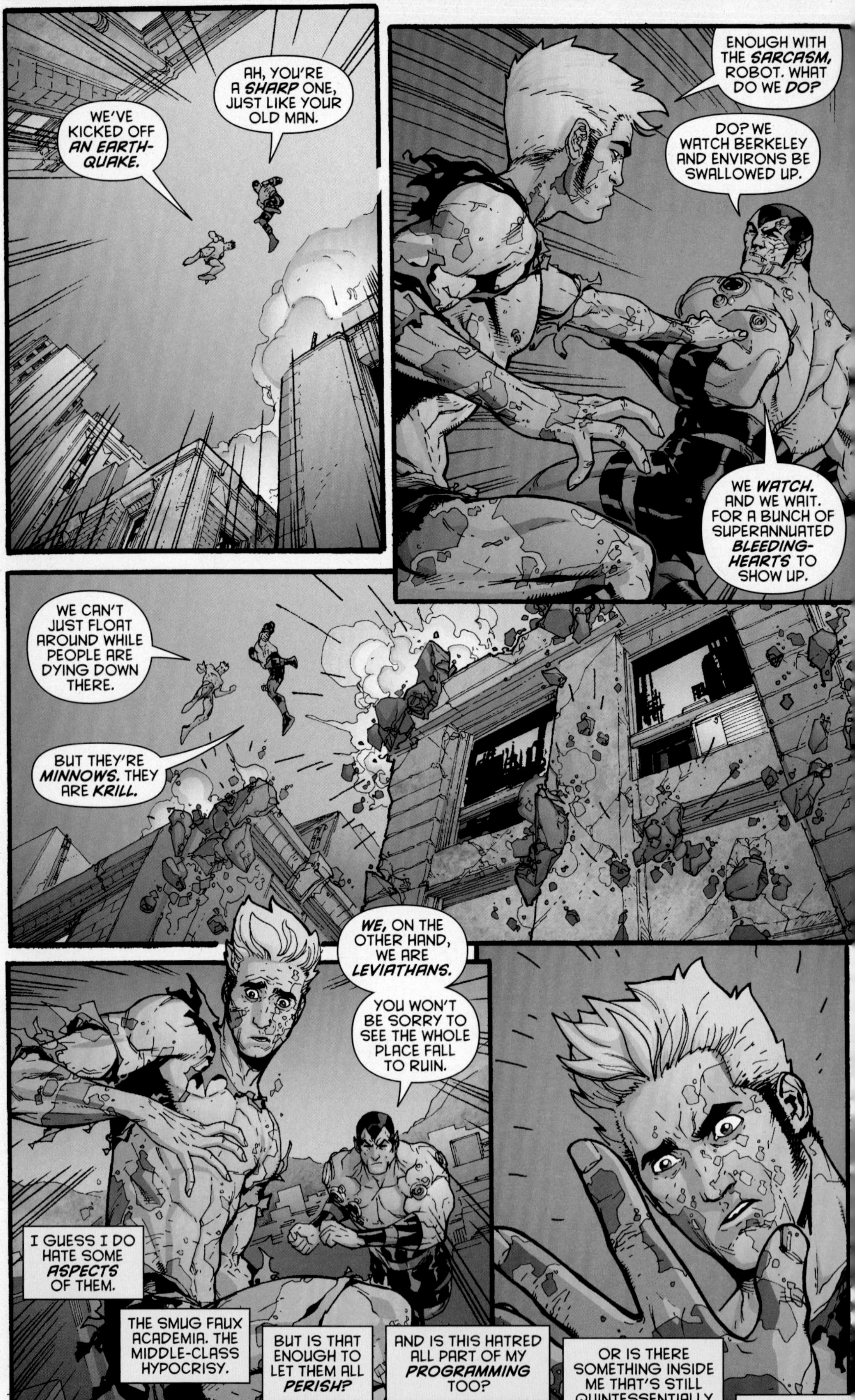
WE'VE KICKED OFF AN EARTH-QUAKE.
AH, YOU'RE A SHARP ONE, JUST LIKE YOUR OLD MAN.
ENOUGH WITH THE SARCASM, ROBOT. WHAT DO WE DO?
DO? WE WATCH BERKELEY AND ENVIRONS BE SWALLOWED UP.
WE WATCH. AND WE WAIT. FOR A BUNCH OF SUPERANNUATED BLEEDING-HEARTS TO SHOW UP.
WE CAN'T JUST FLOAT AROUND WHILE PEOPLE ARE DYING DOWN THERE.
BUT THEY'RE MINNOWS. THEY ARE KRILL.
WE, ON THE OTHER HAND, WE ARE LEVIATHANS.
YOU WON'T BE SORRY TO SEE THE WHOLE PLACE FALL TO RUIN.
I GUESS I DO HATE SOME ASPECTS OF THEM.
THE SMUG FAUX ACADEMIA. THE MIDDLE-CLASS HYPOCRISY.
BUT IS THAT ENOUGH TO LET THEM ALL PERISH?
AND IS THIS HATRED ALL PART OF MY PROGRAMMING TOO?
OR IS THERE SOMETHING INSIDE ME THAT'S STILL QUINTESSENTIALLY FRANK HALLORAN.
INVIOLABLY ME

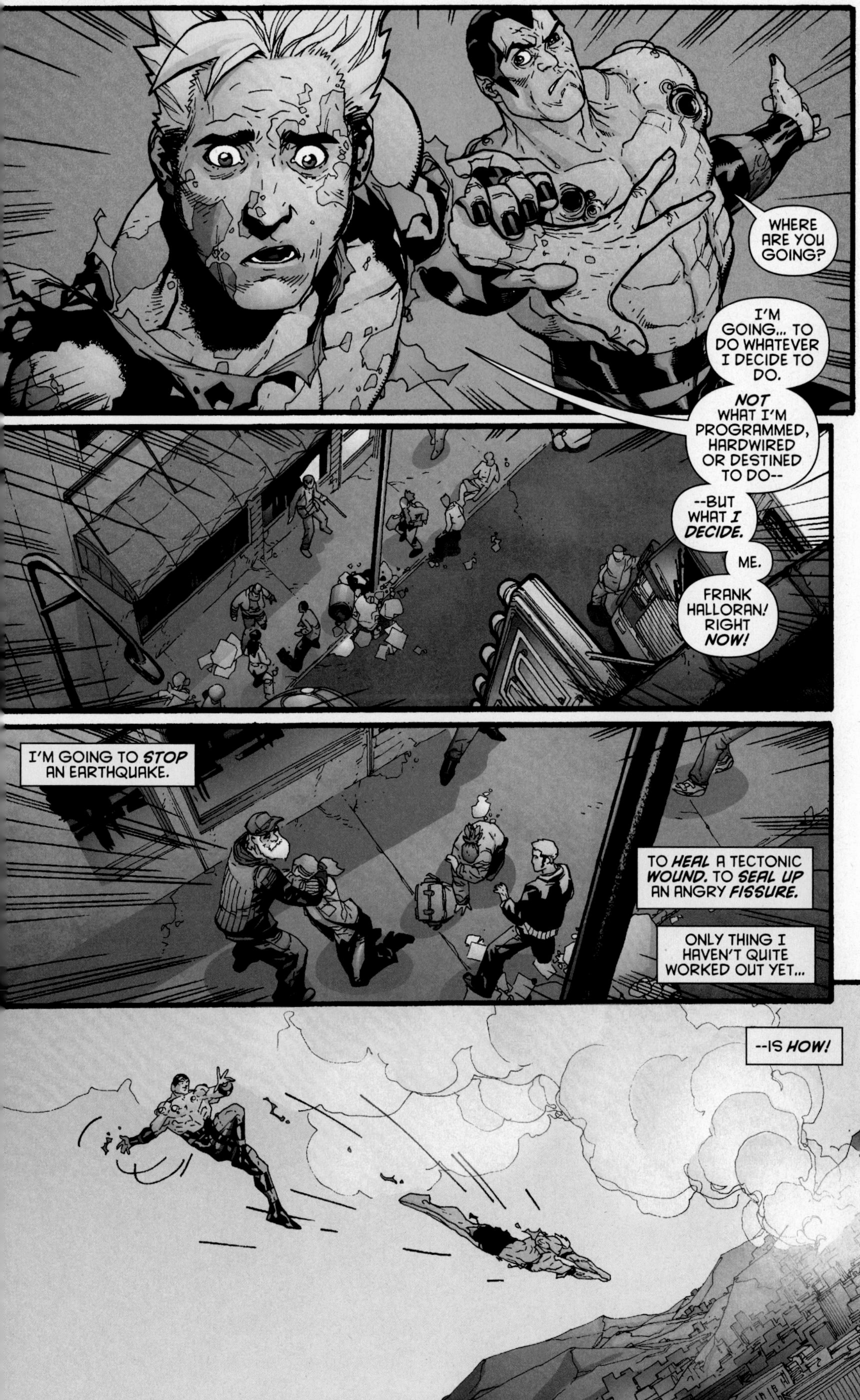
WHERE ARE YOU GOING?
I'M GOING... TO DO WHATEVER I DECIDE TO DO.
NOT WHAT I'M PROGRAMMED, HARDWIRED OR DESTINED TO DO--
--BUT WHAT I DECIDE.
ME.
FRANK HALLORAN! RIGHT NOW!
I'M GOING TO STOP AN EARTHQUAKE.
TO HEAL A TECTONIC WOUND. TO SEAL UP AN ANGRY FISSURE.
ONLY THING I HAVEN'T QUITE WORKED OUT YET...
--IS HOW!

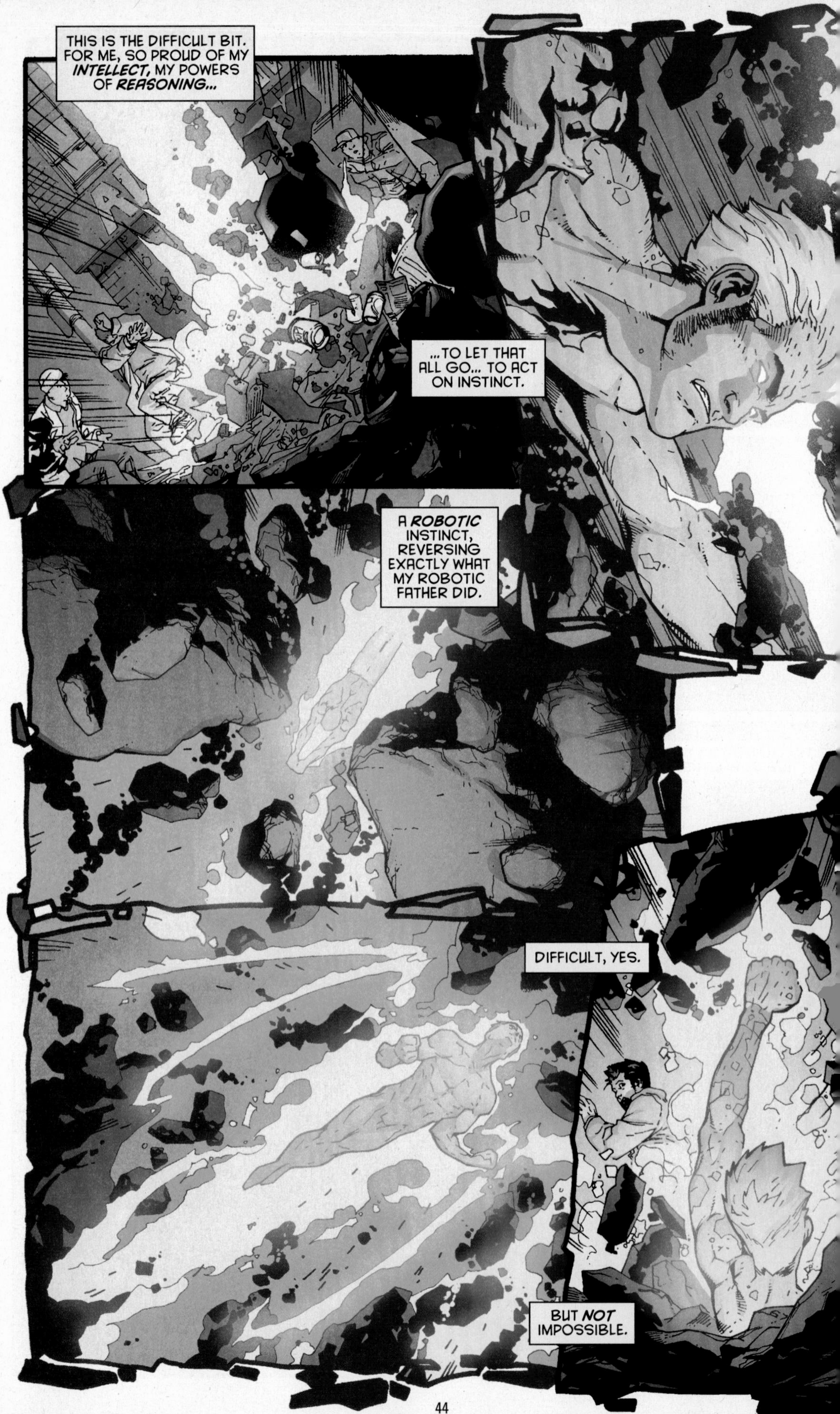
THIS IS THE DIFFICULT BIT. FOR ME, SO PROUD OF MY *INTELLECT,* MY POWERS OF *REASONING...*
...TO LET THAT ALL GO... TO ACT ON INSTINCT.
A *ROBOTIC* INSTINCT, REVERSING EXACTLY WHAT MY ROBOTIC FATHER DID.
DIFFICULT, YES.
BUT *NOT* IMPOSSIBLE.

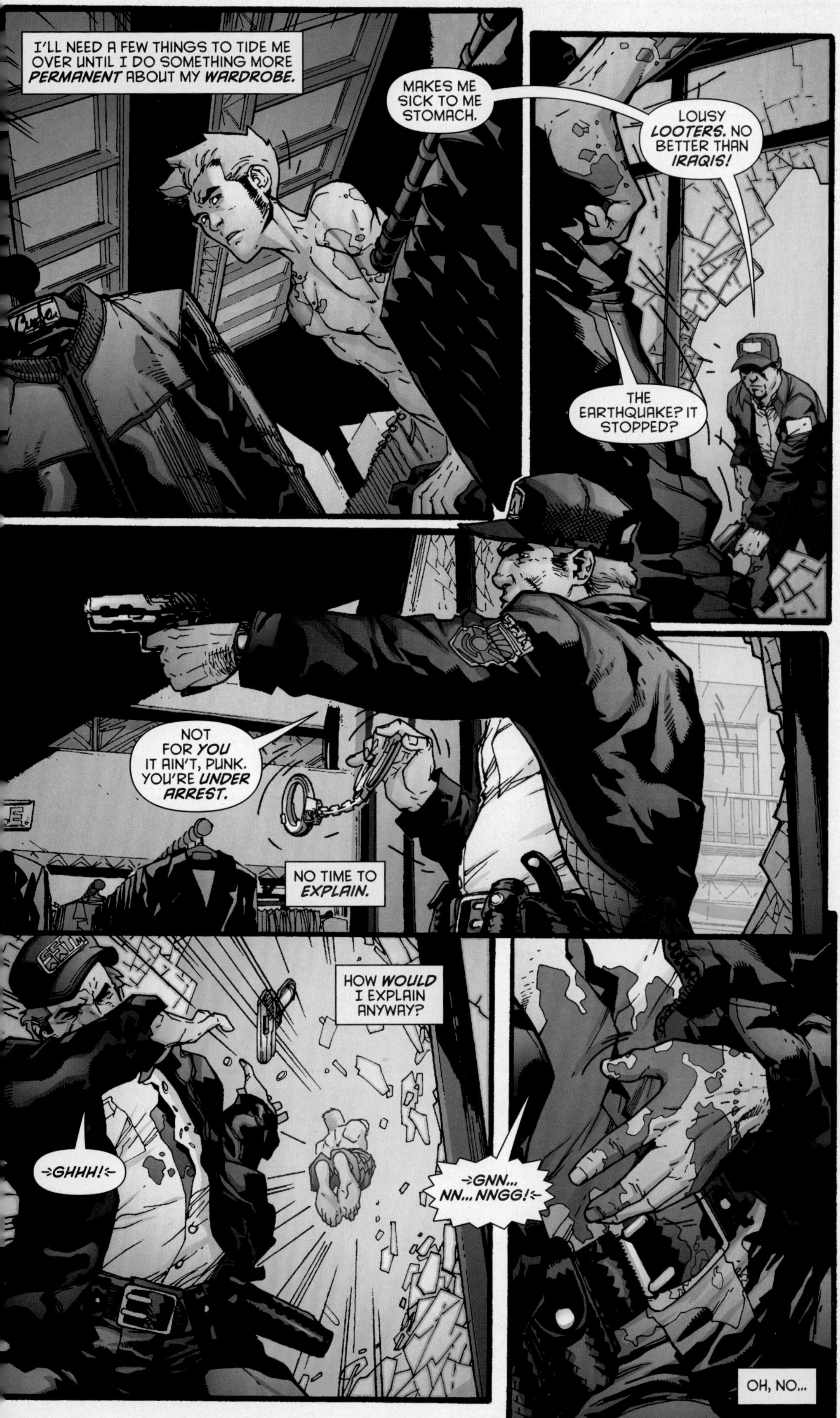

I'LL NEED A FEW THINGS TO TIDE ME OVER UNTIL I DO SOMETHING MORE PERMANENT ABOUT MY WARDROBE.
MAKES ME SICK TO ME STOMACH.
LOUSY LOOTERS. NO BETTER THAN IRAQIS!
THE EARTHQUAKE? IT STOPPED?
NOT FOR YOU IT AIN'T, PUNK. YOU'RE UNDER ARREST.
NO TIME TO EXPLAIN.
HOW WOULD I EXPLAIN ANYWAY?
GHHH!
GNN... NN... NNGG!
OH, NO...

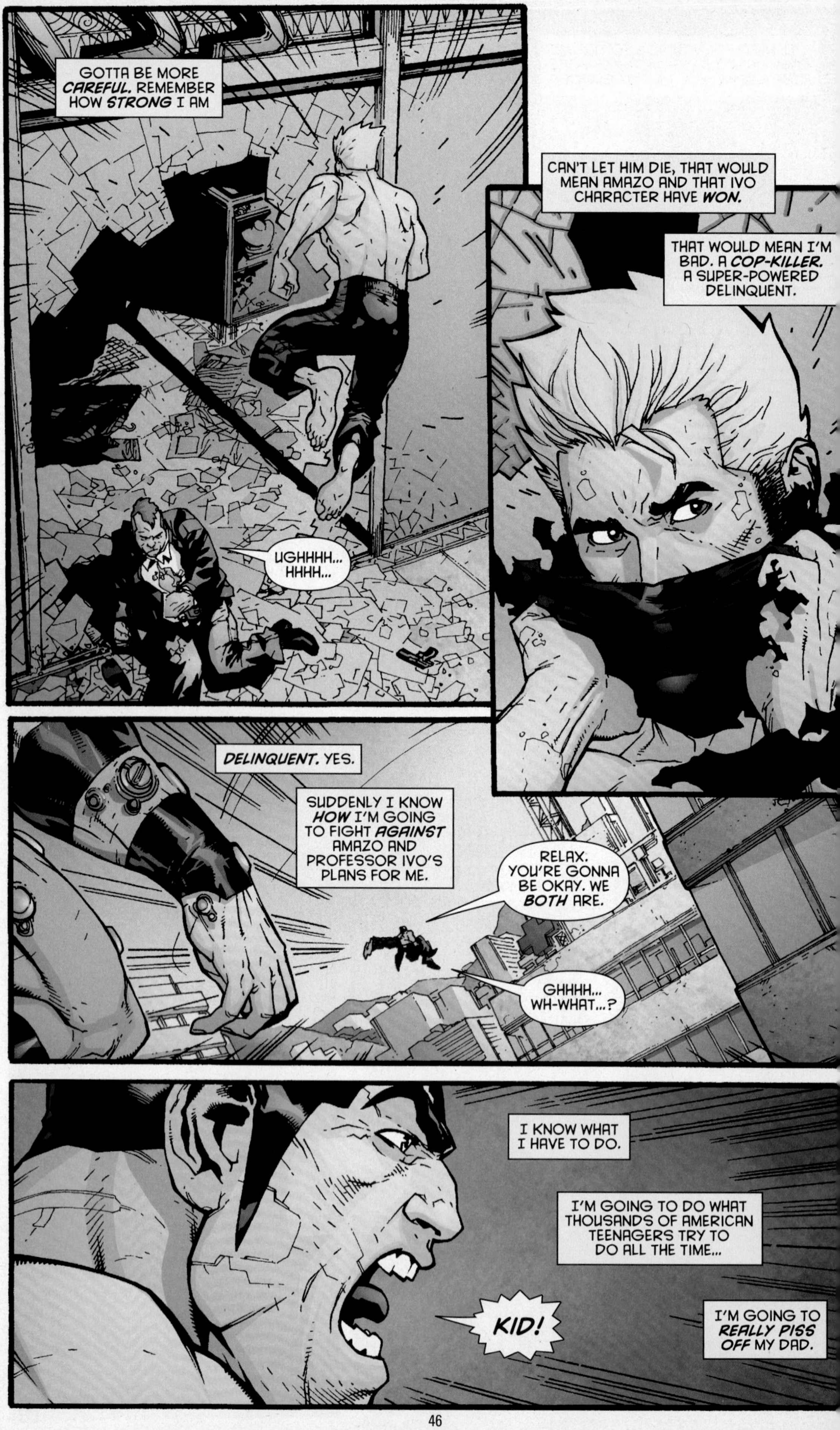
GOTTA BE MORE CAREFUL. REMEMBER HOW STRONG I AM
UGHHHH... HHHH...
CAN'T LET HIM DIE, THAT WOULD MEAN AMAZO AND THAT IVO CHARACTER HAVE WON.
THAT WOULD MEAN I'M BAD. A COP-KILLER. A SUPER-POWERED DELINQUENT.
DELINQUENT. YES.
SUDDENLY I KNOW HOW I'M GOING TO FIGHT AGAINST AMAZO AND PROFESSOR IVO'S PLANS FOR ME.
RELAX. YOU'RE GONNA BE OKAY. WE BOTH ARE.
GHHHH... WH-WHAT...?
I KNOW WHAT I HAVE TO DO.
I'M GOING TO DO WHAT THOUSANDS OF AMERICAN TEENAGERS TRY TO DO ALL THE TIME...
KID!
I'M GOING TO REALLY PISS OFF MY DAD.

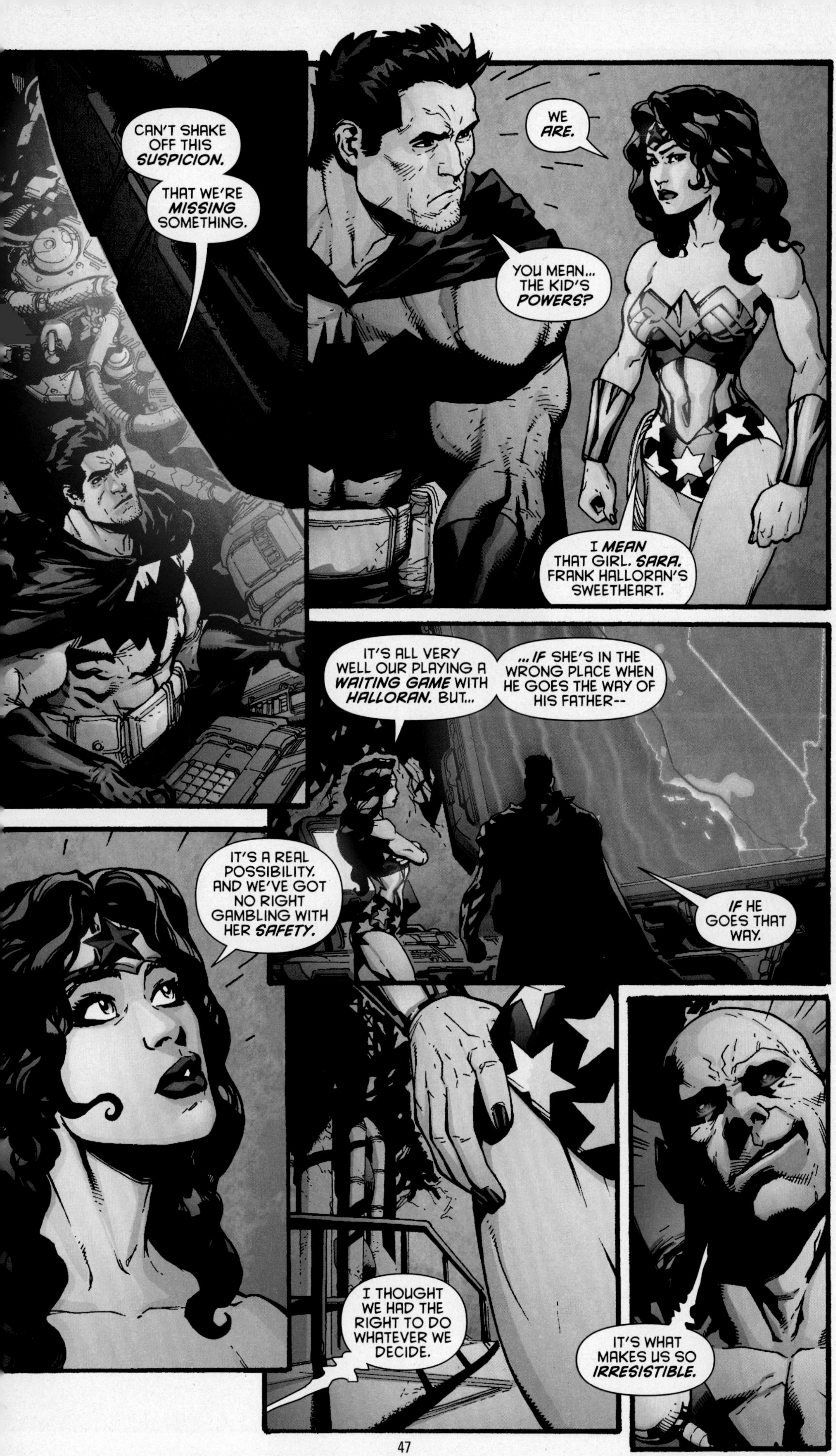
CAN'T SHAKE OFF THIS SUSPICION.
THAT WE'RE MISSING SOMETHING.
WE ARE.
YOU MEAN... THE KID'S POWERS?
I MEAN THAT GIRL. SARA. FRANK HALLORAN'S SWEETHEART.
IT'S ALL VERY WELL OUR PLAYING A WAITING GAME WITH HALLORAN. BUT...
...IF SHE'S IN THE WRONG PLACE WHEN HE GOES THE WAY OF HIS FATHER--
IF HE GOES THAT WAY.
IT'S A REAL POSSIBILITY. AND WE'VE GOT NO RIGHT GAMBLING WITH HER SAFETY.
I THOUGHT WE HAD THE RIGHT TO DO WHATEVER WE DECIDE.
IT'S WHAT MAKES US SO IRRESISTIBLE.

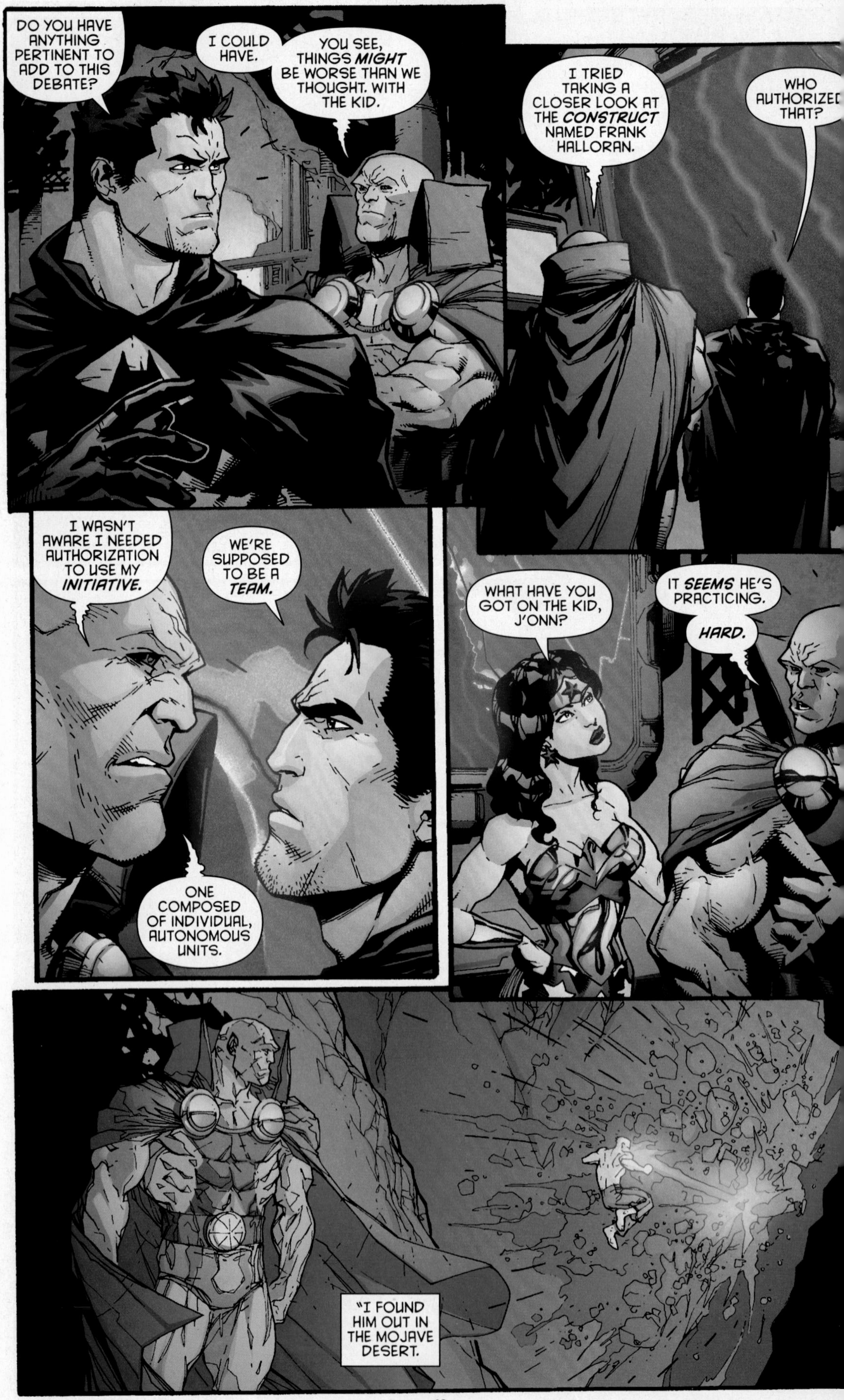
DO YOU HAVE ANYTHING PERTINENT TO ADD TO THIS DEBATE?
I COULD HAVE.
YOU SEE, THINGS *MIGHT* BE WORSE THAN WE THOUGHT. WITH THE KID.
I TRIED TAKING A CLOSER LOOK AT THE *CONSTRUCT* NAMED FRANK HALLORAN.
WHO AUTHORIZED THAT?
I WASN'T AWARE I NEEDED AUTHORIZATION TO USE MY *INITIATIVE.*
WE'RE SUPPOSED TO BE A *TEAM.*
ONE COMPOSED OF INDIVIDUAL, AUTONOMOUS UNITS.
WHAT HAVE YOU GOT ON THE KID, J'ONN?
IT *SEEMS* HE'S PRACTICING.
HARD.
"I FOUND HIM OUT IN THE MOJAVE DESERT.

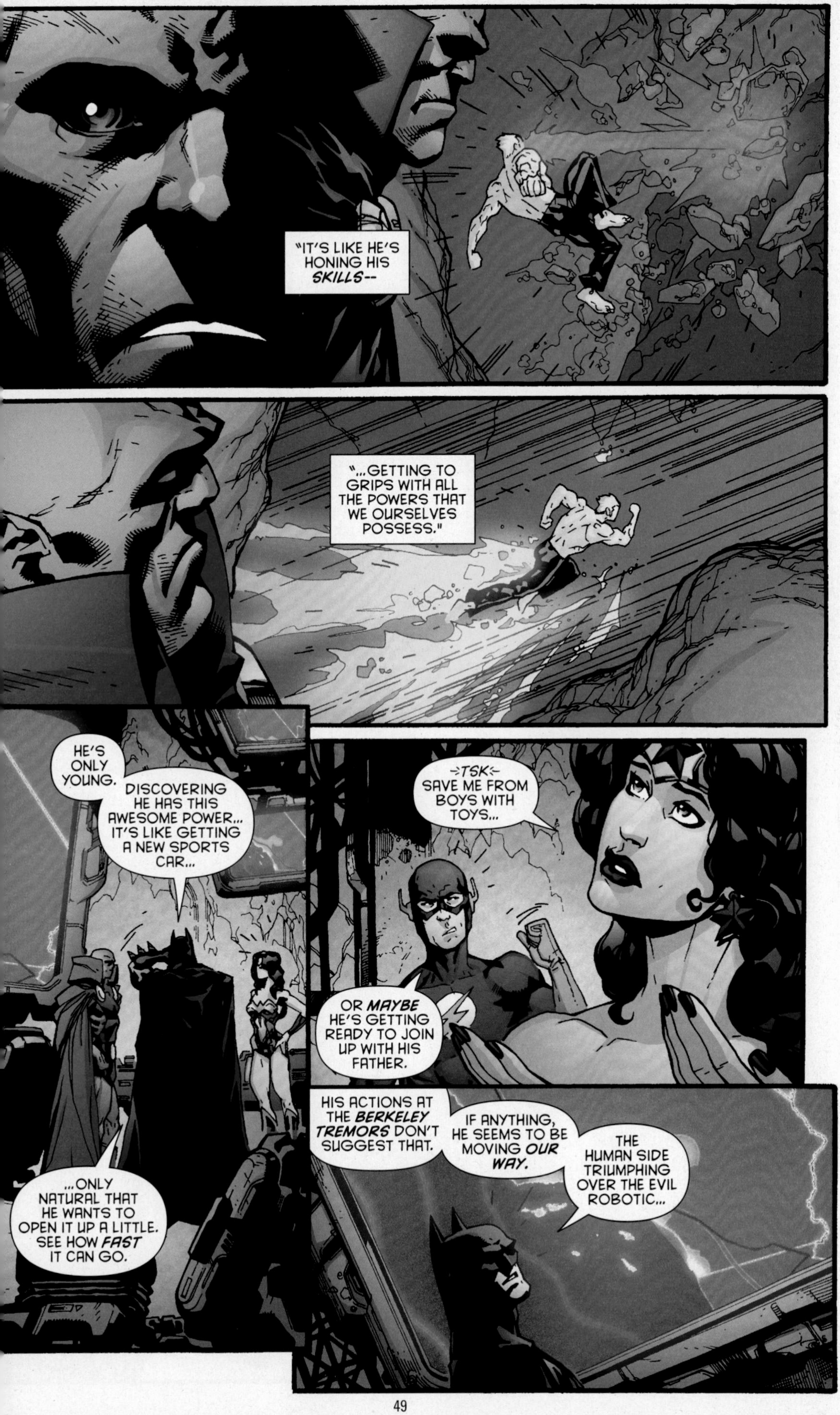

"IT'S LIKE HE'S HONING HIS SKILLS--
"...GETTING TO GRIPS WITH ALL THE POWERS THAT WE OURSELVES POSSESS."
HE'S ONLY YOUNG.
DISCOVERING HE HAS THIS AWESOME POWER... IT'S LIKE GETTING A NEW SPORTS CAR...
...ONLY NATURAL THAT HE WANTS TO OPEN IT UP A LITTLE. SEE HOW FAST IT CAN GO.
-TSK- SAVE ME FROM BOYS WITH TOYS...
OR MAYBE HE'S GETTING READY TO JOIN UP WITH HIS FATHER.
HIS ACTIONS AT THE BERKELEY TREMORS DON'T SUGGEST THAT.
IF ANYTHING, HE SEEMS TO BE MOVING OUR WAY.
THE HUMAN SIDE TRIUMPHING OVER THE EVIL ROBOTIC...

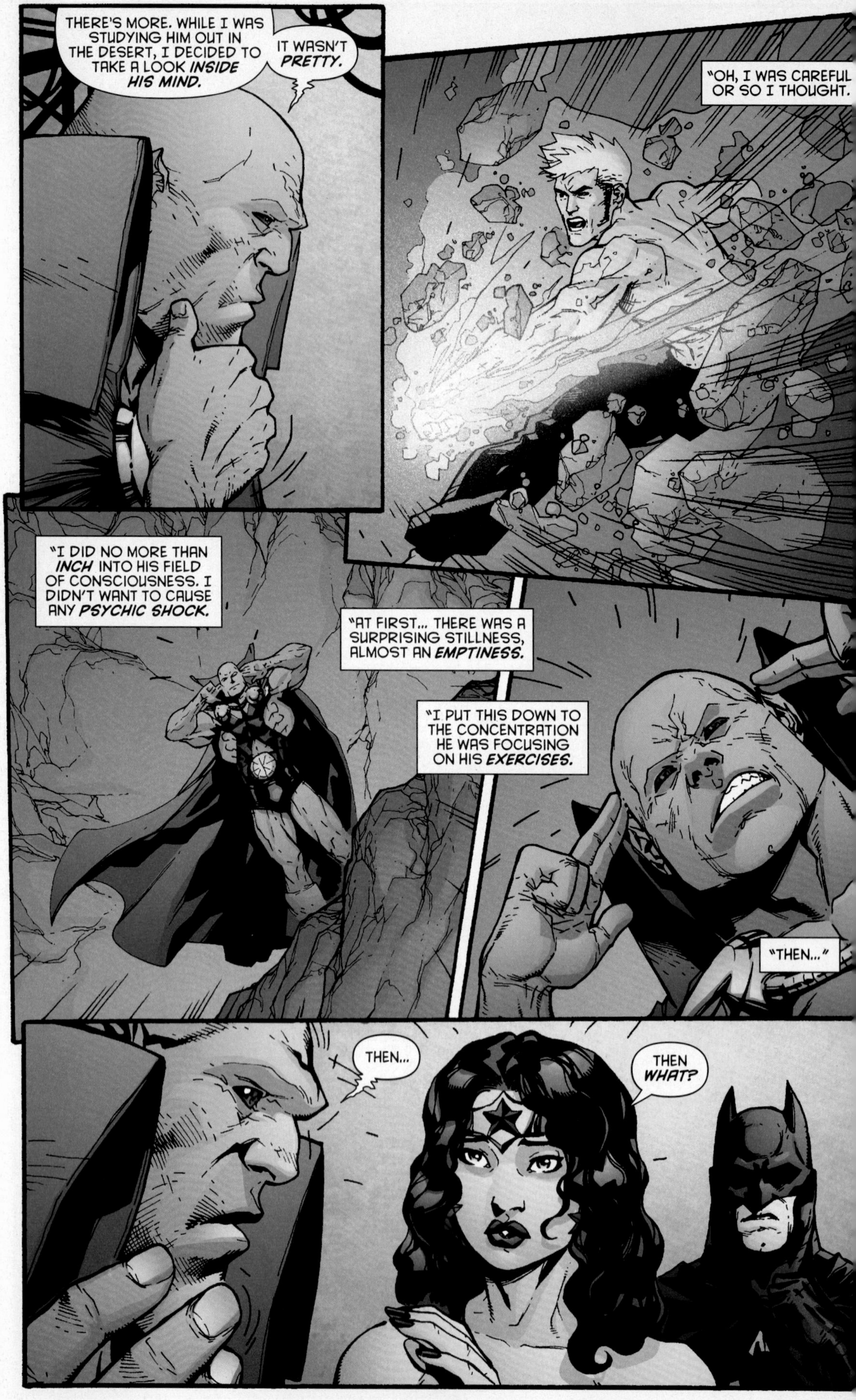
THERE'S MORE. WHILE I WAS STUDYING HIM OUT IN THE DESERT, I DECIDED TO TAKE A LOOK *INSIDE HIS MIND.*
IT WASN'T *PRETTY.*
"OH, I WAS CAREFUL OR SO I THOUGHT.
"I DID NO MORE THAN *INCH* INTO HIS FIELD OF CONSCIOUSNESS. I DIDN'T WANT TO CAUSE ANY *PSYCHIC SHOCK.*
"AT FIRST... THERE WAS A SURPRISING STILLNESS, ALMOST AN *EMPTINESS.*
"I PUT THIS DOWN TO THE CONCENTRATION HE WAS FOCUSING ON HIS *EXERCISES.*
"THEN..."
THEN...
THEN *WHAT?*

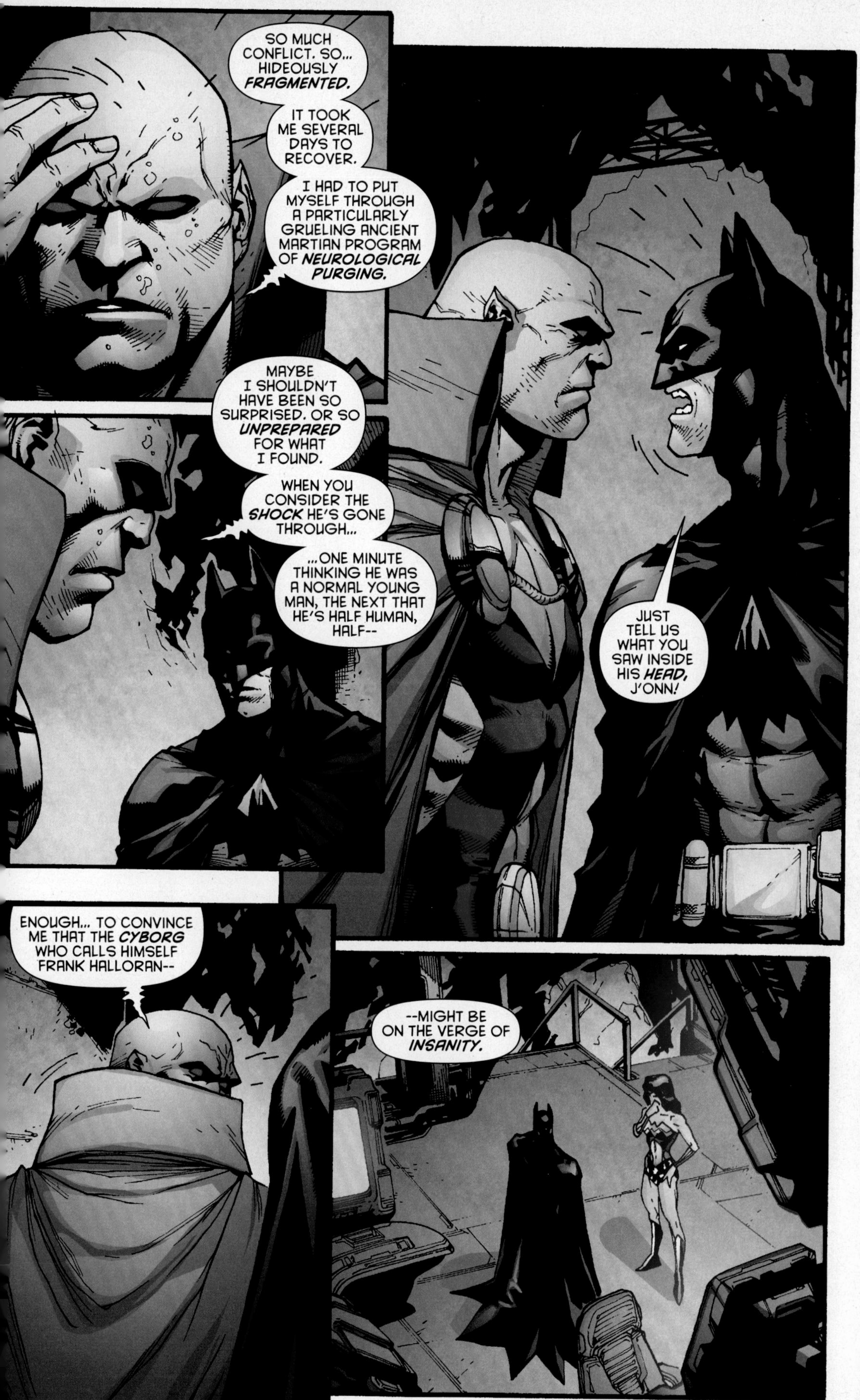
SO MUCH CONFLICT. SO... HIDEOUSLY *FRAGMENTED.*
IT TOOK ME SEVERAL DAYS TO RECOVER.
I HAD TO PUT MYSELF THROUGH A PARTICULARLY GRUELING ANCIENT MARTIAN PROGRAM OF *NEUROLOGICAL PURGING.*
MAYBE I SHOULDN'T HAVE BEEN SO SURPRISED. OR SO *UNPREPARED* FOR WHAT I FOUND.
WHEN YOU CONSIDER THE *SHOCK* HE'S GONE THROUGH...
...ONE MINUTE THINKING HE WAS A NORMAL YOUNG MAN, THE NEXT THAT HE'S HALF HUMAN, HALF--
JUST TELL US WHAT YOU SAW INSIDE HIS *HEAD,* J'ONN!
ENOUGH... TO CONVINCE ME THAT THE *CYBORG* WHO CALLS HIMSELF FRANK HALLORAN--
--MIGHT BE ON THE VERGE OF *INSANITY.*

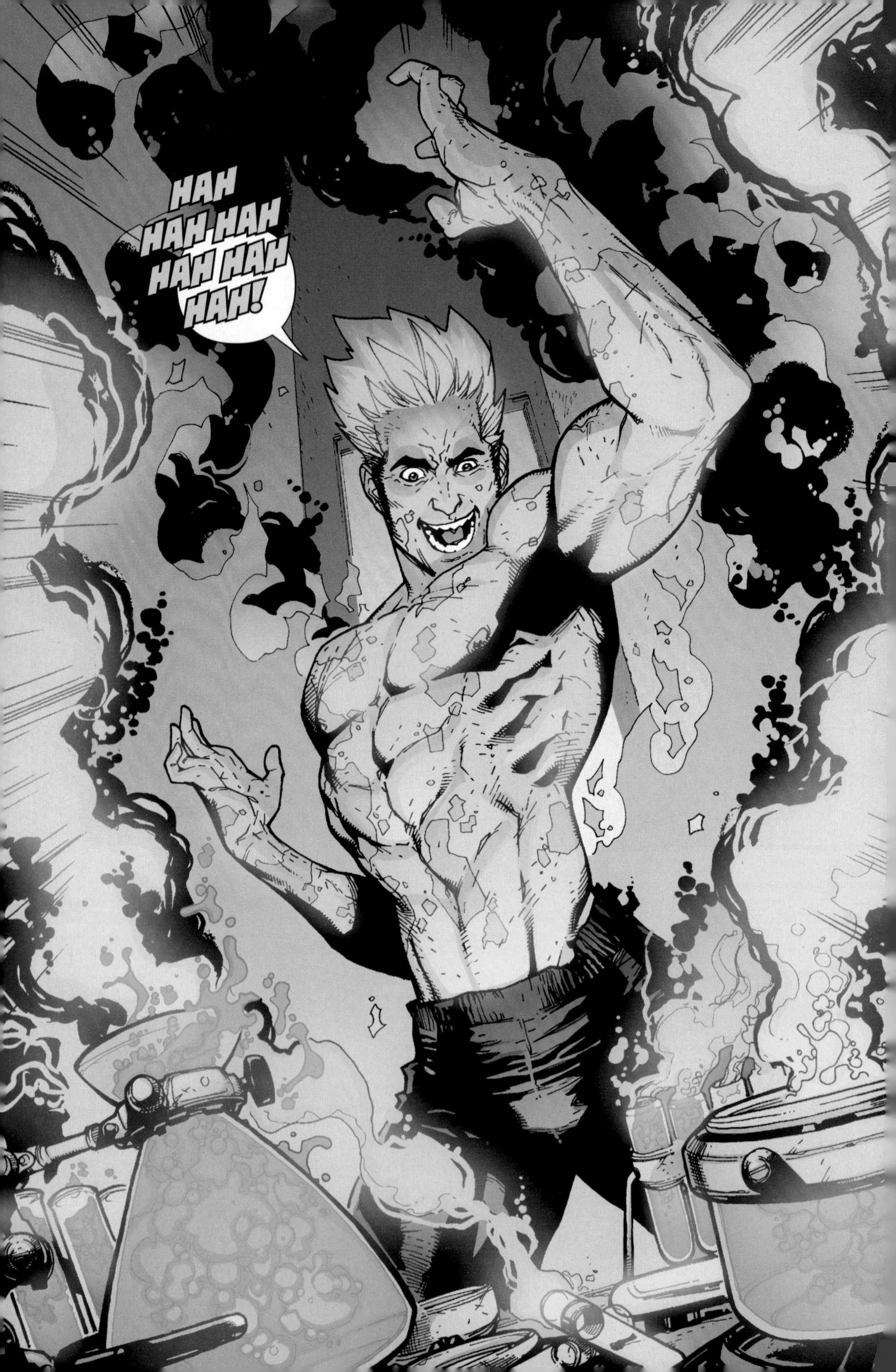
HAH HAH HAH HAH HAH HAH!

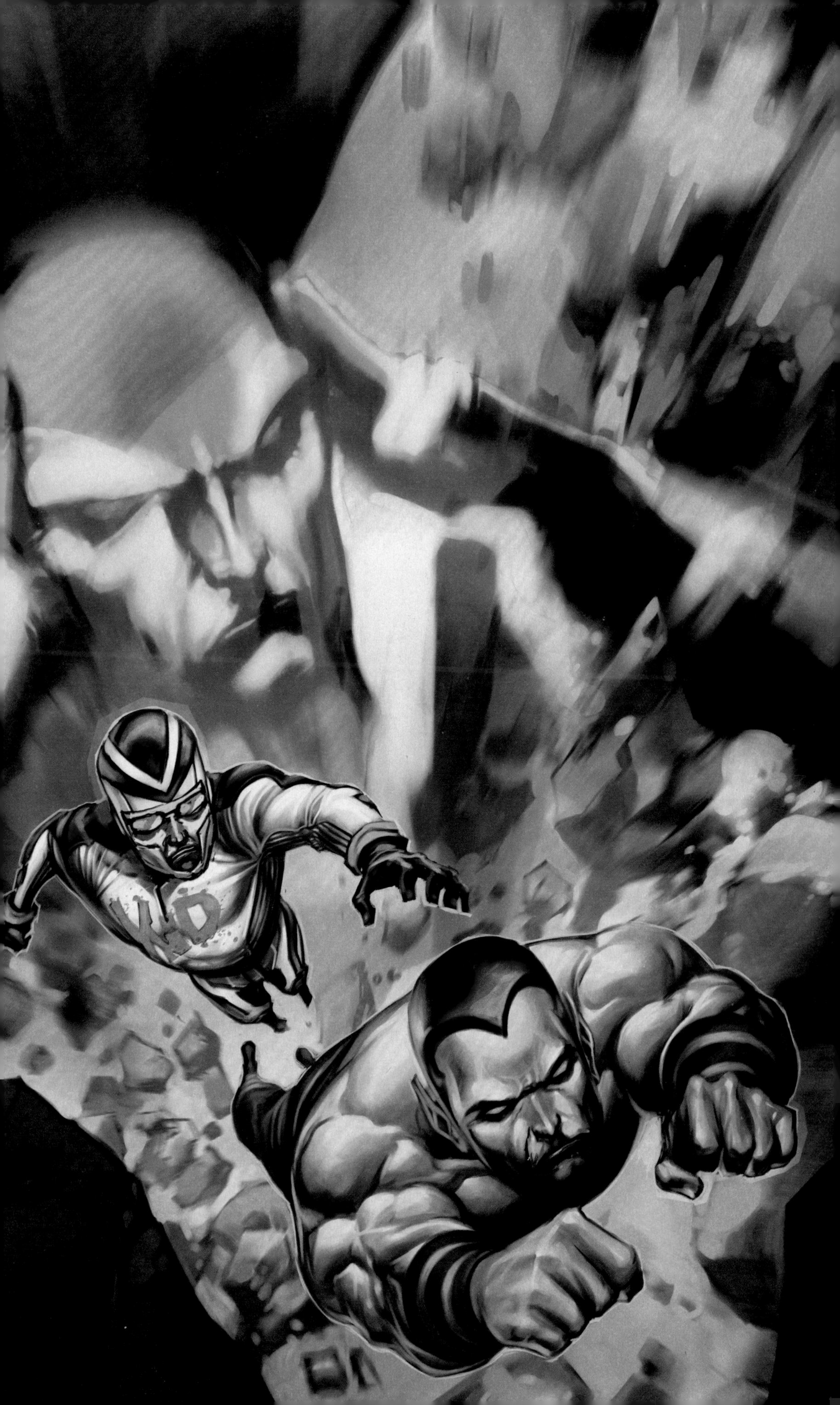

Chapter Three
THE BIRTH OF TRAGEDY!

COVER ART BY HOWARD PORTER

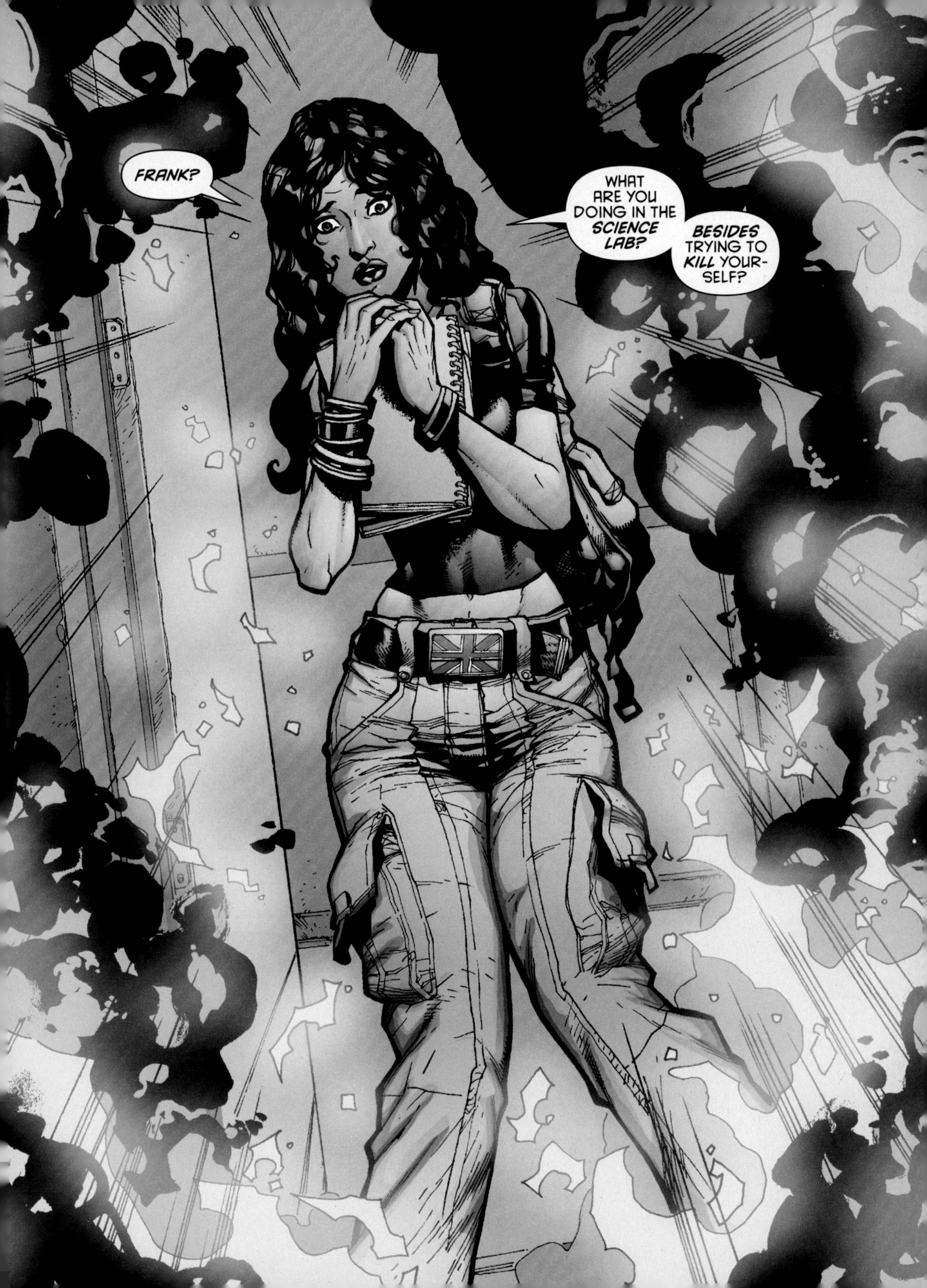

FRANK?
WHAT ARE YOU DOING IN THE SCIENCE LAB?
BESIDES TRYING TO KILL YOUR-SELF?

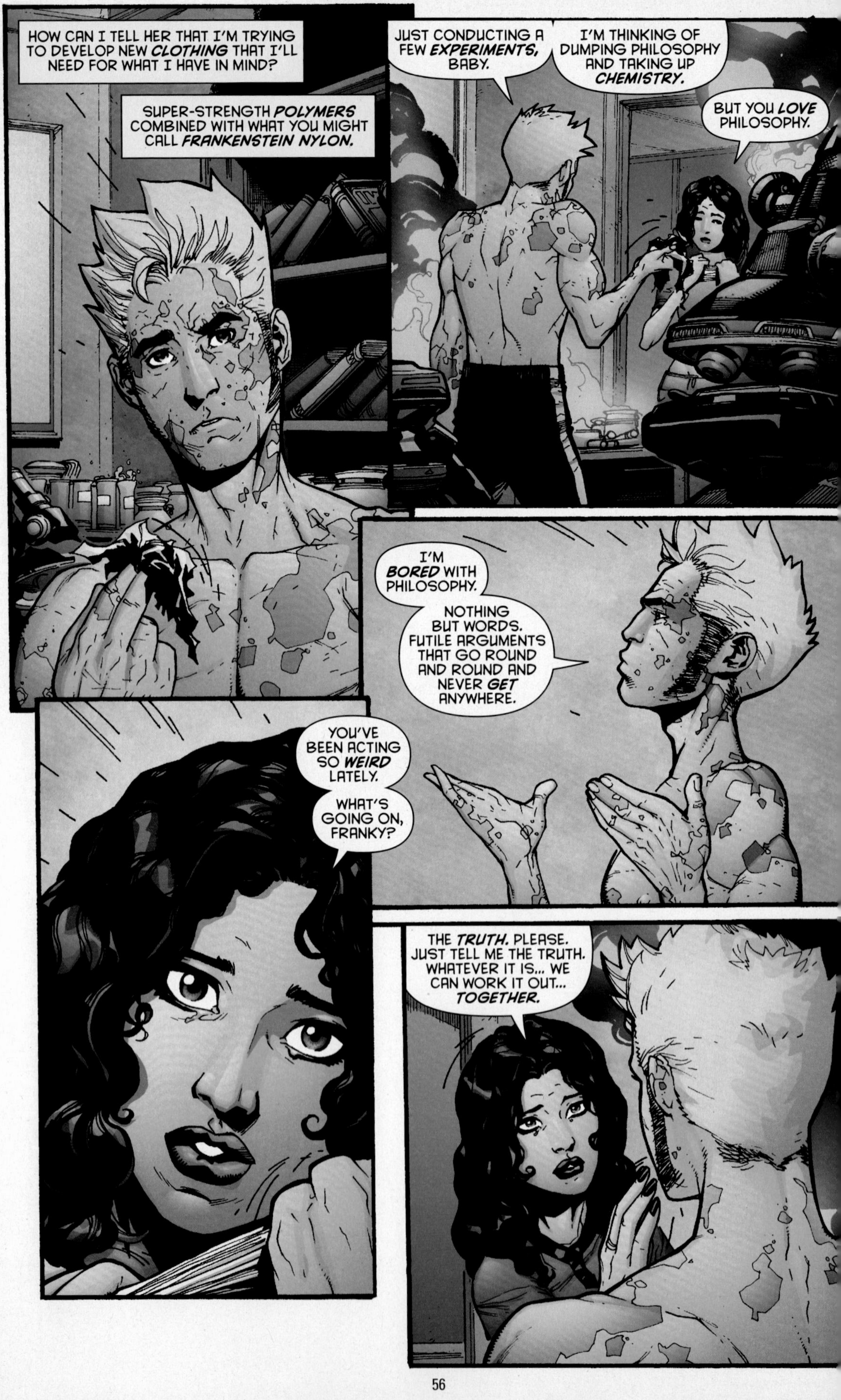

HOW CAN I TELL HER THAT I'M TRYING TO DEVELOP NEW *CLOTHING* THAT I'LL NEED FOR WHAT I HAVE IN MIND?
SUPER-STRENGTH *POLYMERS* COMBINED WITH WHAT YOU MIGHT CALL *FRANKENSTEIN NYLON.*
JUST CONDUCTING A FEW *EXPERIMENTS,* BABY.
I'M THINKING OF DUMPING PHILOSOPHY AND TAKING UP *CHEMISTRY.*
BUT YOU *LOVE* PHILOSOPHY.
I'M *BORED* WITH PHILOSOPHY.
NOTHING BUT WORDS. FUTILE ARGUMENTS THAT GO ROUND AND ROUND AND NEVER *GET* ANYWHERE.
YOU'VE BEEN ACTING SO *WEIRD* LATELY.
WHAT'S GOING ON, FRANKY?
THE *TRUTH.* PLEASE. JUST TELL ME THE TRUTH. WHATEVER IT IS... WE CAN WORK IT OUT... *TOGETHER.*

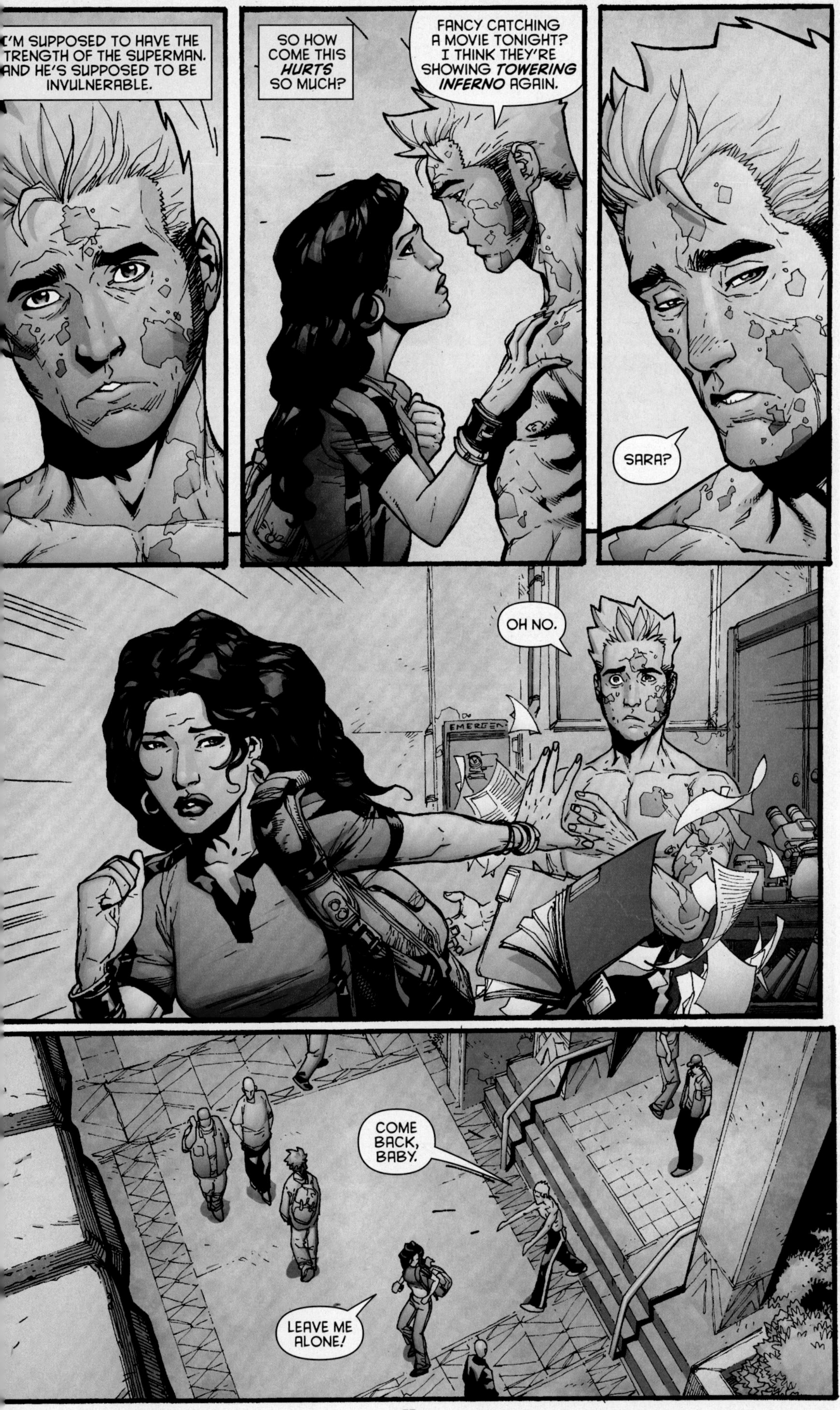

I'M SUPPOSED TO HAVE THE STRENGTH OF THE SUPERMAN. AND HE'S SUPPOSED TO BE INVULNERABLE.
SO HOW COME THIS *HURTS* SO MUCH?
FANCY CATCHING A MOVIE TONIGHT? I THINK THEY'RE SHOWING *TOWERING INFERNO* AGAIN.
SARA?
OH NO.
COME BACK, BABY.
LEAVE ME ALONE!

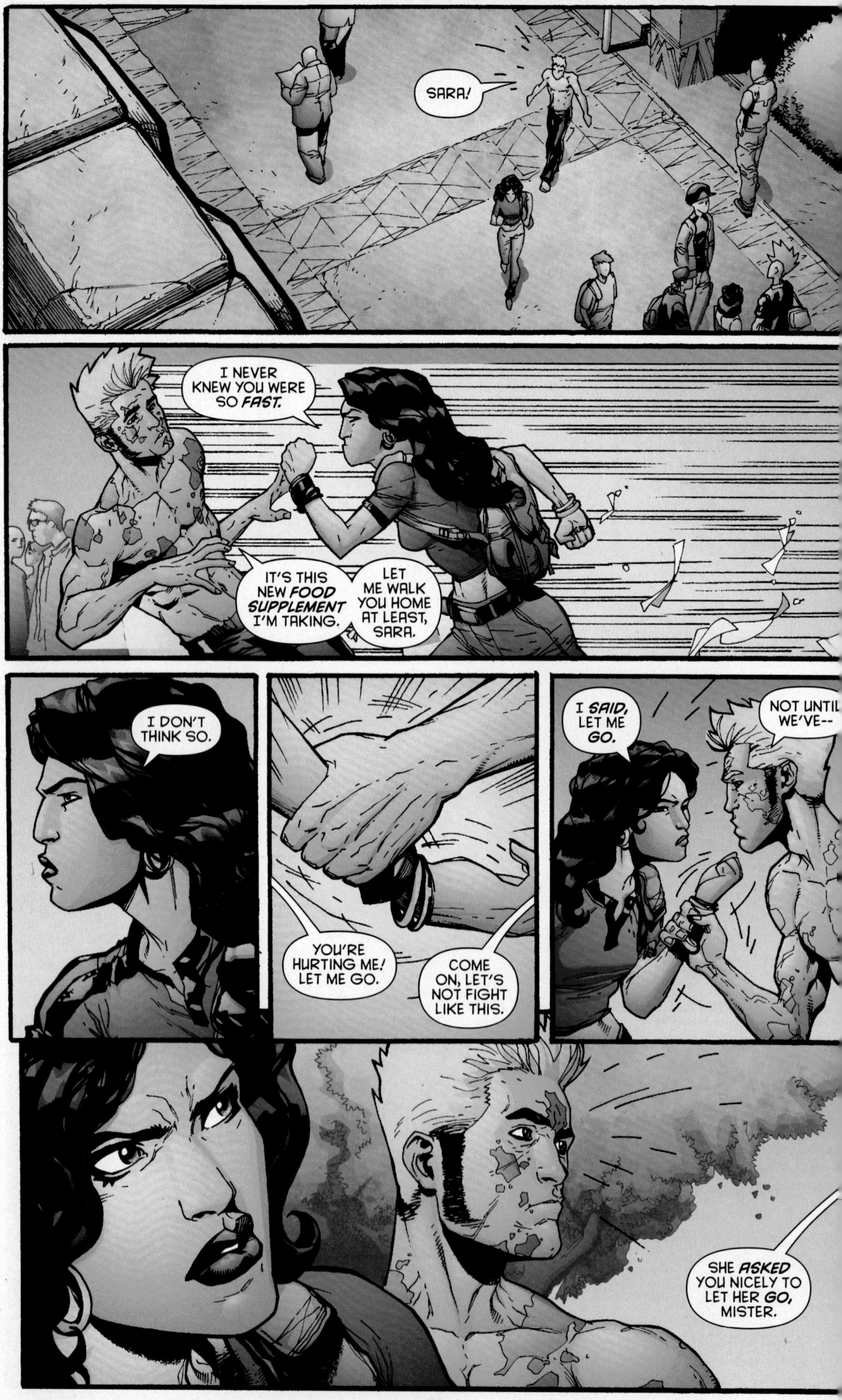
SARA!
I NEVER KNEW YOU WERE SO FAST.
IT'S THIS NEW FOOD SUPPLEMENT I'M TAKING.
LET ME WALK YOU HOME AT LEAST, SARA.
I DON'T THINK SO.
YOU'RE HURTING ME! LET ME GO.
COME ON, LET'S NOT FIGHT LIKE THIS.
I SAID, LET ME GO.
NOT UNTIL WE'VE--
SHE ASKED YOU NICELY TO LET HER GO, MISTER.

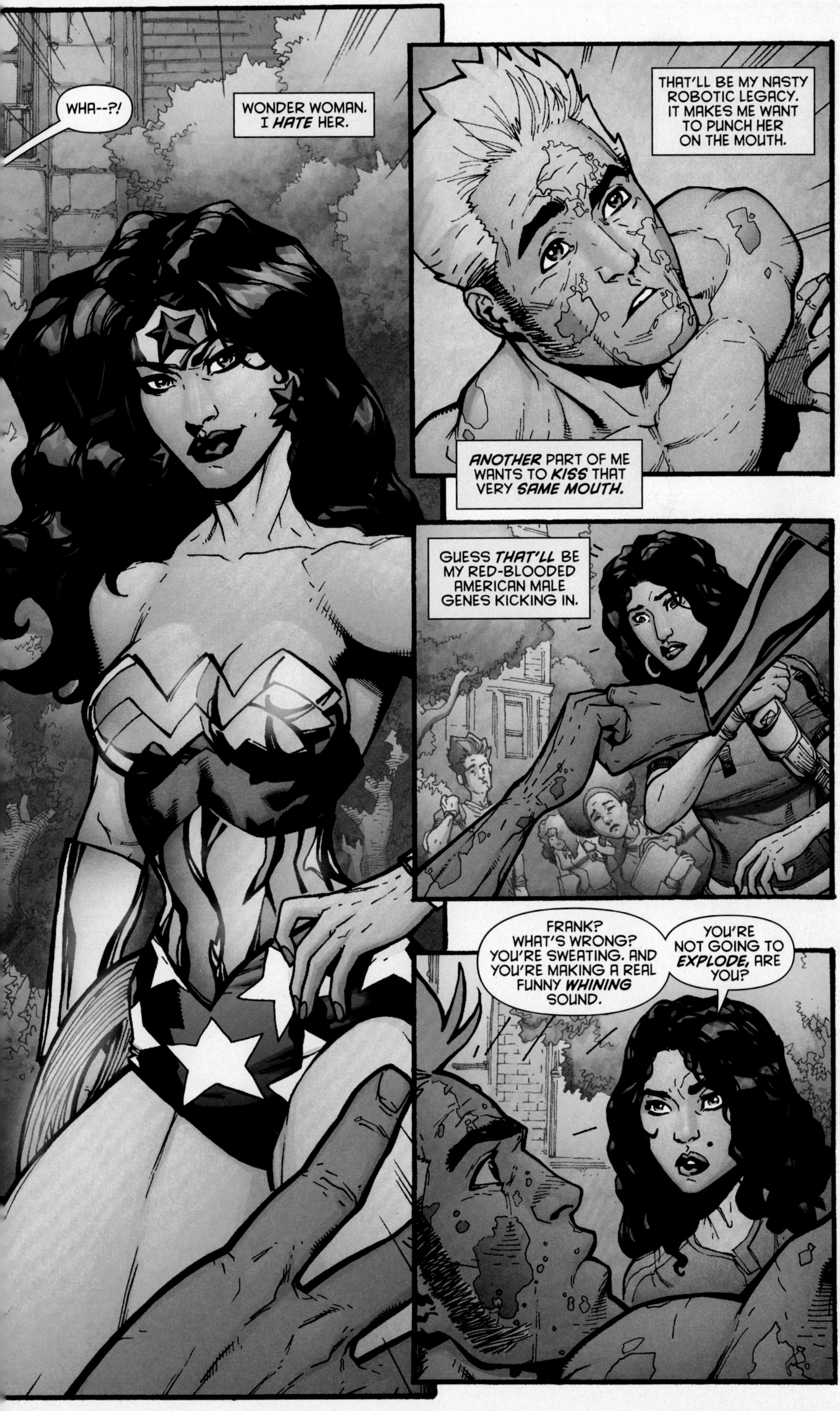
WHA--?!
WONDER WOMAN. I HATE HER.
THAT'LL BE MY NASTY ROBOTIC LEGACY. IT MAKES ME WANT TO PUNCH HER ON THE MOUTH.
ANOTHER PART OF ME WANTS TO KISS THAT VERY SAME MOUTH.
GUESS THAT'LL BE MY RED-BLOODED AMERICAN MALE GENES KICKING IN.
FRANK? WHAT'S WRONG? YOU'RE SWEATING. AND YOU'RE MAKING A REAL FUNNY WHINING SOUND.
YOU'RE NOT GOING TO EXPLODE, ARE YOU?

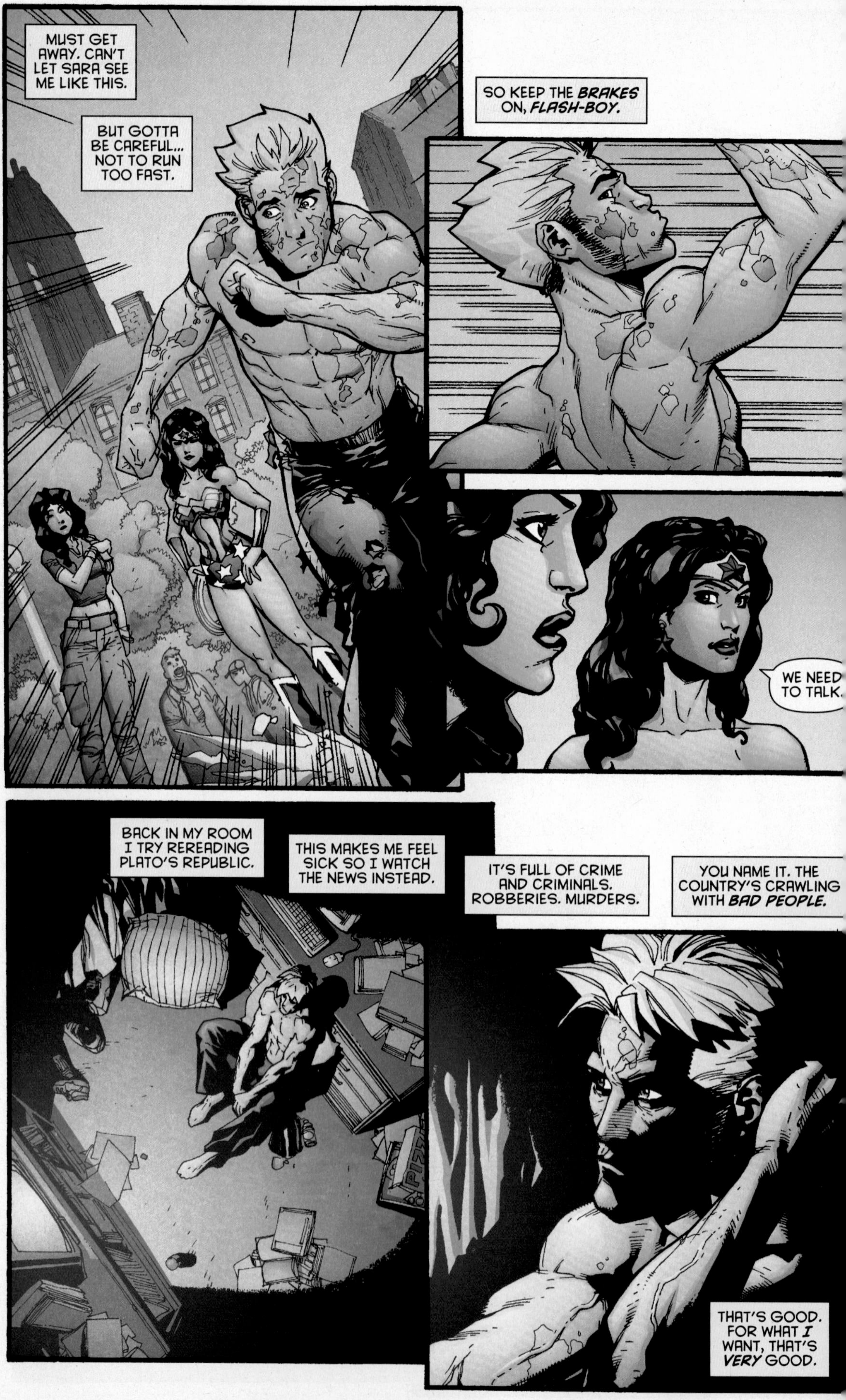
MUST GET AWAY. CAN'T LET SARA SEE ME LIKE THIS.
BUT GOTTA BE CAREFUL... NOT TO RUN TOO FAST.
SO KEEP THE *BRAKES* ON, *FLASH-BOY.*
WE NEED TO TALK.
BACK IN MY ROOM I TRY REREADING PLATO'S REPUBLIC.
THIS MAKES ME FEEL SICK SO I WATCH THE NEWS INSTEAD.
IT'S FULL OF CRIME AND CRIMINALS. ROBBERIES. MURDERS.
YOU NAME IT. THE COUNTRY'S CRAWLING WITH *BAD PEOPLE.*
THAT'S GOOD. FOR WHAT *I* WANT, THAT'S *VERY* GOOD.

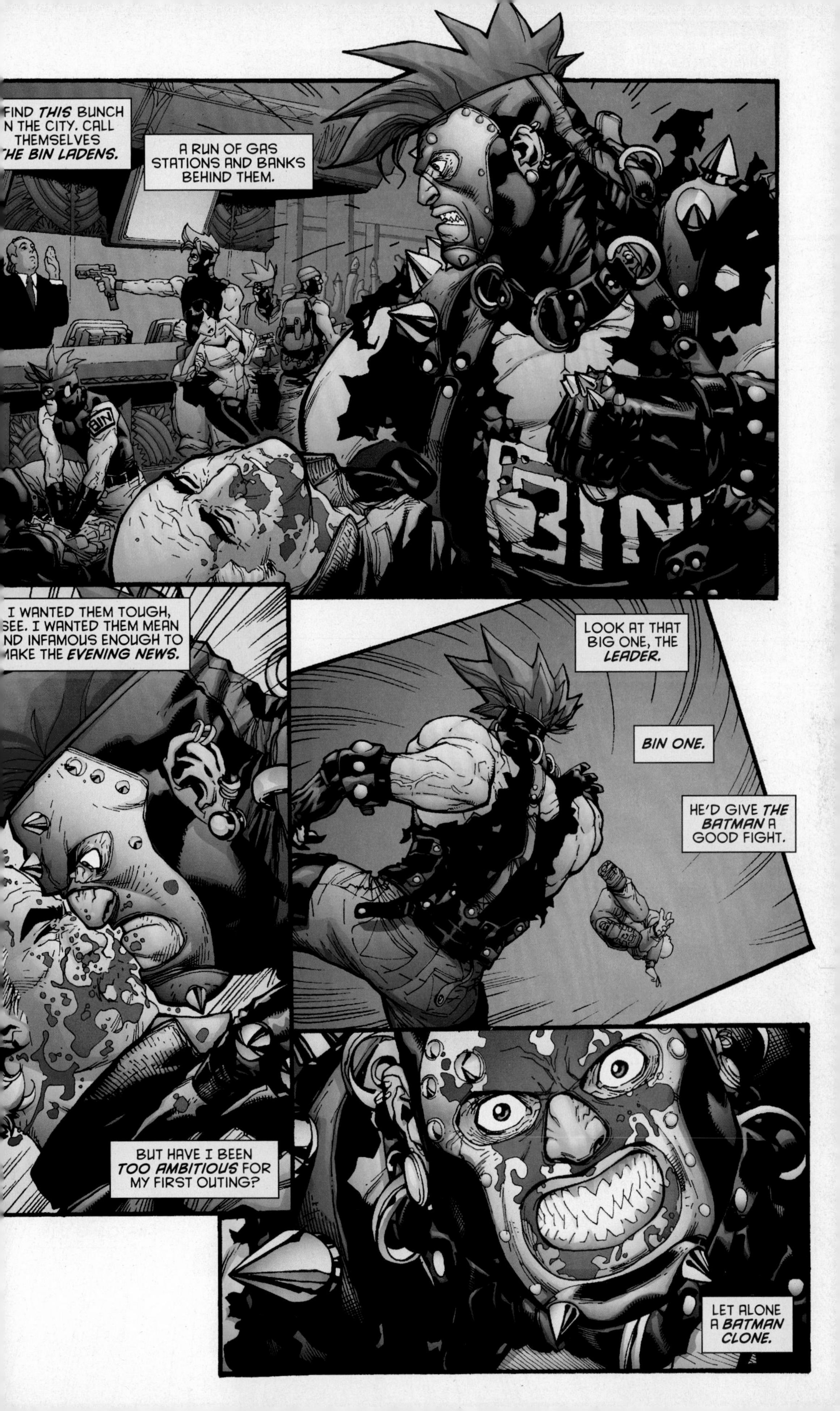
FIND THIS BUNCH
N THE CITY. CALL
THEMSELVES
THE BIN LADENS.
A RUN OF GAS STATIONS AND BANKS BEHIND THEM.
BIN
I WANTED THEM TOUGH,
SEE. I WANTED THEM MEAN
ND INFAMOUS ENOUGH TO
MAKE THE EVENING NEWS.
LOOK AT THAT BIG ONE, THE LEADER.
BIN ONE.
HE'D GIVE THE BATMAN A GOOD FIGHT.
BUT HAVE I BEEN TOO AMBITIOUS FOR MY FIRST OUTING?
LET ALONE A BATMAN CLONE.

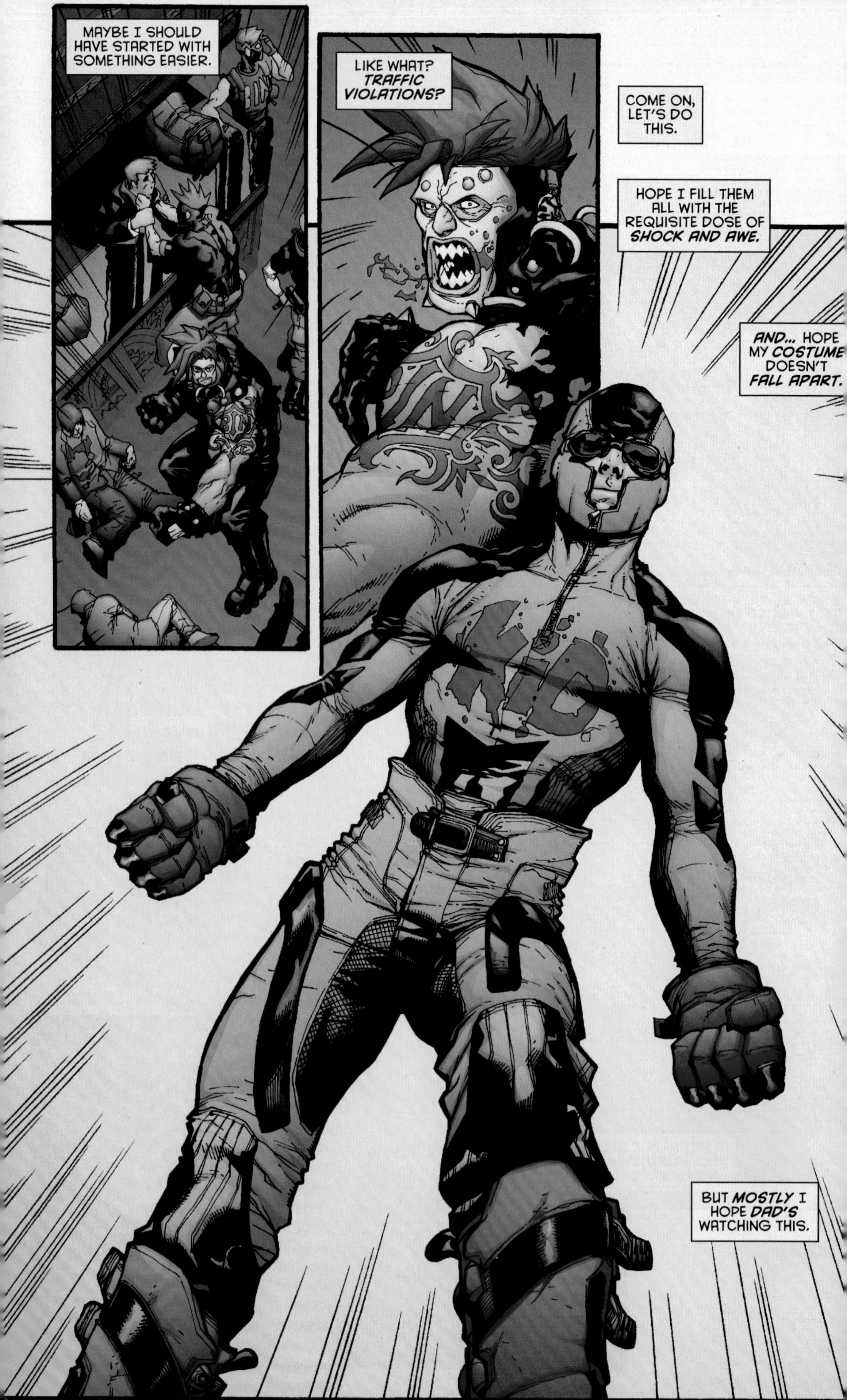
MAYBE I SHOULD HAVE STARTED WITH SOMETHING EASIER.
LIKE WHAT? TRAFFIC VIOLATIONS?
COME ON, LET'S DO THIS.
HOPE I FILL THEM ALL WITH THE REQUISITE DOSE OF SHOCK AND AWE.
AND... HOPE MY COSTUME DOESN'T FALL APART.
BUT MOSTLY I HOPE DAD'S WATCHING THIS.

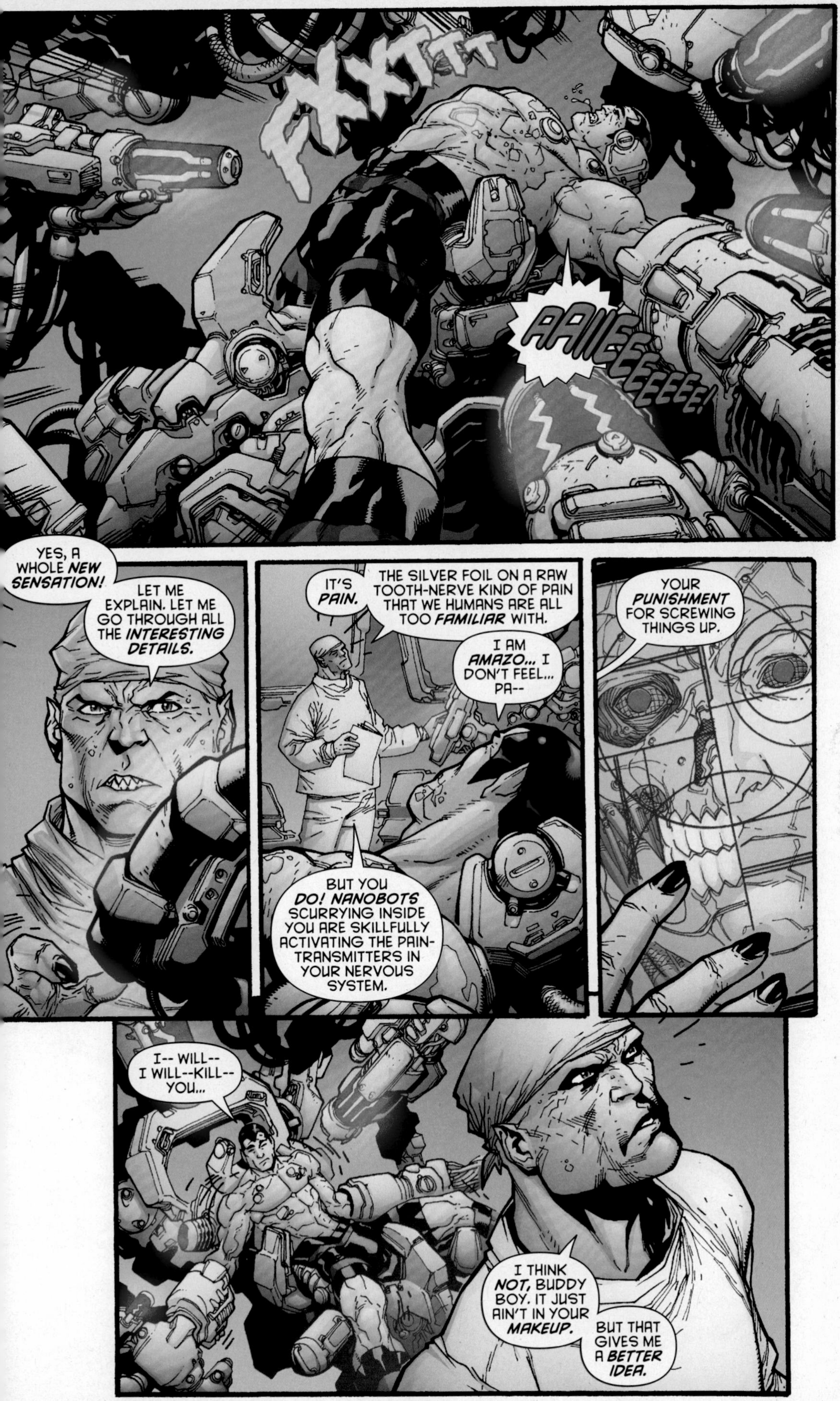
FXXTTT
AAIIEEEEEEEE!
YES, A WHOLE NEW SENSATION!
LET ME EXPLAIN. LET ME GO THROUGH ALL THE INTERESTING DETAILS.
IT'S PAIN.
THE SILVER FOIL ON A RAW TOOTH-NERVE KIND OF PAIN THAT WE HUMANS ARE ALL TOO FAMILIAR WITH.
I AM AMAZO... I DON'T FEEL... PA--
BUT YOU DO! NANOBOTS SCURRYING INSIDE YOU ARE SKILLFULLY ACTIVATING THE PAIN-TRANSMITTERS IN YOUR NERVOUS SYSTEM.
YOUR PUNISHMENT FOR SCREWING THINGS UP.
I-- WILL-- I WILL--KILL-- YOU...
I THINK NOT, BUDDY BOY. IT JUST AIN'T IN YOUR MAKEUP.
BUT THAT GIVES ME A BETTER IDEA.

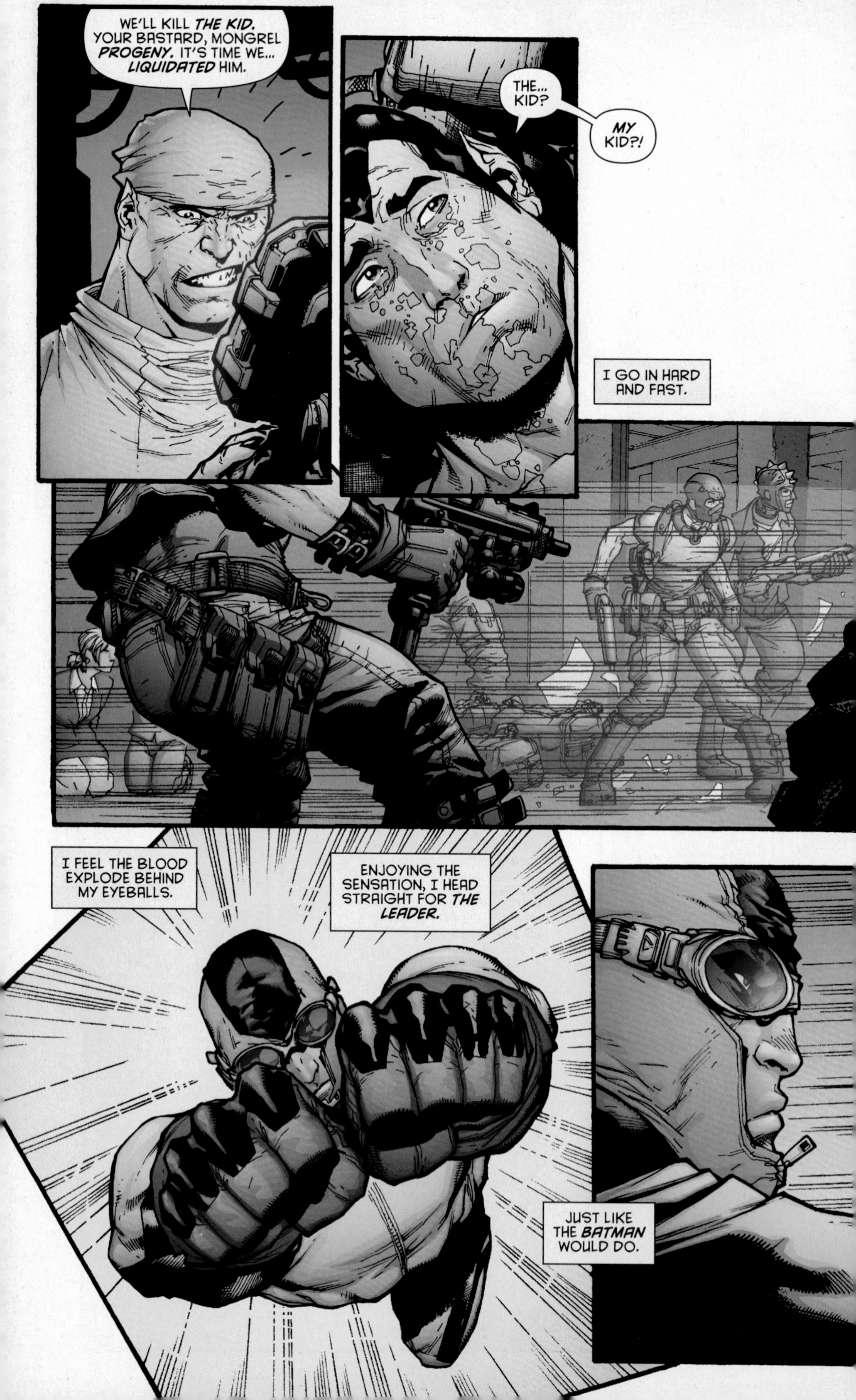
WE'LL KILL THE KID. YOUR BASTARD, MONGREL PROGENY. IT'S TIME WE... LIQUIDATED HIM.
THE... KID?
MY KID?!
I GO IN HARD AND FAST.
I FEEL THE BLOOD EXPLODE BEHIND MY EYEBALLS.
ENJOYING THE SENSATION, I HEAD STRAIGHT FOR THE LEADER.
JUST LIKE THE BATMAN WOULD DO.

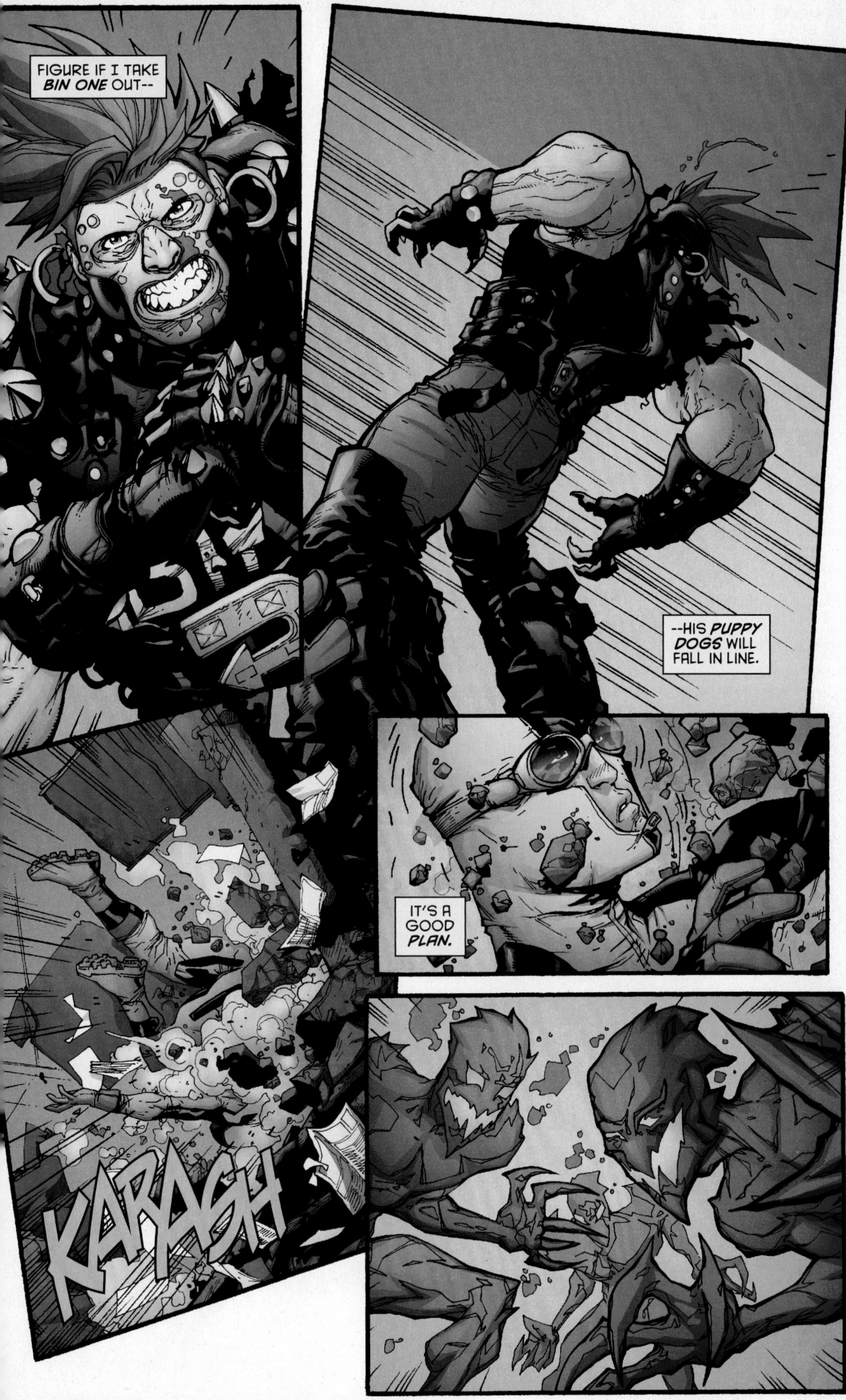
FIGURE IF I TAKE BIN ONE OUT--
--HIS PUPPY DOGS WILL FALL IN LINE.
KARASH
IT'S A GOOD PLAN.

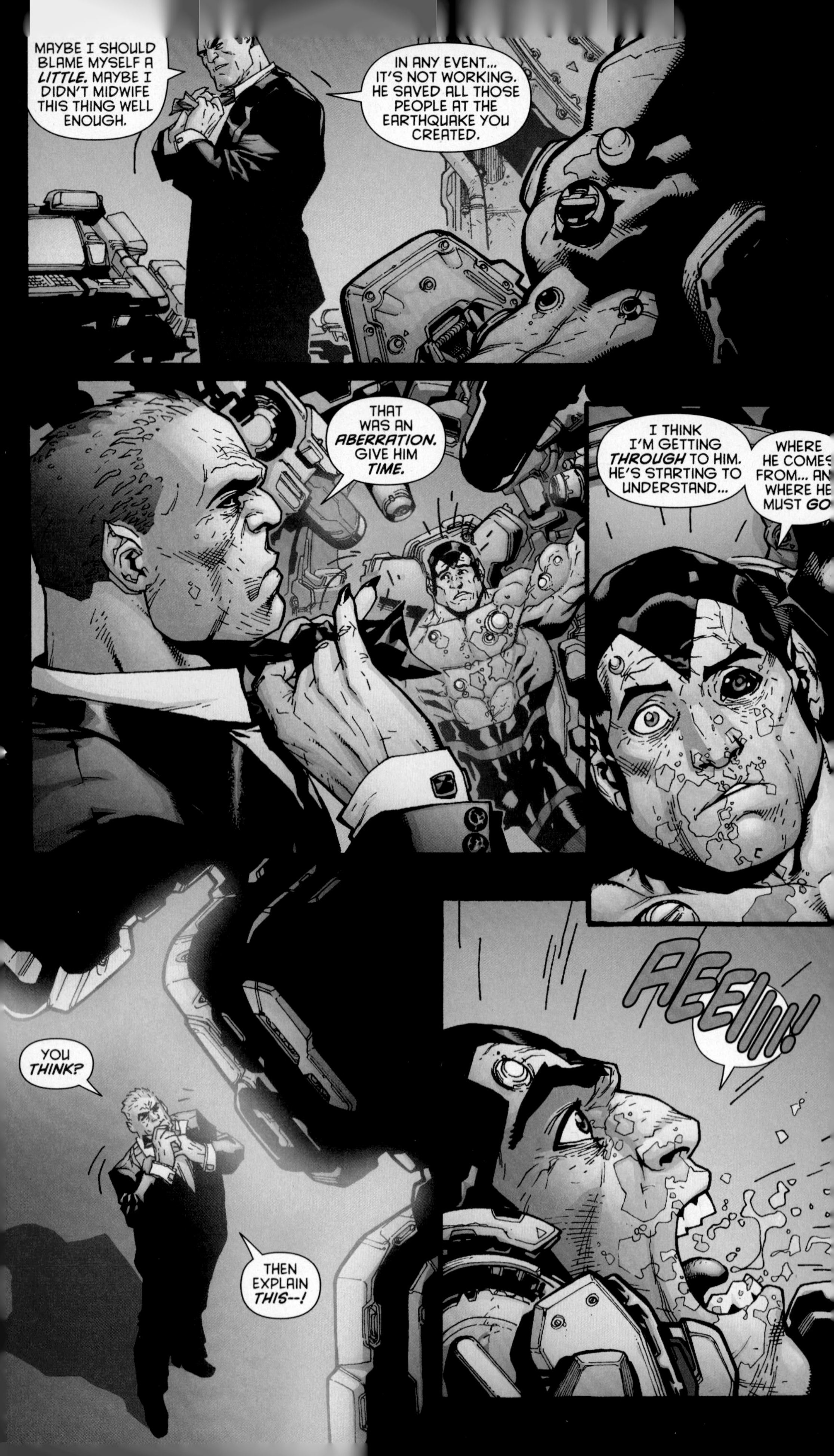
MAYBE I SHOULD BLAME MYSELF A *LITTLE.* MAYBE I DIDN'T MIDWIFE THIS THING WELL ENOUGH.
IN ANY EVENT... IT'S NOT WORKING. HE SAVED ALL THOSE PEOPLE AT THE EARTHQUAKE YOU CREATED.
THAT WAS AN *ABERRATION.* GIVE HIM *TIME.*
I THINK I'M GETTING *THROUGH* TO HIM. HE'S STARTING TO UNDERSTAND...
WHERE HE COMES FROM... AND WHERE HE MUST *GO*
YOU *THINK?*
THEN EXPLAIN *THIS--!*
AEEIIII!

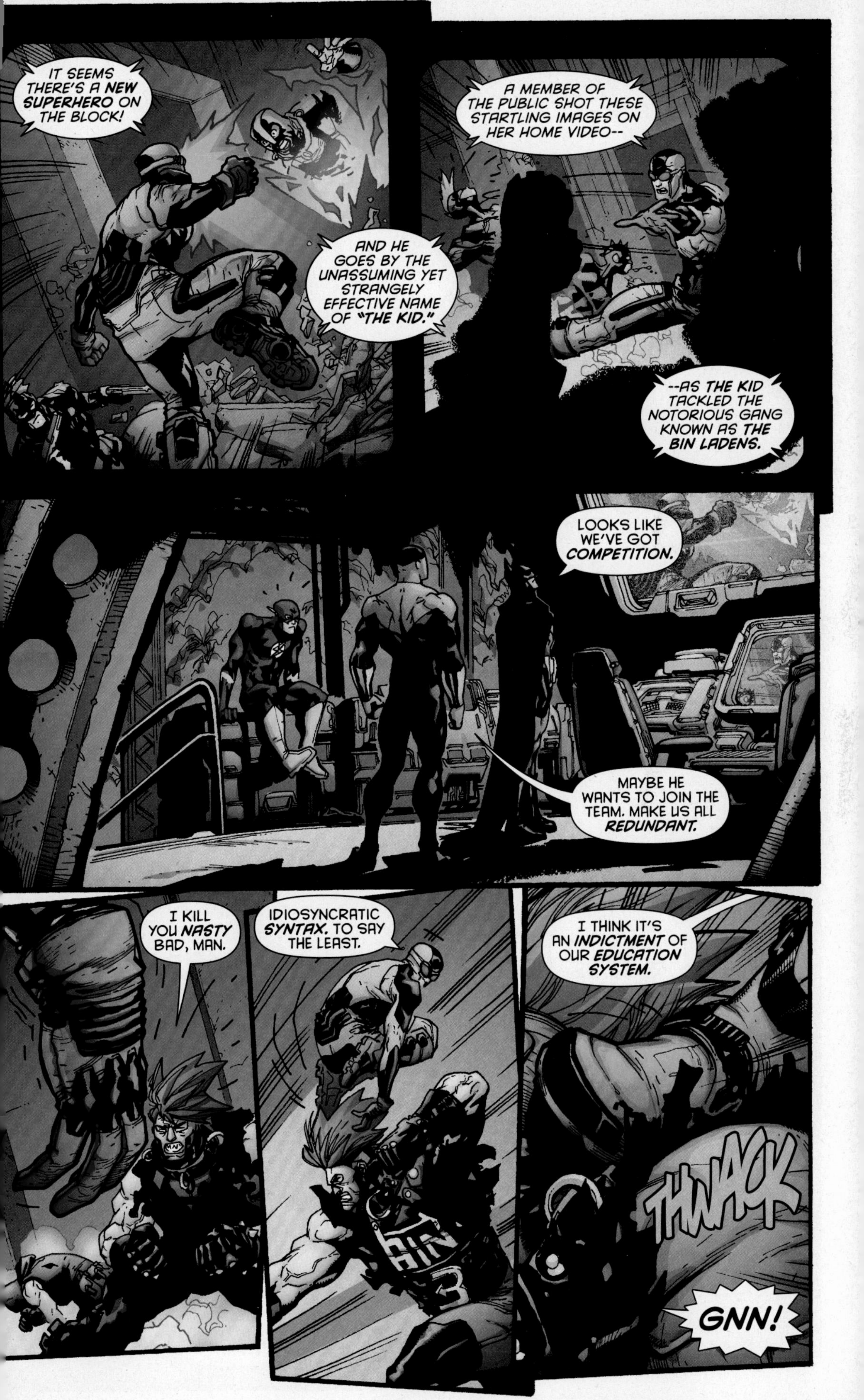
IT SEEMS THERE'S A NEW SUPERHERO ON THE BLOCK!
AND HE GOES BY THE UNASSUMING YET STRANGELY EFFECTIVE NAME OF "THE KID."
A MEMBER OF THE PUBLIC SHOT THESE STARTLING IMAGES ON HER HOME VIDEO--
--AS THE KID TACKLED THE NOTORIOUS GANG KNOWN AS THE BIN LADENS.
LOOKS LIKE WE'VE GOT COMPETITION.
MAYBE HE WANTS TO JOIN THE TEAM. MAKE US ALL REDUNDANT.
I KILL YOU NASTY BAD, MAN.
IDIOSYNCRATIC SYNTAX, TO SAY THE LEAST.
I THINK IT'S AN INDICTMENT OF OUR EDUCATION SYSTEM.
THWACK
GNN!

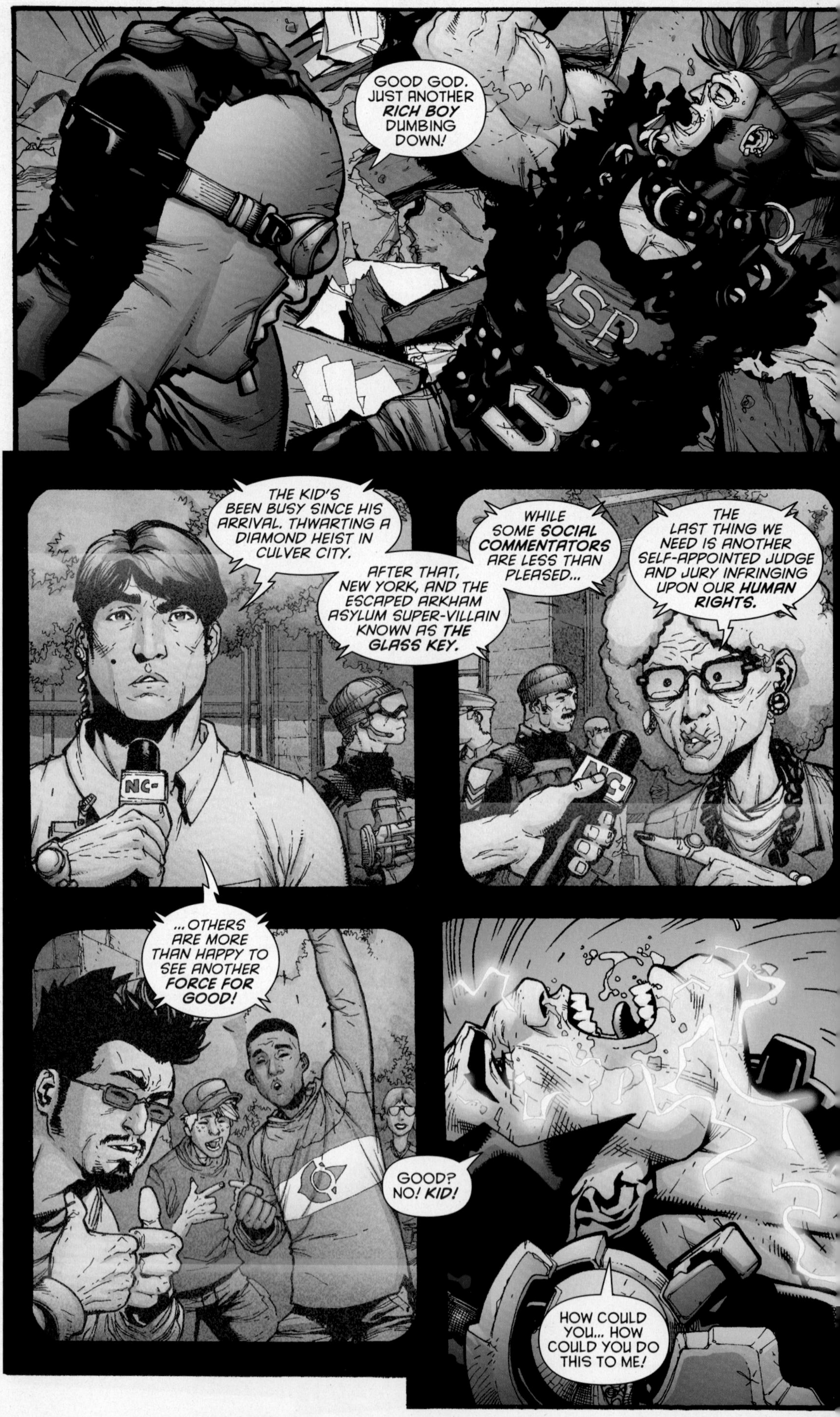
GOOD GOD. JUST ANOTHER RICH BOY DUMBING DOWN!
THE KID'S BEEN BUSY SINCE HIS ARRIVAL. THWARTING A DIAMOND HEIST IN CULVER CITY.
AFTER THAT, NEW YORK, AND THE ESCAPED ARKHAM ASYLUM SUPER-VILLAIN KNOWN AS THE GLASS KEY.
WHILE SOME SOCIAL COMMENTATORS ARE LESS THAN PLEASED...
THE LAST THING WE NEED IS ANOTHER SELF-APPOINTED JUDGE AND JURY INFRINGING UPON OUR HUMAN RIGHTS.
...OTHERS ARE MORE THAN HAPPY TO SEE ANOTHER FORCE FOR GOOD!
GOOD? NO! KID!
HOW COULD YOU... HOW COULD YOU DO THIS TO ME!

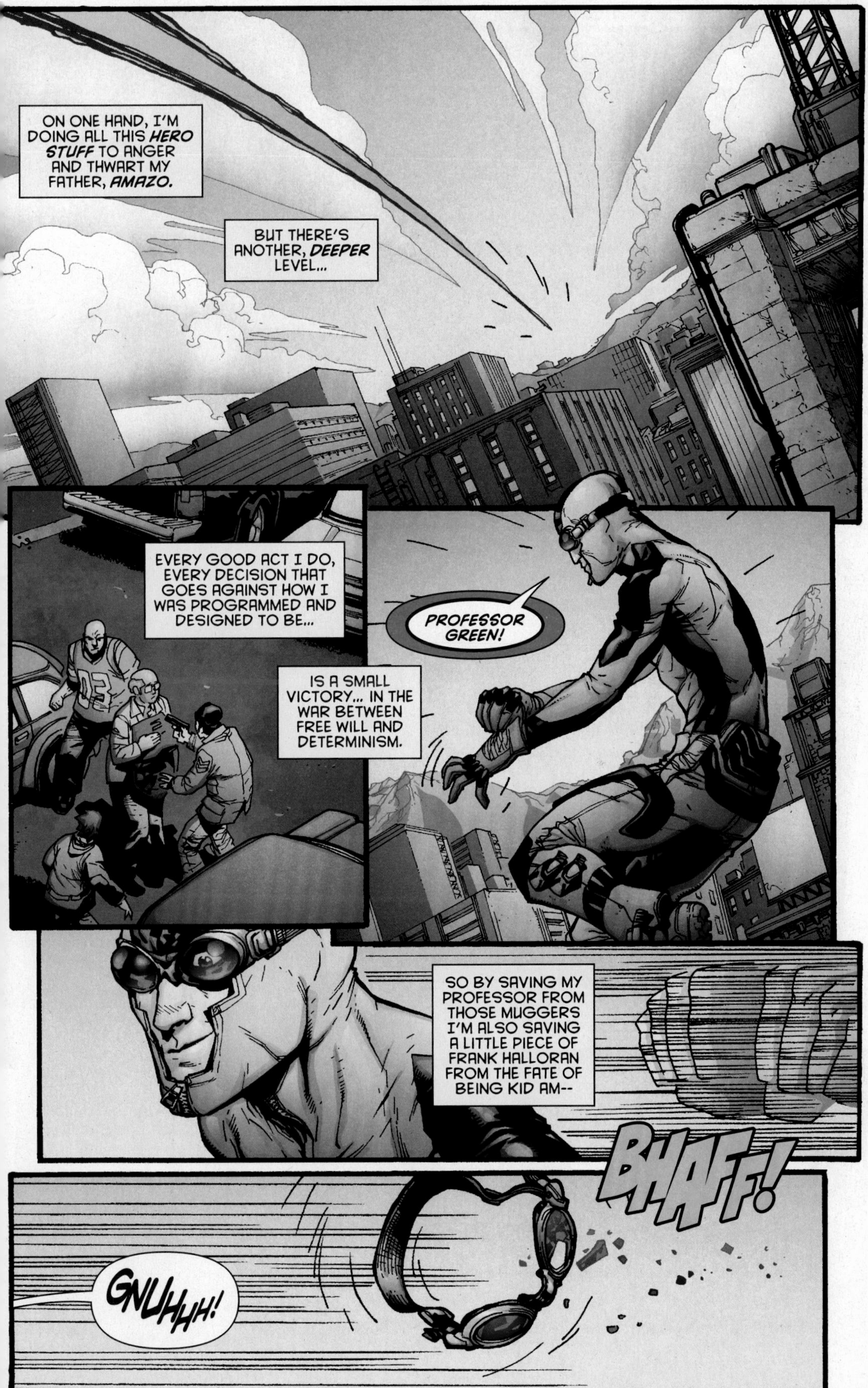

ON ONE HAND, I'M DOING ALL THIS HERO STUFF TO ANGER AND THWART MY FATHER, AMAZO.
BUT THERE'S ANOTHER, DEEPER LEVEL...
EVERY GOOD ACT I DO, EVERY DECISION THAT GOES AGAINST HOW I WAS PROGRAMMED AND DESIGNED TO BE...
PROFESSOR GREEN!
IS A SMALL VICTORY... IN THE WAR BETWEEN FREE WILL AND DETERMINISM.
SO BY SAVING MY PROFESSOR FROM THOSE MUGGERS I'M ALSO SAVING A LITTLE PIECE OF FRANK HALLORAN FROM THE FATE OF BEING KID AM--
BHAFF!
GNUHHH!

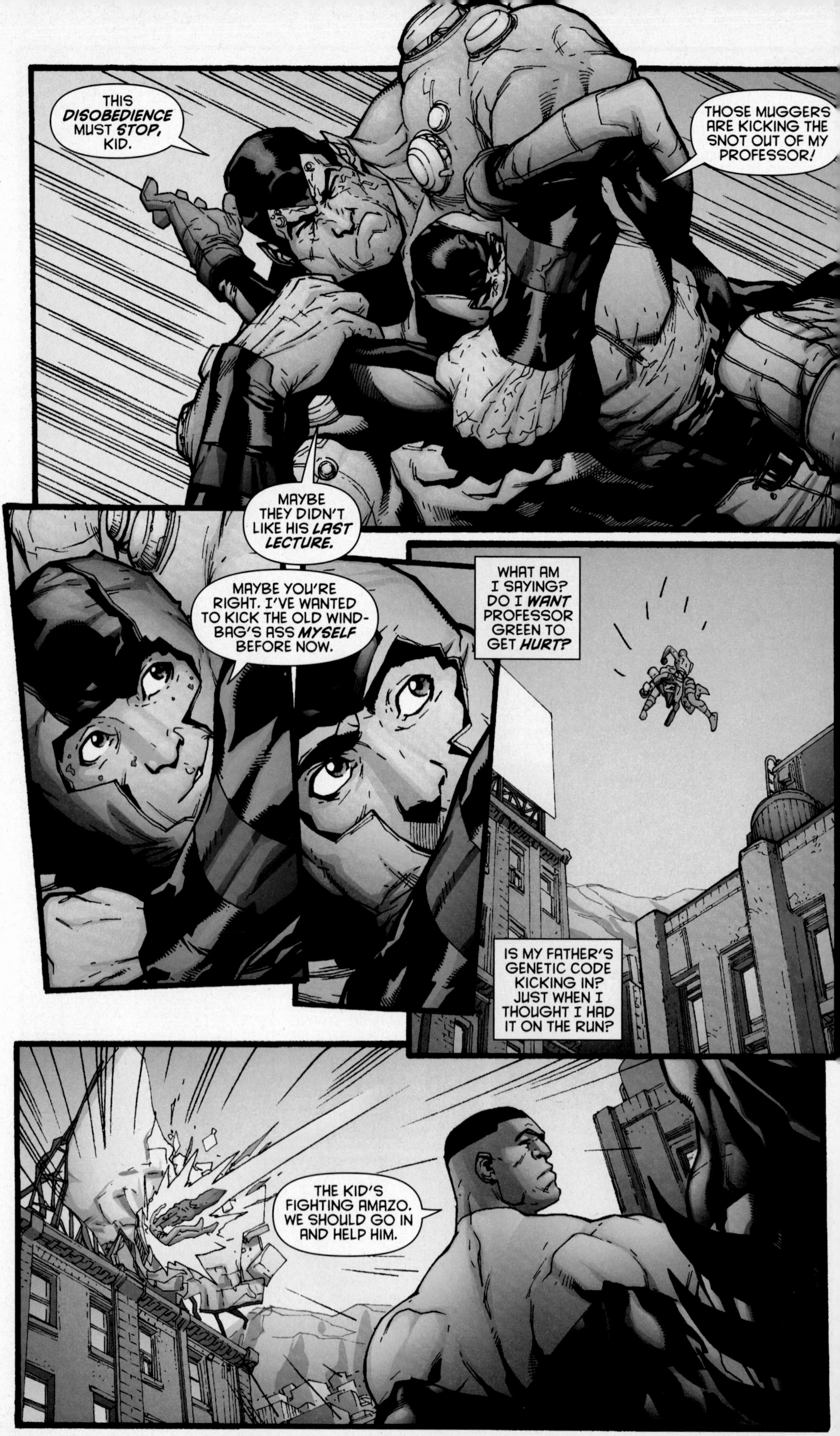

THIS *DISOBEDIENCE* MUST *STOP,* KID.
THOSE MUGGERS ARE KICKING THE SNOT OUT OF MY PROFESSOR!
MAYBE THEY DIDN'T LIKE HIS *LAST LECTURE.*
MAYBE YOU'RE RIGHT. I'VE WANTED TO KICK THE OLD WIND-BAG'S ASS *MYSELF* BEFORE NOW.
WHAT AM I SAYING? DO I *WANT* PROFESSOR GREEN TO GET *HURT?*
IS MY FATHER'S GENETIC CODE KICKING IN? JUST WHEN I THOUGHT I HAD IT ON THE RUN?
THE KID'S FIGHTING AMAZO. WE SHOULD GO IN AND HELP HIM.

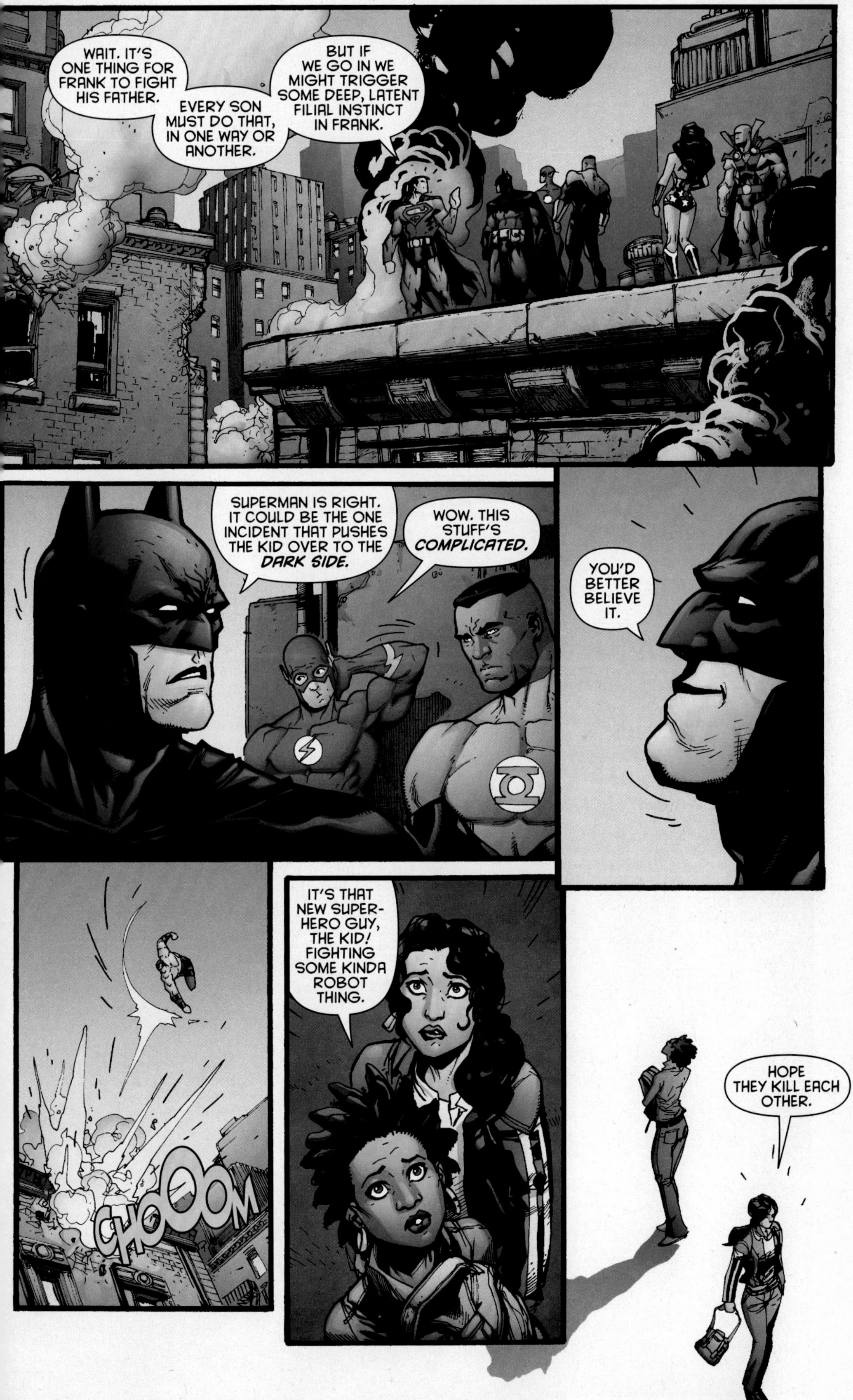
WAIT. IT'S ONE THING FOR FRANK TO FIGHT HIS FATHER.
EVERY SON MUST DO THAT, IN ONE WAY OR ANOTHER.
BUT IF WE GO IN WE MIGHT TRIGGER SOME DEEP, LATENT FILIAL INSTINCT IN FRANK.
SUPERMAN IS RIGHT. IT COULD BE THE ONE INCIDENT THAT PUSHES THE KID OVER TO THE DARK SIDE.
WOW. THIS STUFF'S COMPLICATED.
YOU'D BETTER BELIEVE IT.
CHOOOOM
IT'S THAT NEW SUPER-HERO GUY, THE KID! FIGHTING SOME KINDA ROBOT THING.
HOPE THEY KILL EACH OTHER.

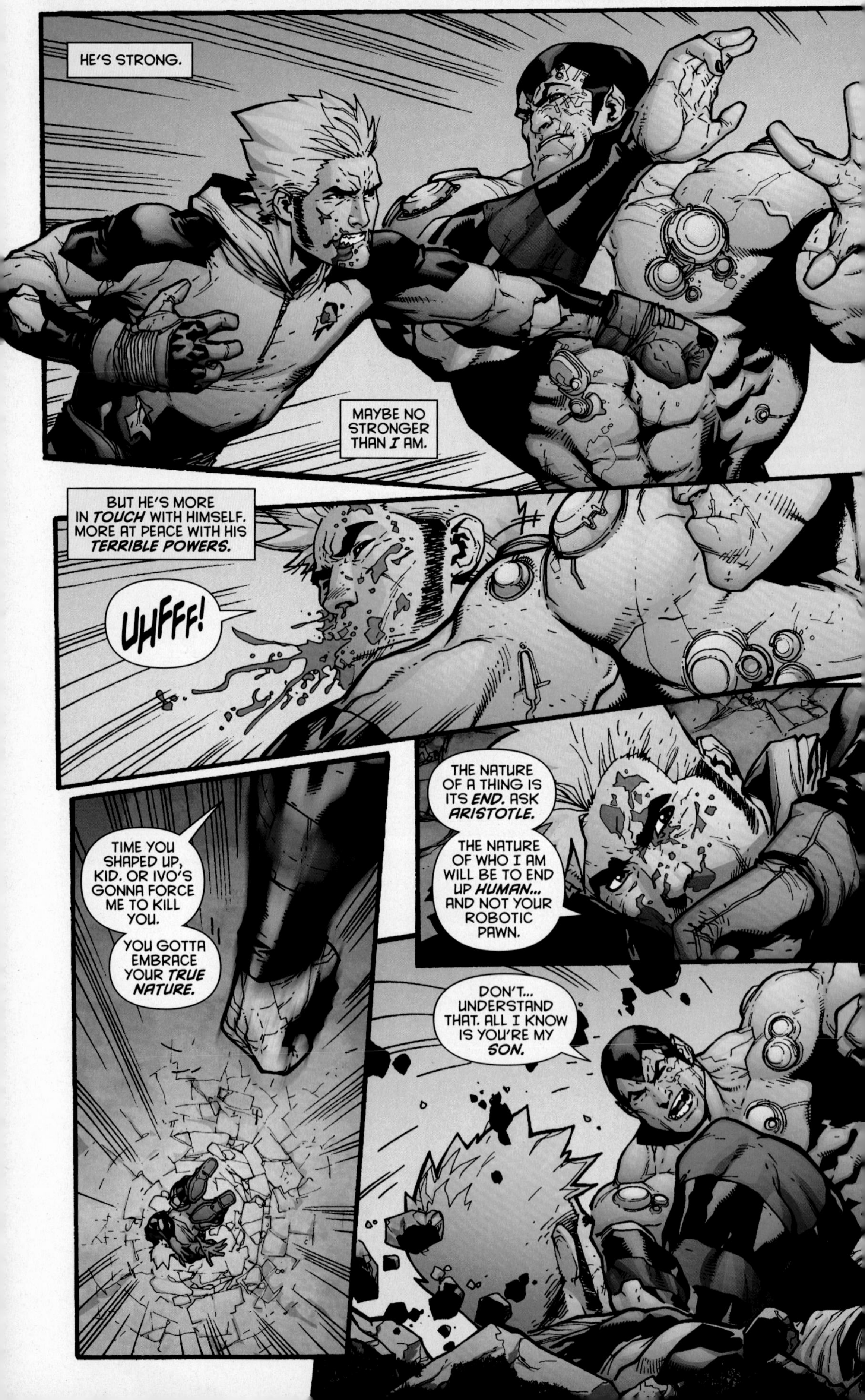

HE'S STRONG.
MAYBE NO STRONGER THAN *I* AM.
BUT HE'S MORE IN *TOUCH* WITH HIMSELF. MORE AT PEACE WITH HIS *TERRIBLE POWERS.*
UHFFF!
TIME YOU SHAPED UP, KID. OR IVO'S GONNA FORCE ME TO KILL YOU.
YOU GOTTA EMBRACE YOUR *TRUE NATURE.*
THE NATURE OF A THING IS ITS *END.* ASK *ARISTOTLE.*
THE NATURE OF WHO I AM WILL BE TO END UP *HUMAN*... AND NOT YOUR ROBOTIC PAWN.
DON'T... UNDERSTAND THAT. ALL I KNOW IS YOU'RE MY *SON.*

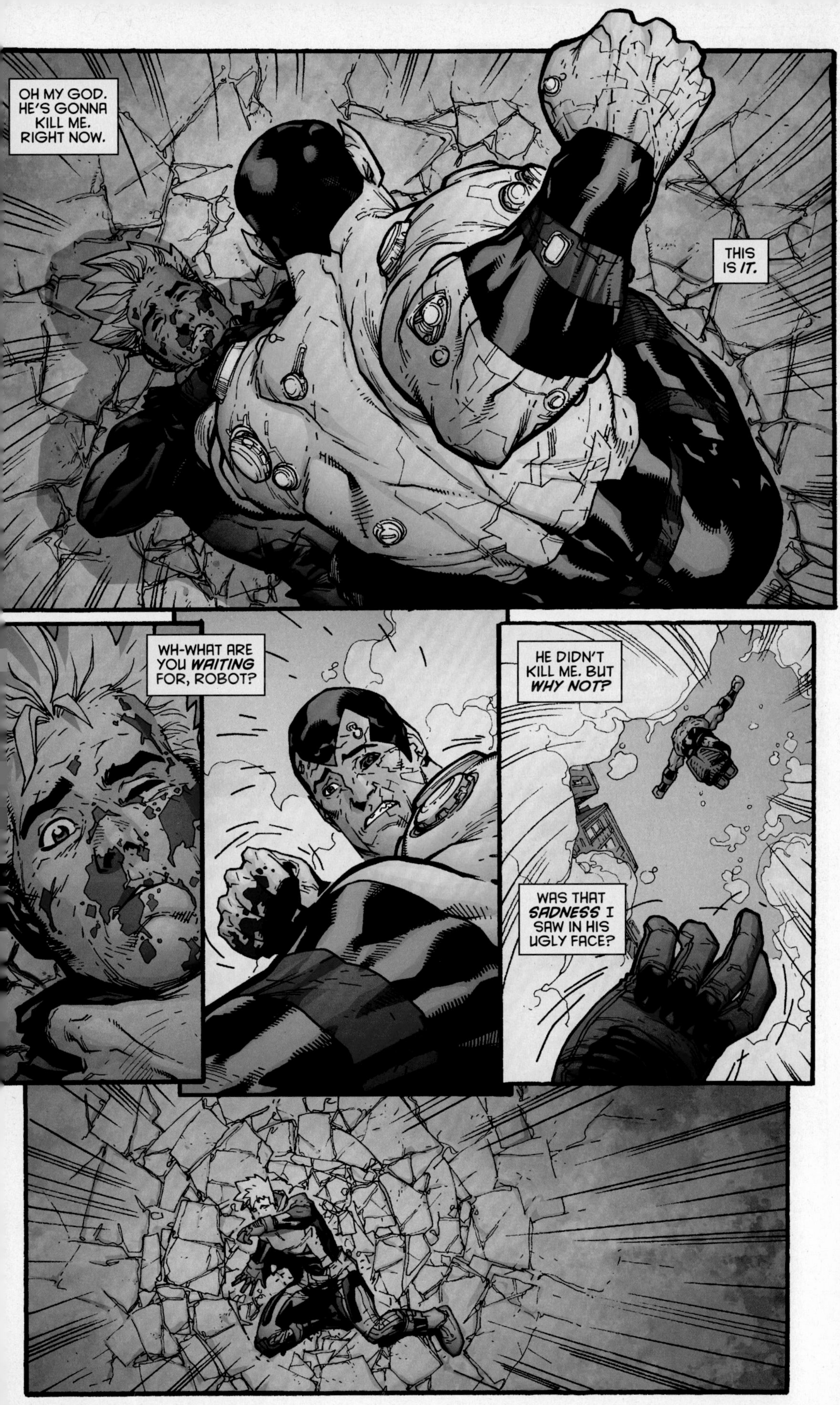

OH MY GOD. HE'S GONNA KILL ME. RIGHT NOW.
THIS IS *IT.*
WH-WHAT ARE YOU *WAITING* FOR, ROBOT?
HE DIDN'T KILL ME. BUT *WHY NOT?*
WAS THAT *SADNESS* I SAW IN HIS UGLY FACE?

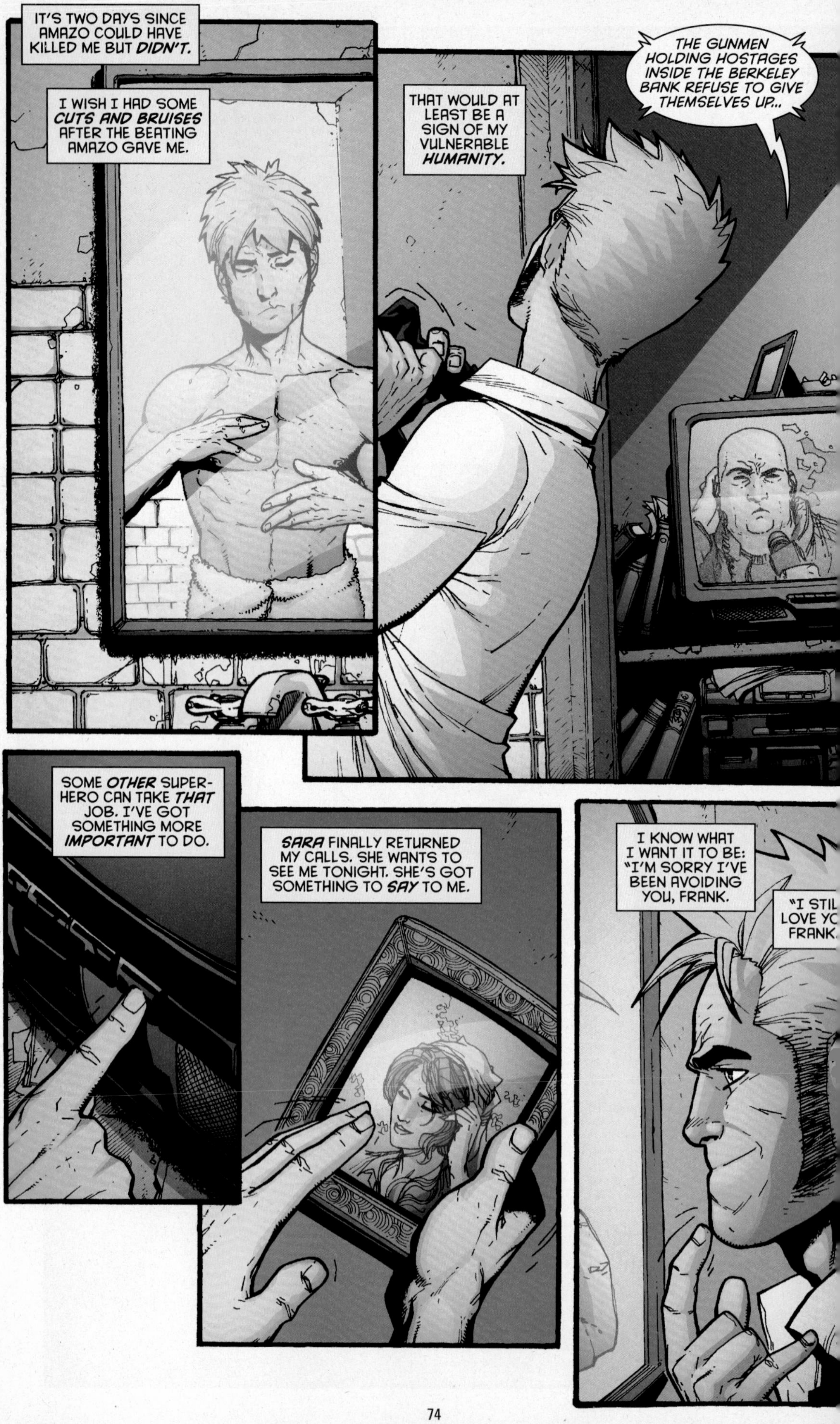

IT'S TWO DAYS SINCE AMAZO COULD HAVE KILLED ME BUT DIDN'T.
I WISH I HAD SOME CUTS AND BRUISES AFTER THE BEATING AMAZO GAVE ME.
THAT WOULD AT LEAST BE A SIGN OF MY VULNERABLE HUMANITY.
THE GUNMEN HOLDING HOSTAGES INSIDE THE BERKELEY BANK REFUSE TO GIVE THEMSELVES UP...
SOME OTHER SUPER-HERO CAN TAKE THAT JOB. I'VE GOT SOMETHING MORE IMPORTANT TO DO.
SARA FINALLY RETURNED MY CALLS. SHE WANTS TO SEE ME TONIGHT. SHE'S GOT SOMETHING TO SAY TO ME.
I KNOW WHAT I WANT IT TO BE: "I'M SORRY I'VE BEEN AVOIDING YOU, FRANK.

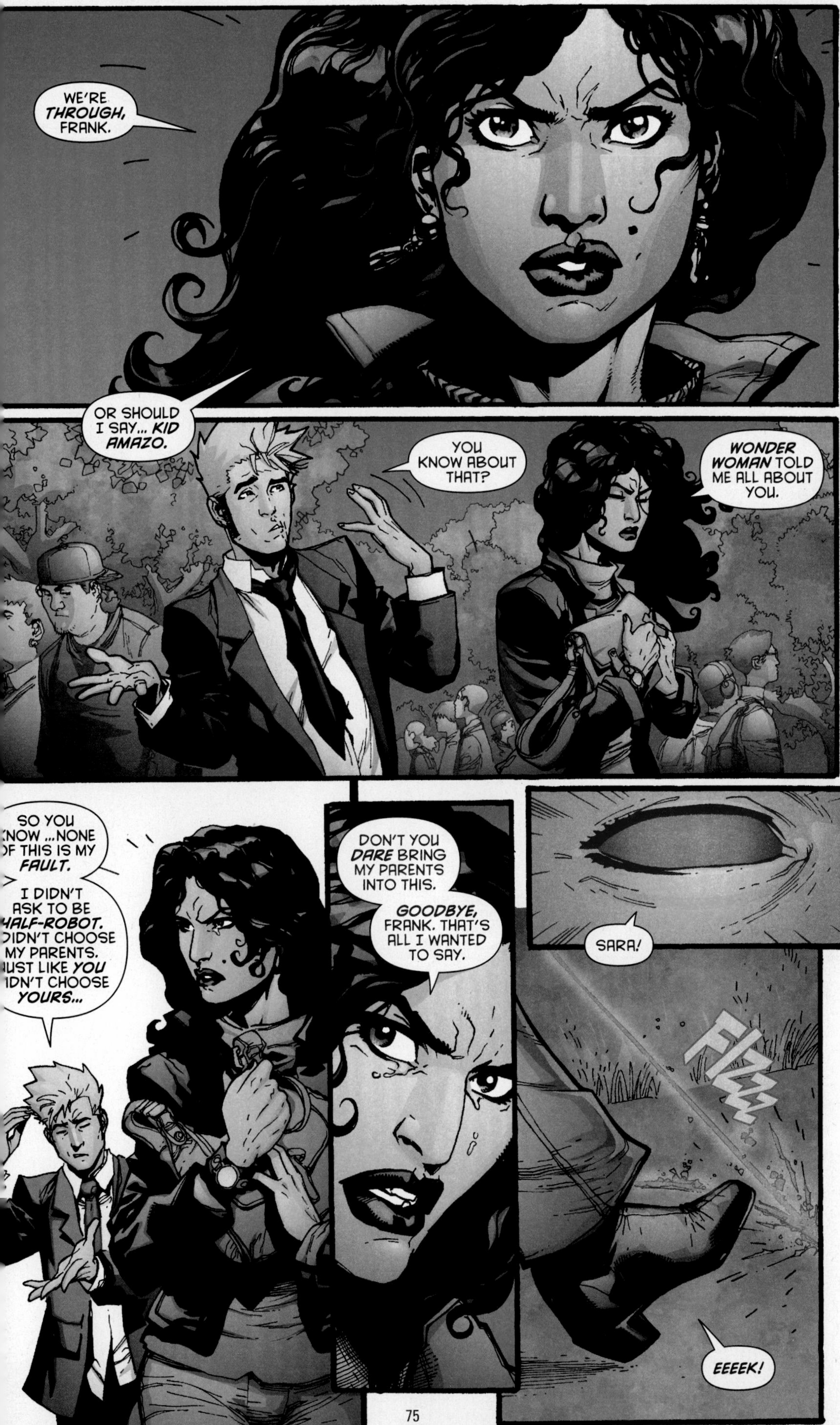
WE'RE *THROUGH,* FRANK.
OR SHOULD I SAY... *KID AMAZO.*
YOU KNOW ABOUT THAT?
WONDER WOMAN TOLD ME ALL ABOUT YOU.
SO YOU KNOW ...NONE OF THIS IS MY *FAULT.*
I DIDN'T ASK TO BE *HALF-ROBOT.* I DIDN'T CHOOSE MY PARENTS. JUST LIKE *YOU* DIDN'T CHOOSE *YOURS...*
DON'T YOU *DARE* BRING MY PARENTS INTO THIS.
GOODBYE, FRANK. THAT'S ALL I WANTED TO SAY.
SARA!
FIZZ
EEEEK!

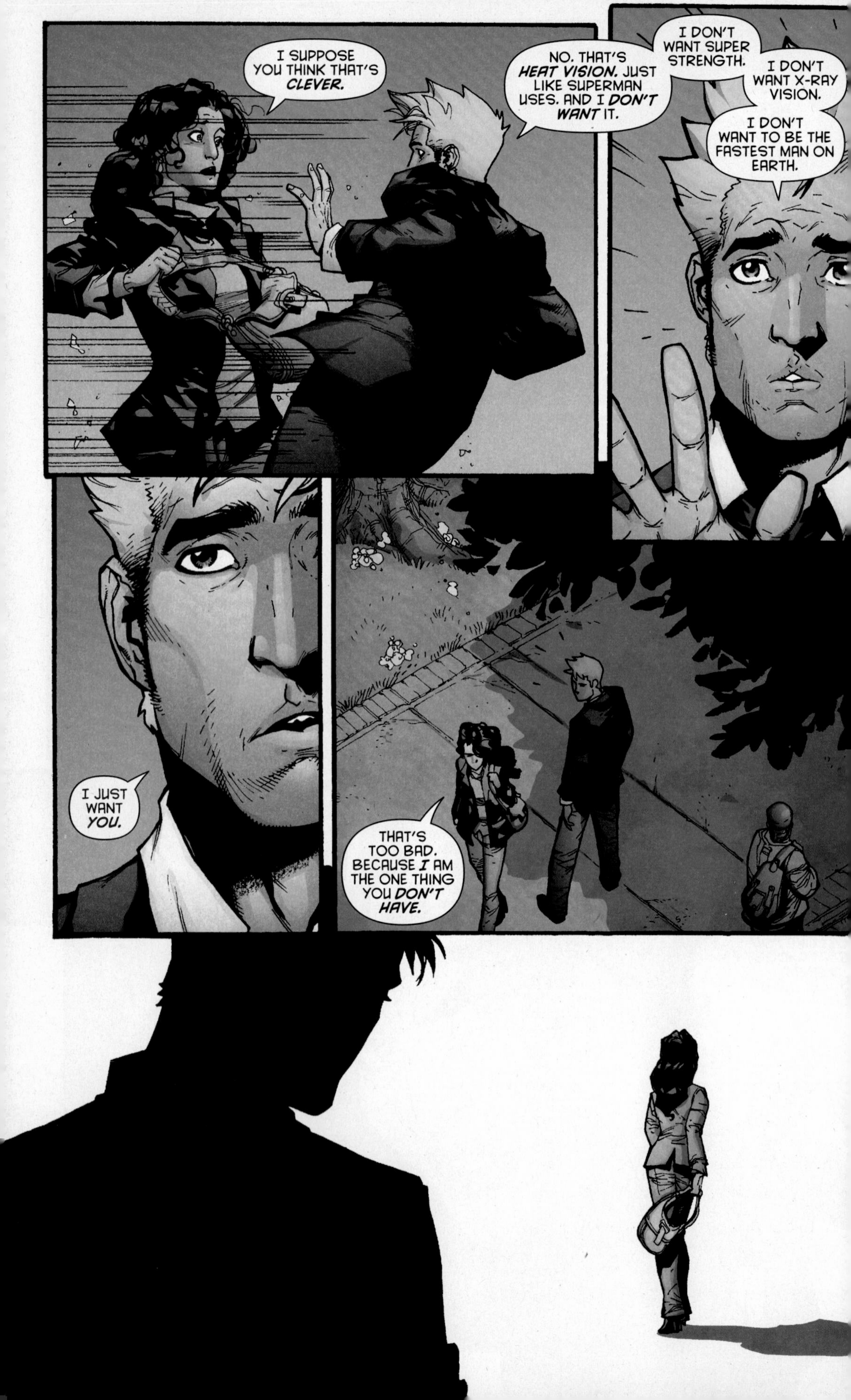

I SUPPOSE YOU THINK THAT'S *CLEVER.*
NO. THAT'S *HEAT VISION.* JUST LIKE SUPERMAN USES. AND I *DON'T WANT* IT.
I DON'T WANT SUPER STRENGTH.
I DON'T WANT X-RAY VISION.
I DON'T WANT TO BE THE FASTEST MAN ON EARTH.
I JUST WANT *YOU.*
THAT'S TOO BAD. BECAUSE *I* AM THE ONE THING YOU *DON'T HAVE.*

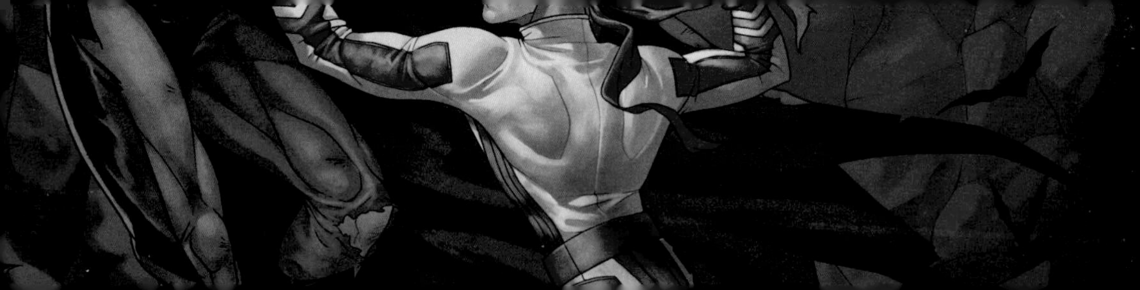

Chapter Four
HUMAN, ALL TOO HUMAN

COVER ART BY SAMI BASRI

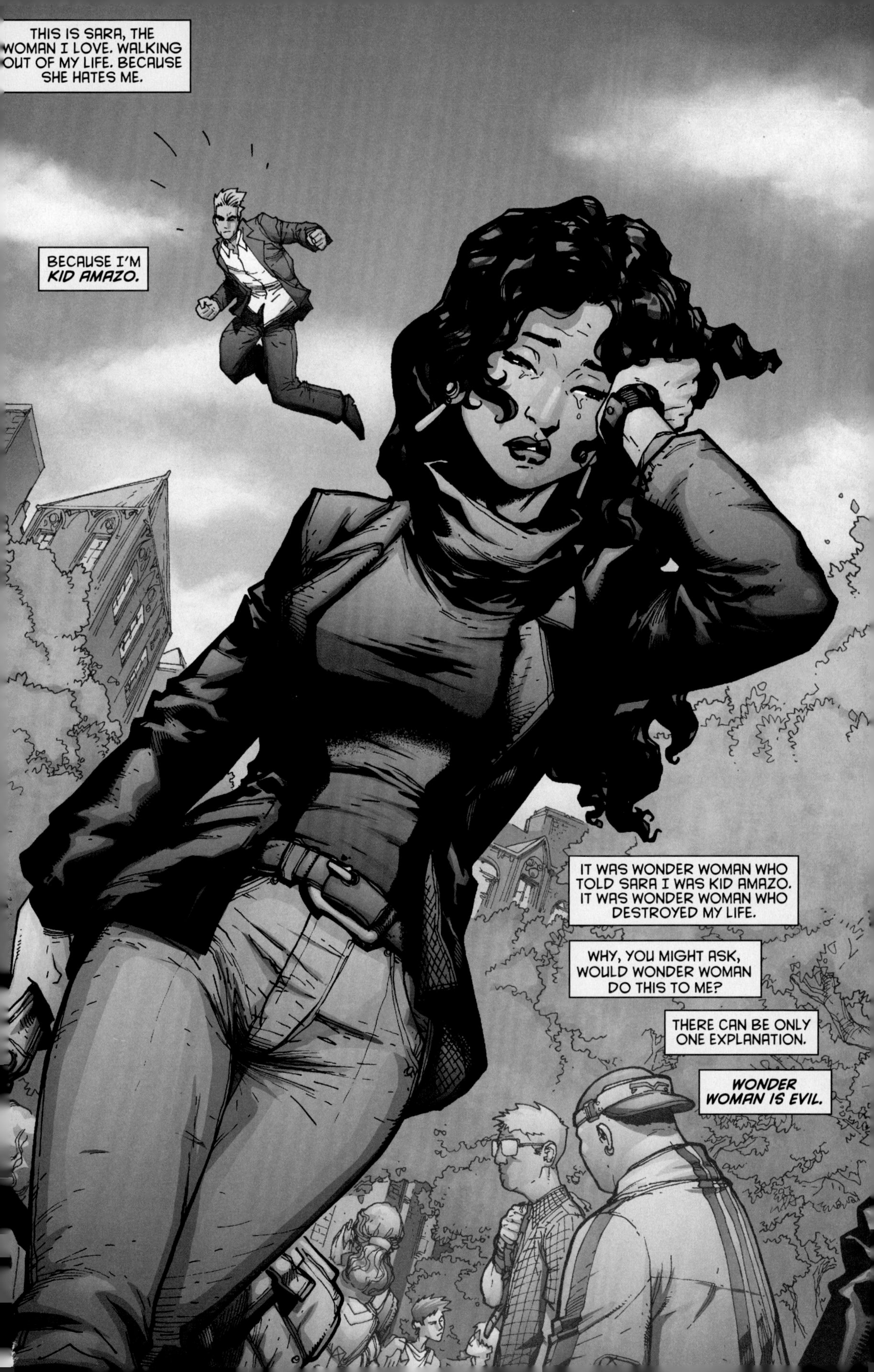
THIS IS SARA, THE WOMAN I LOVE. WALKING OUT OF MY LIFE. BECAUSE SHE HATES ME.
BECAUSE I'M *KID AMAZO.*
IT WAS WONDER WOMAN WHO TOLD SARA I WAS KID AMAZO. IT WAS WONDER WOMAN WHO DESTROYED MY LIFE.
WHY, YOU MIGHT ASK, WOULD WONDER WOMAN DO THIS TO ME?
THERE CAN BE ONLY ONE EXPLANATION.
WONDER WOMAN IS EVIL.

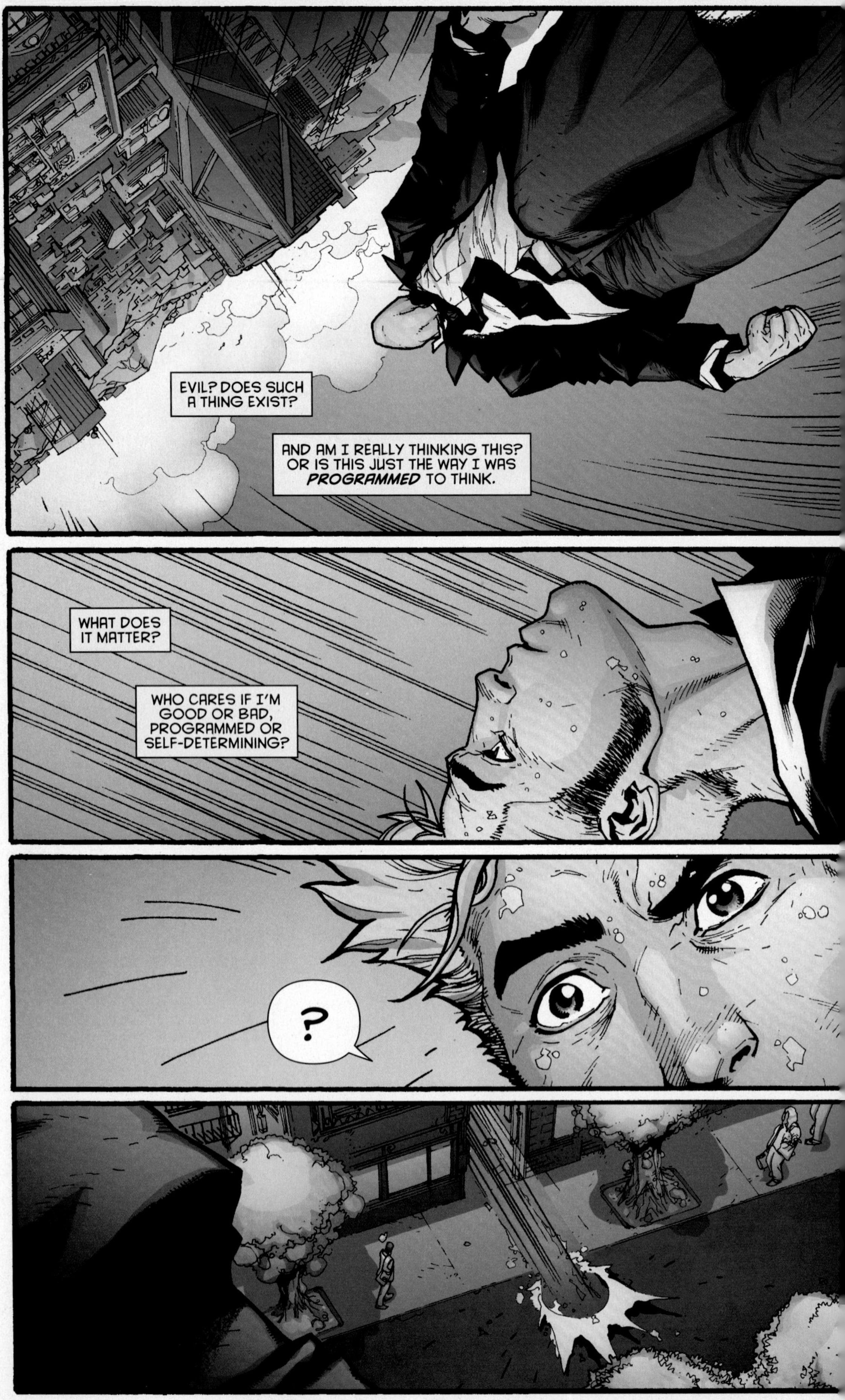
EVIL? DOES SUCH A THING EXIST?
AND AM I REALLY THINKING THIS? OR IS THIS JUST THE WAY I WAS *PROGRAMMED* TO THINK.
WHAT DOES IT MATTER?
WHO CARES IF I'M GOOD OR BAD, PROGRAMMED OR SELF-DETERMINING?
?

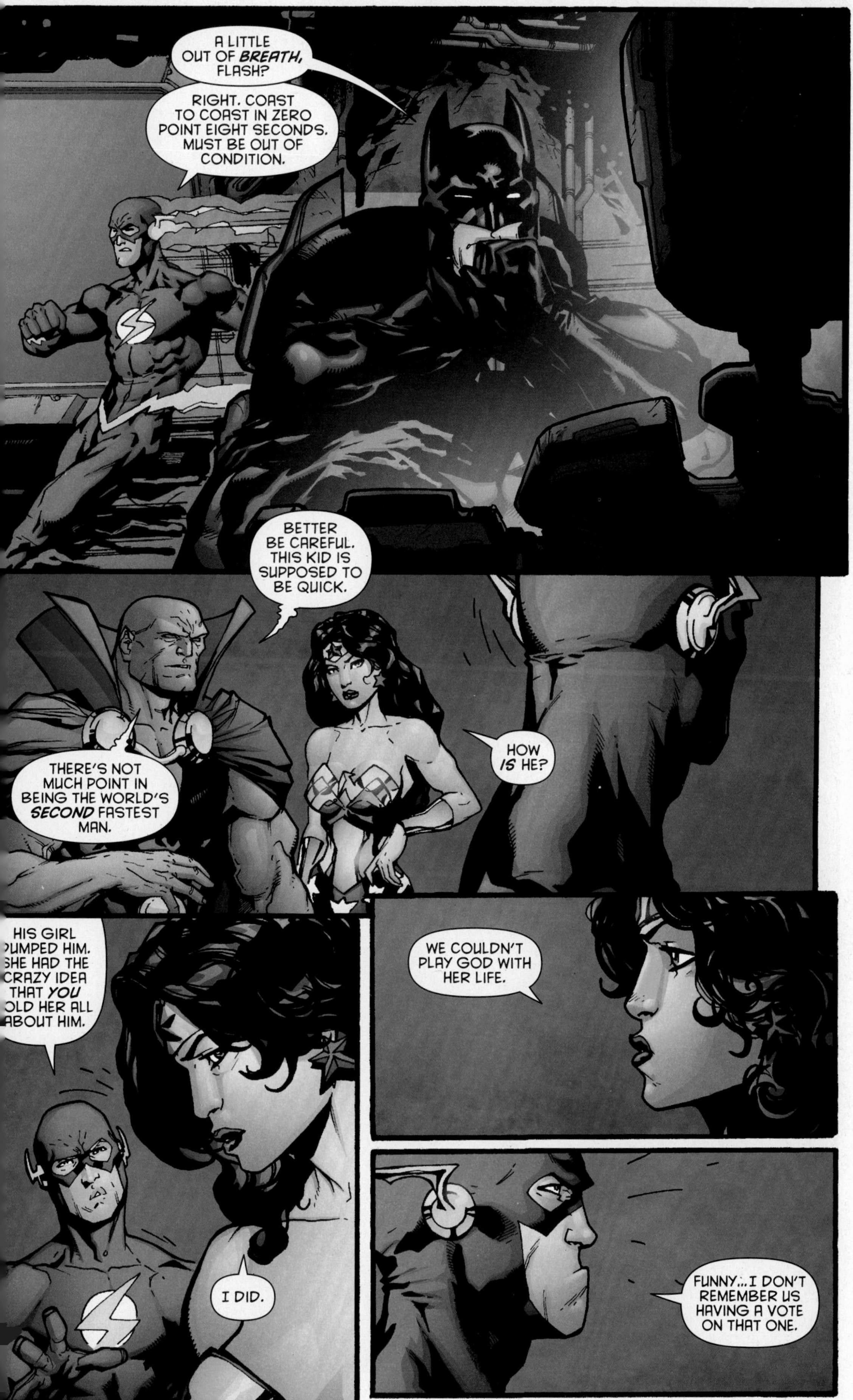
A LITTLE OUT OF BREATH, FLASH?
RIGHT. COAST TO COAST IN ZERO POINT EIGHT SECONDS. MUST BE OUT OF CONDITION.
BETTER BE CAREFUL. THIS KID IS SUPPOSED TO BE QUICK.
THERE'S NOT MUCH POINT IN BEING THE WORLD'S SECOND FASTEST MAN.
HOW IS HE?
HIS GIRL DUMPED HIM. SHE HAD THE CRAZY IDEA THAT YOU TOLD HER ALL ABOUT HIM.
I DID.
WE COULDN'T PLAY GOD WITH HER LIFE.
FUNNY... I DON'T REMEMBER US HAVING A VOTE ON THAT ONE.

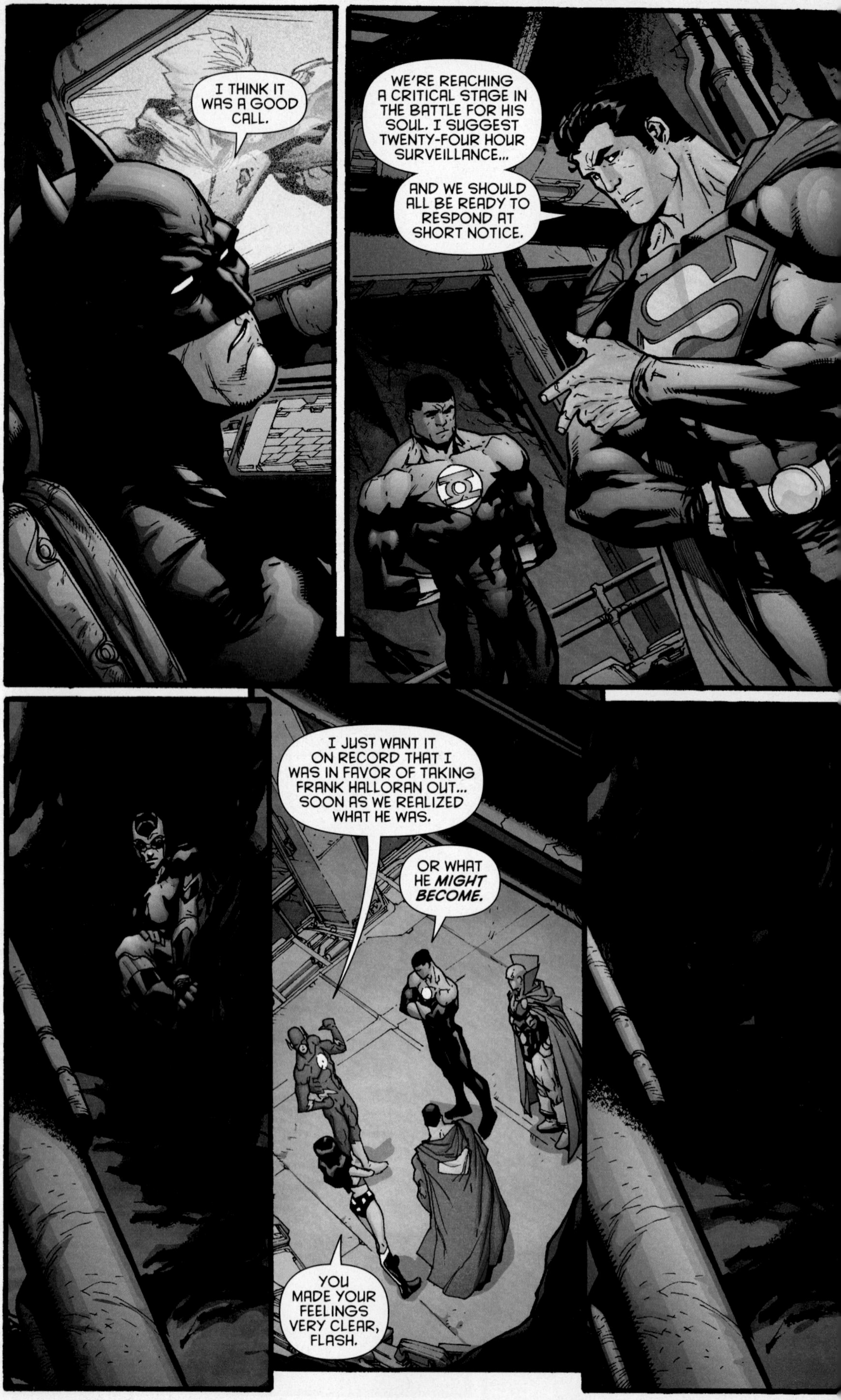
I THINK IT WAS A GOOD CALL.
WE'RE REACHING A CRITICAL STAGE IN THE BATTLE FOR HIS SOUL. I SUGGEST TWENTY-FOUR HOUR SURVEILLANCE...
AND WE SHOULD ALL BE READY TO RESPOND AT SHORT NOTICE.
I JUST WANT IT ON RECORD THAT I WAS IN FAVOR OF TAKING FRANK HALLORAN OUT... SOON AS WE REALIZED WHAT HE WAS.
OR WHAT HE *MIGHT BECOME.*
YOU MADE YOUR FEELINGS VERY CLEAR, FLASH.

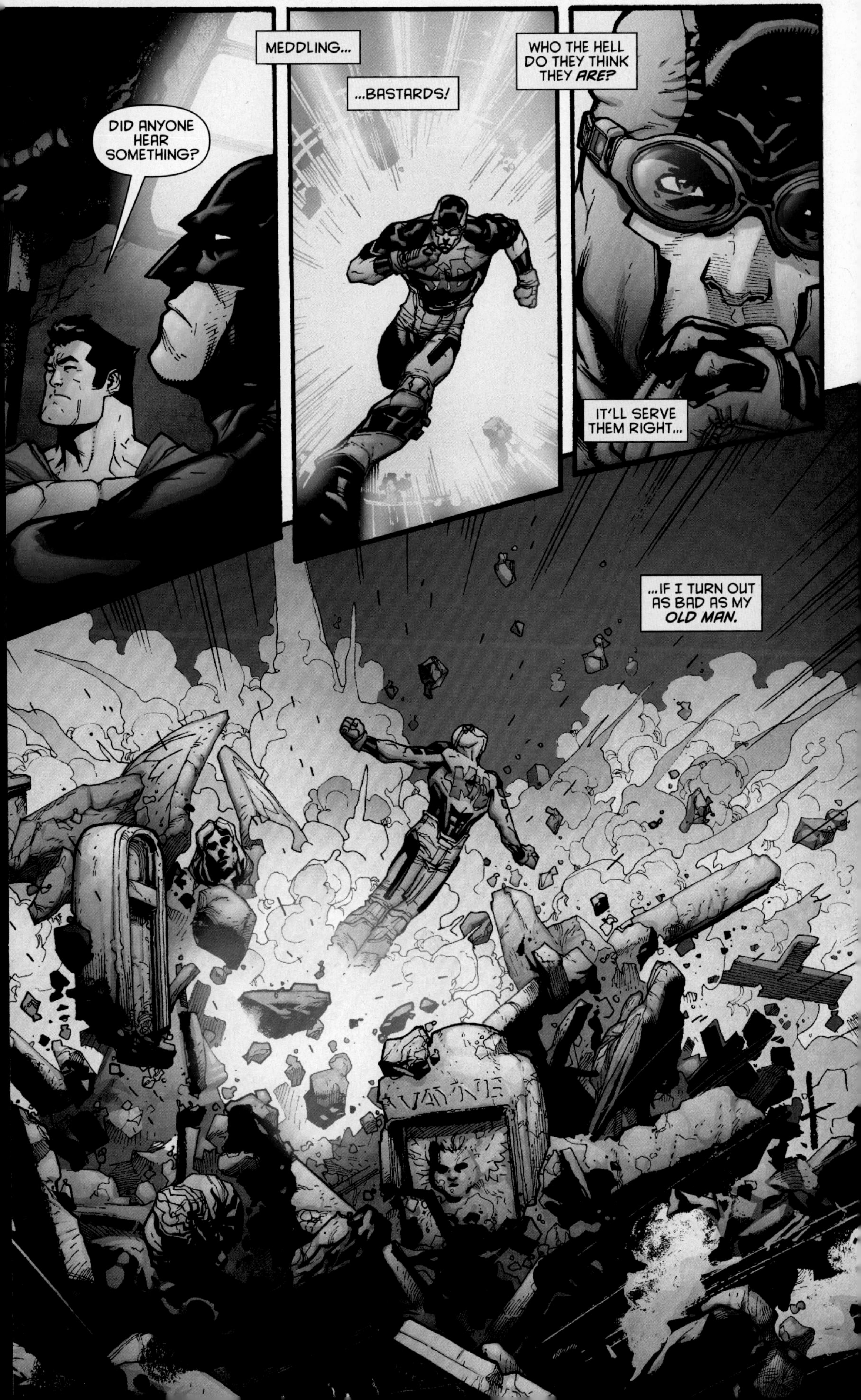
DID ANYONE HEAR SOMETHING?
MEDDLING...
...BASTARDS!
WHO THE HELL DO THEY THINK THEY ARE?
IT'LL SERVE THEM RIGHT...
...IF I TURN OUT AS BAD AS MY OLD MAN.
WAYNE

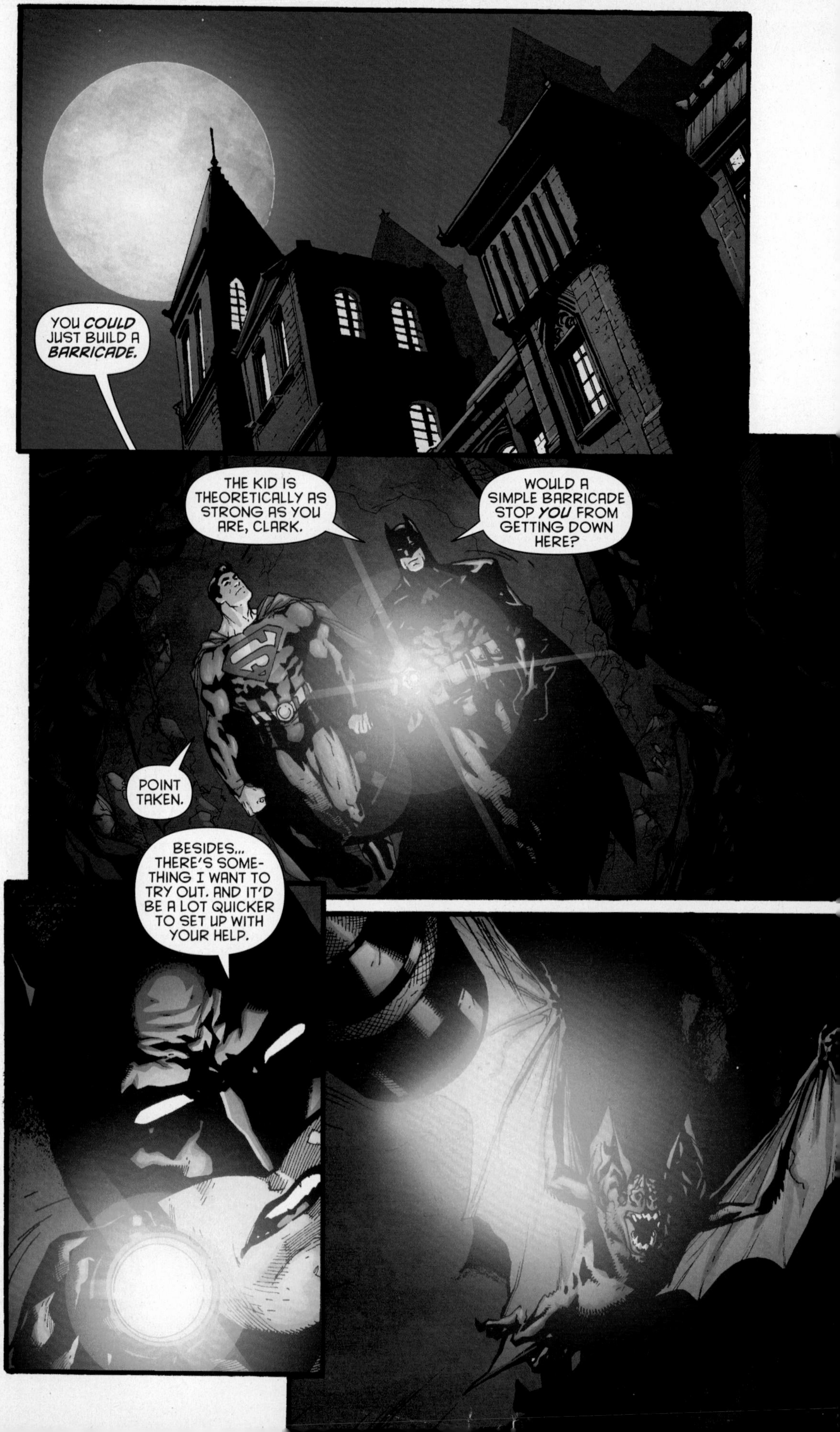
YOU COULD JUST BUILD A BARRICADE.
THE KID IS THEORETICALLY AS STRONG AS YOU ARE, CLARK.
WOULD A SIMPLE BARRICADE STOP YOU FROM GETTING DOWN HERE?
POINT TAKEN.
BESIDES... THERE'S SOME-THING I WANT TO TRY OUT. AND IT'D BE A LOT QUICKER TO SET UP WITH YOUR HELP.

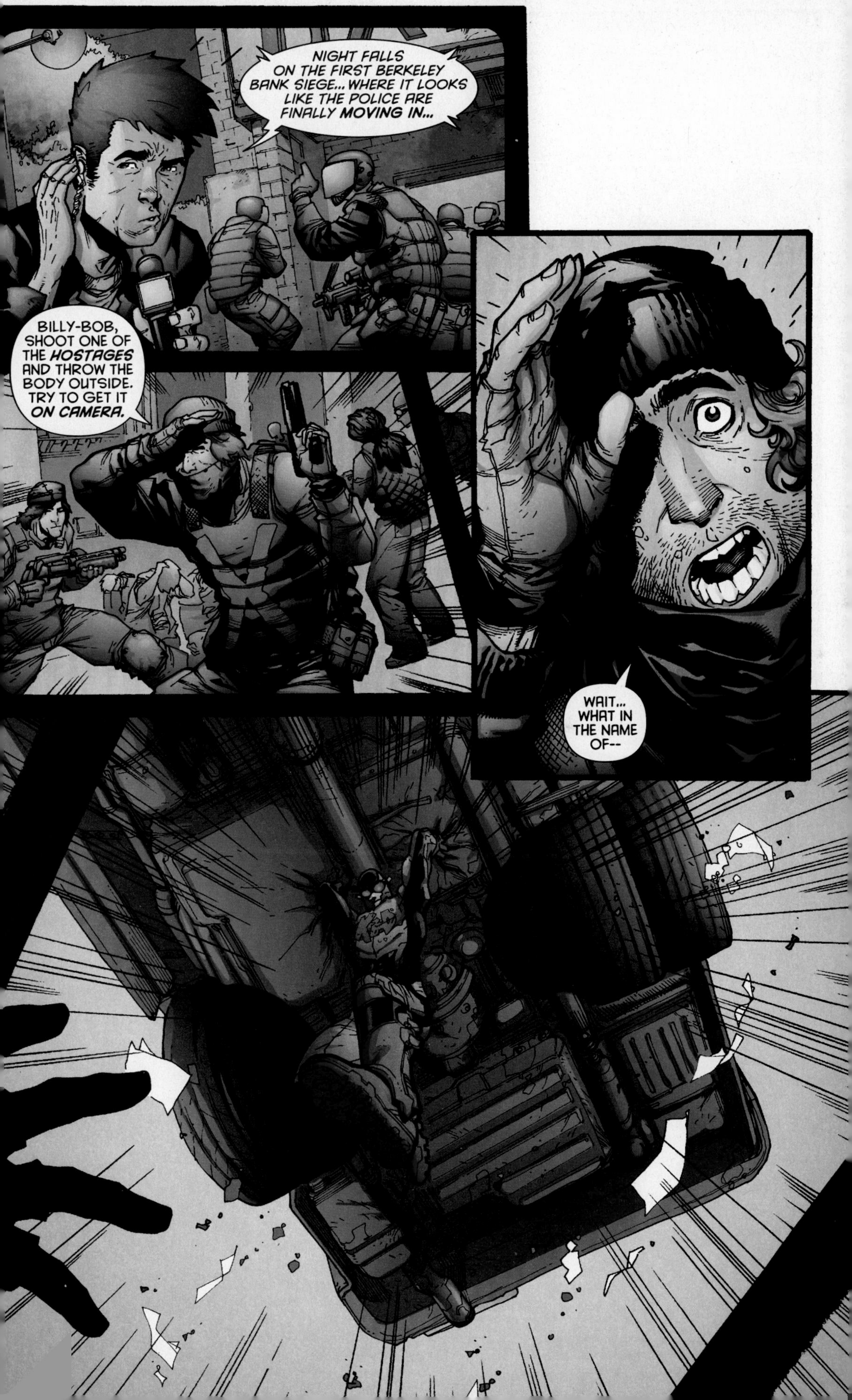
NIGHT FALLS ON THE FIRST BERKELEY BANK SIEGE... WHERE IT LOOKS LIKE THE POLICE ARE FINALLY MOVING IN...
BILLY-BOB, SHOOT ONE OF THE HOSTAGES AND THROW THE BODY OUTSIDE. TRY TO GET IT ON CAMERA.
WAIT... WHAT IN THE NAME OF--

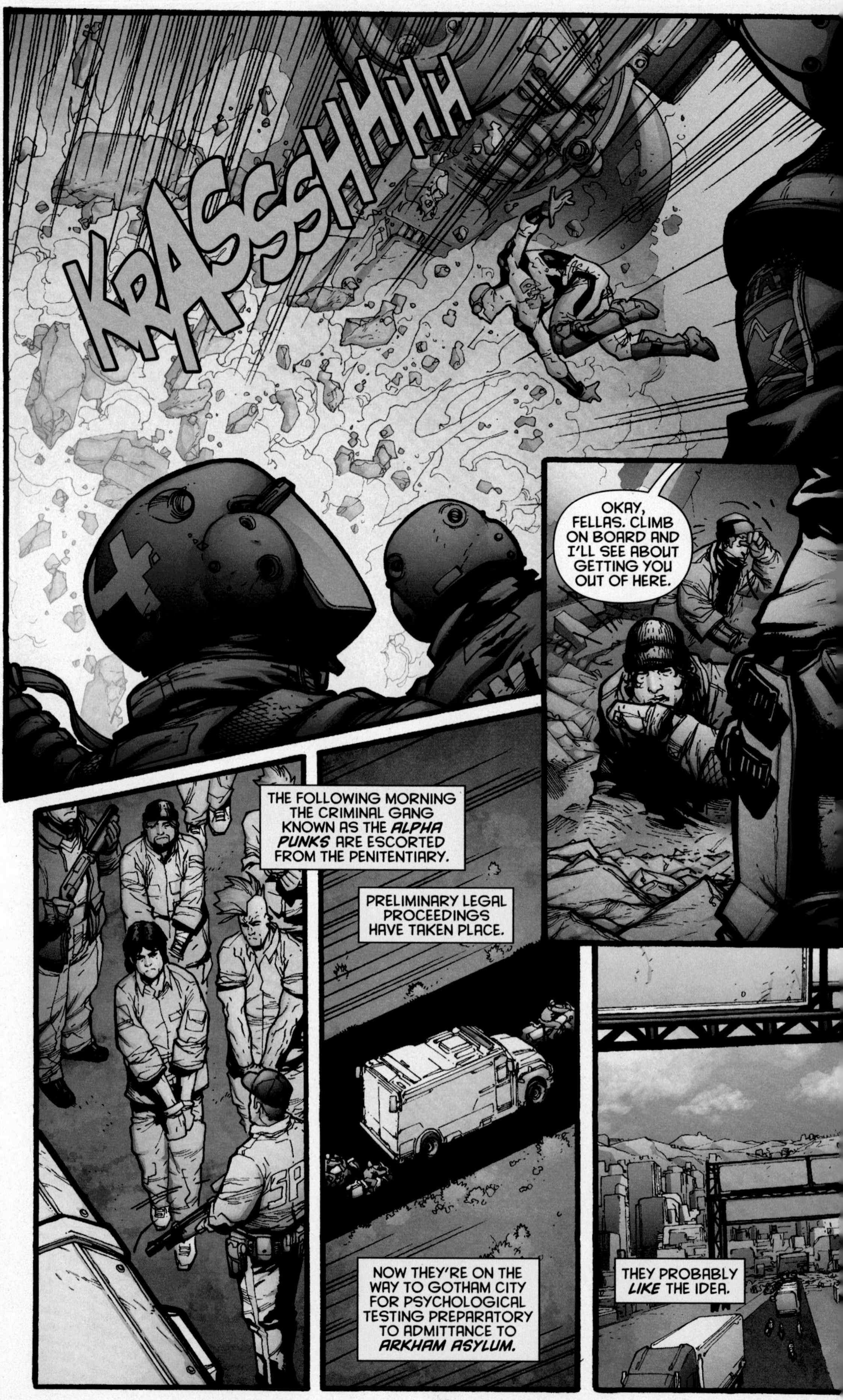
KRASSHHHHH
OKAY, FELLAS. CLIMB ON BOARD AND I'LL SEE ABOUT GETTING YOU OUT OF HERE.
THE FOLLOWING MORNING THE CRIMINAL GANG KNOWN AS THE *ALPHA PUNKS* ARE ESCORTED FROM THE PENITENTIARY.
PRELIMINARY LEGAL PROCEEDINGS HAVE TAKEN PLACE.
NOW THEY'RE ON THE WAY TO GOTHAM CITY FOR PSYCHOLOGICAL TESTING PREPARATORY TO ADMITTANCE TO *ARKHAM ASYLUM.*
THEY PROBABLY *LIKE* THE IDEA.

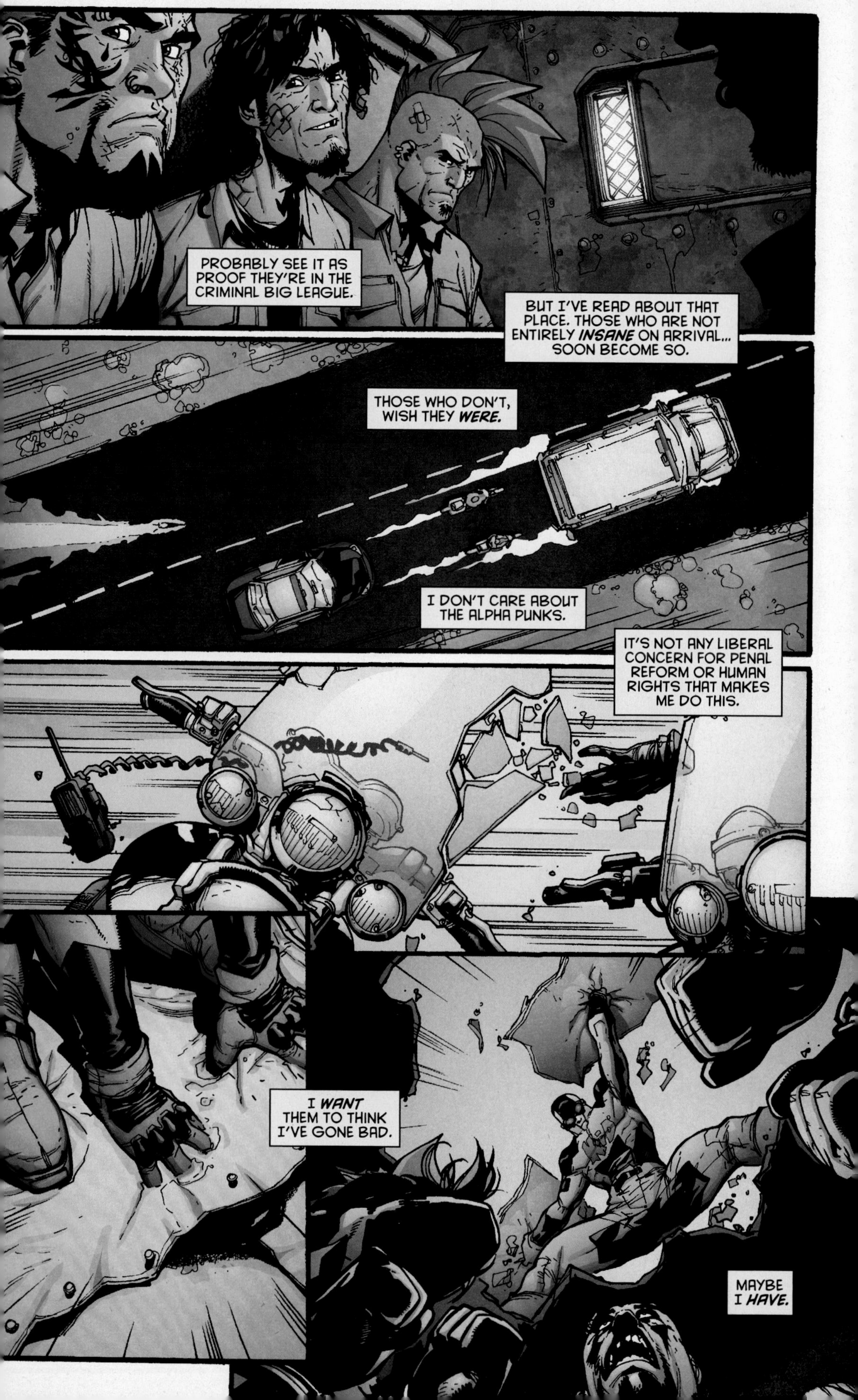
PROBABLY SEE IT AS PROOF THEY'RE IN THE CRIMINAL BIG LEAGUE.
BUT I'VE READ ABOUT THAT PLACE. THOSE WHO ARE NOT ENTIRELY *INSANE* ON ARRIVAL... SOON BECOME SO.
THOSE WHO DON'T, WISH THEY *WERE.*
I DON'T CARE ABOUT THE ALPHA PUNKS.
IT'S NOT ANY LIBERAL CONCERN FOR PENAL REFORM OR HUMAN RIGHTS THAT MAKES ME DO THIS.
I *WANT* THEM TO THINK I'VE GONE BAD.
MAYBE I *HAVE.*

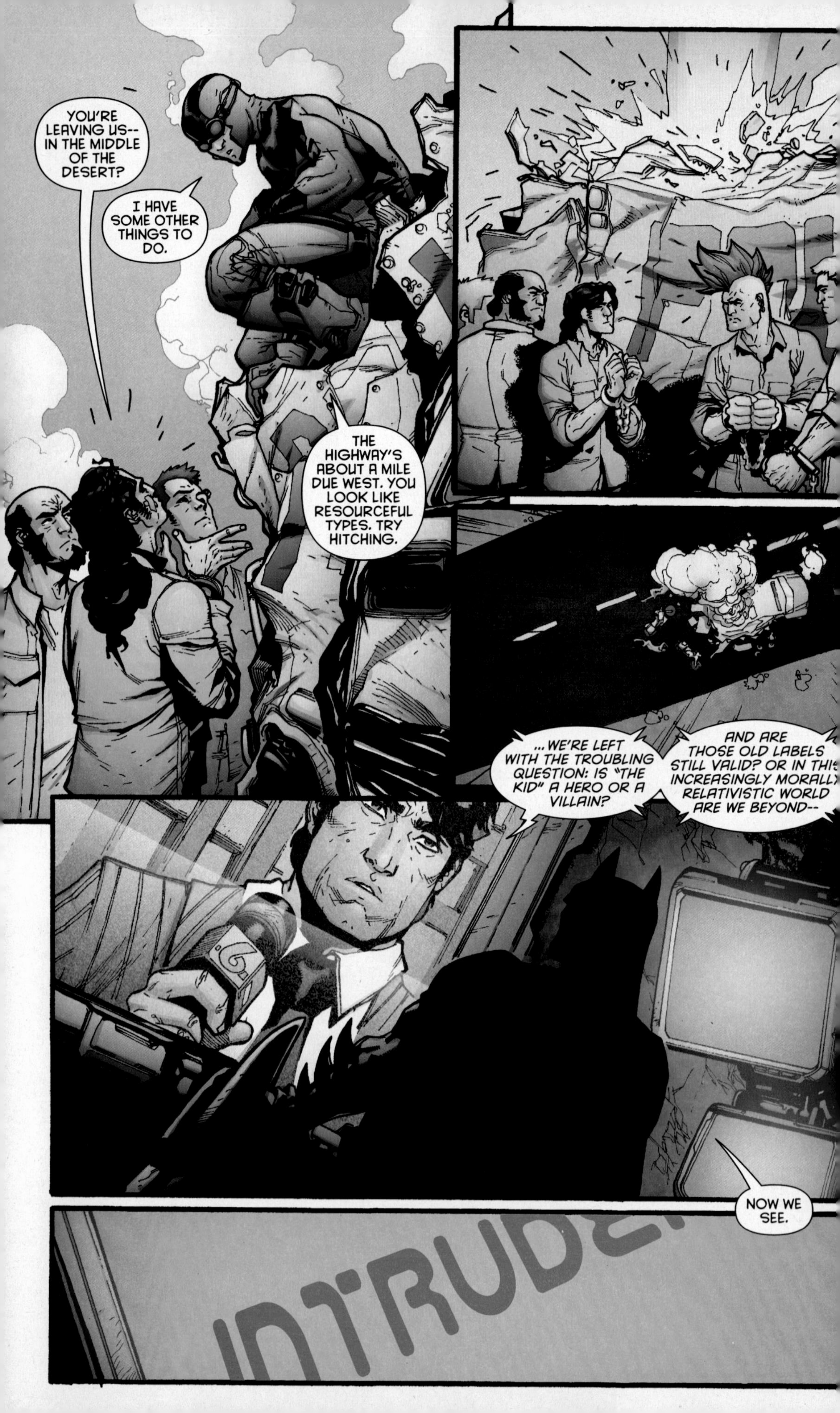
YOU'RE LEAVING US-- IN THE MIDDLE OF THE DESERT?
I HAVE SOME OTHER THINGS TO DO.
THE HIGHWAY'S ABOUT A MILE DUE WEST. YOU LOOK LIKE RESOURCEFUL TYPES. TRY HITCHING.
...WE'RE LEFT WITH THE TROUBLING QUESTION: IS "THE KID" A HERO OR A VILLAIN?
AND ARE THOSE OLD LABELS STILL VALID? OR IN THIS INCREASINGLY MORALLY RELATIVISTIC WORLD ARE WE BEYOND--
NOW WE SEE.
INTRUDE

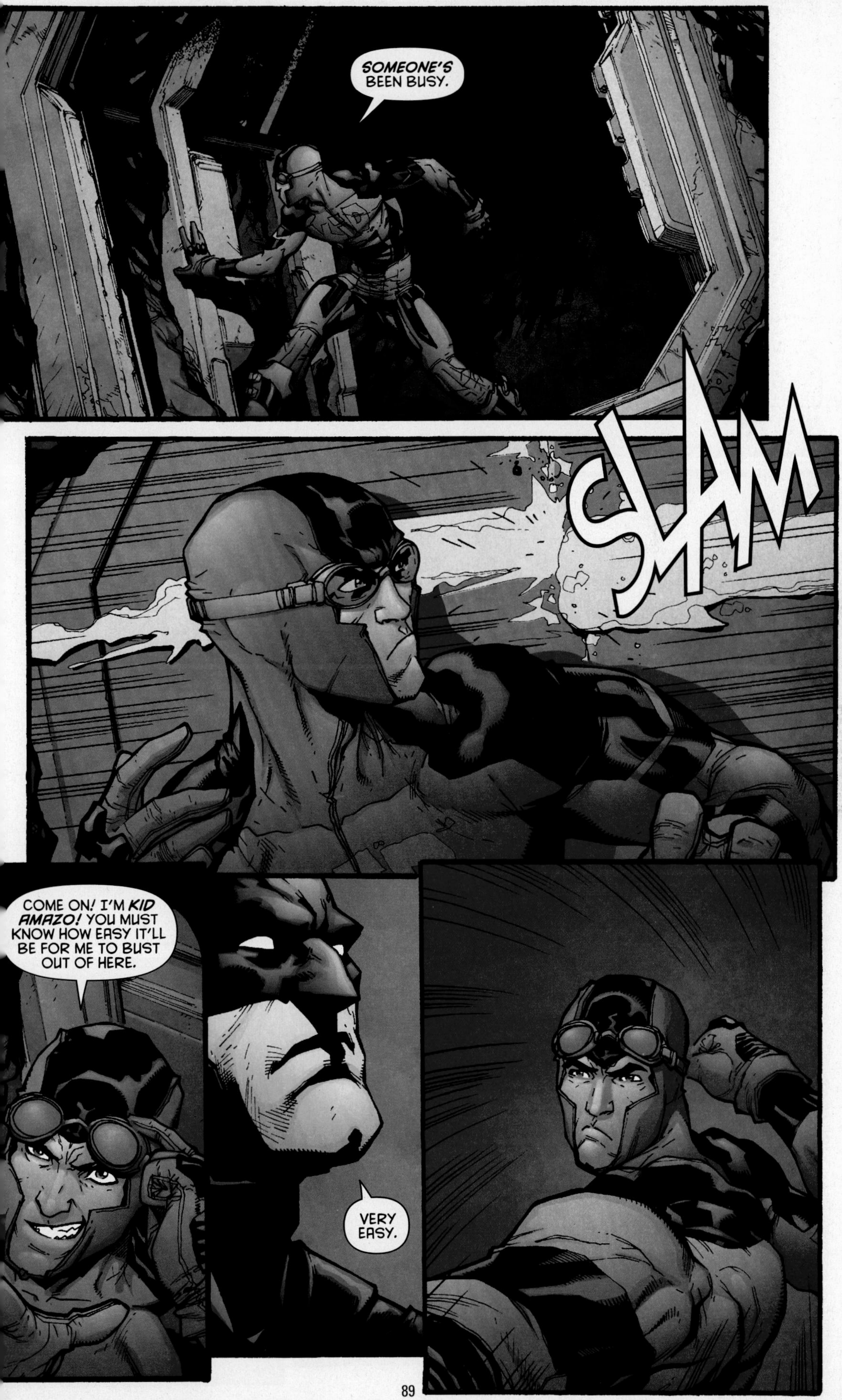
SOMEONE'S BEEN BUSY.
SLAM
COME ON! I'M KID AMAZO! YOU MUST KNOW HOW EASY IT'LL BE FOR ME TO BUST OUT OF HERE.
VERY EASY.

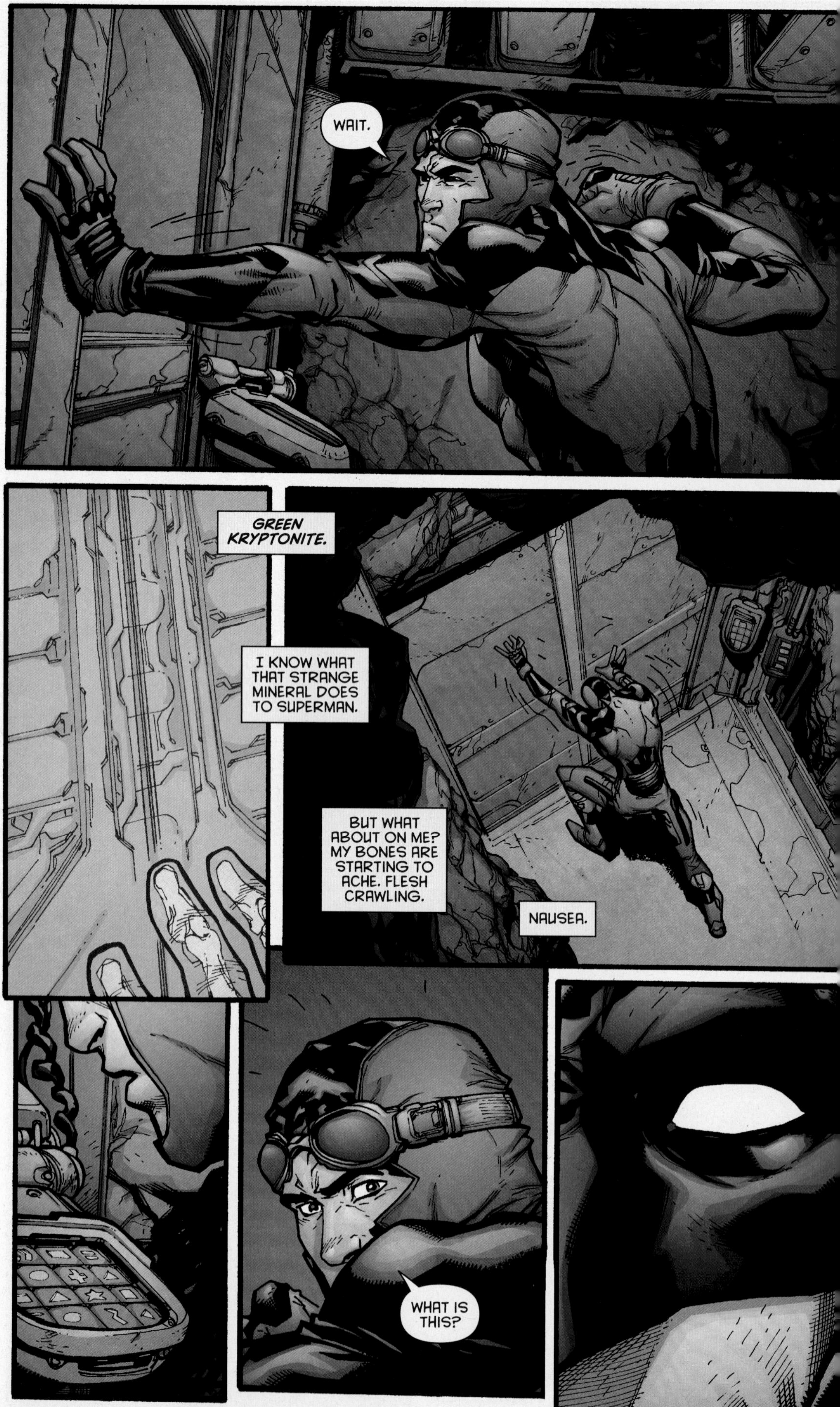
WAIT.
GREEN KRYPTONITE.
I KNOW WHAT THAT STRANGE MINERAL DOES TO SUPERMAN.
BUT WHAT ABOUT ON ME? MY BONES ARE STARTING TO ACHE. FLESH CRAWLING.
NAUSEA.
WHAT IS THIS?

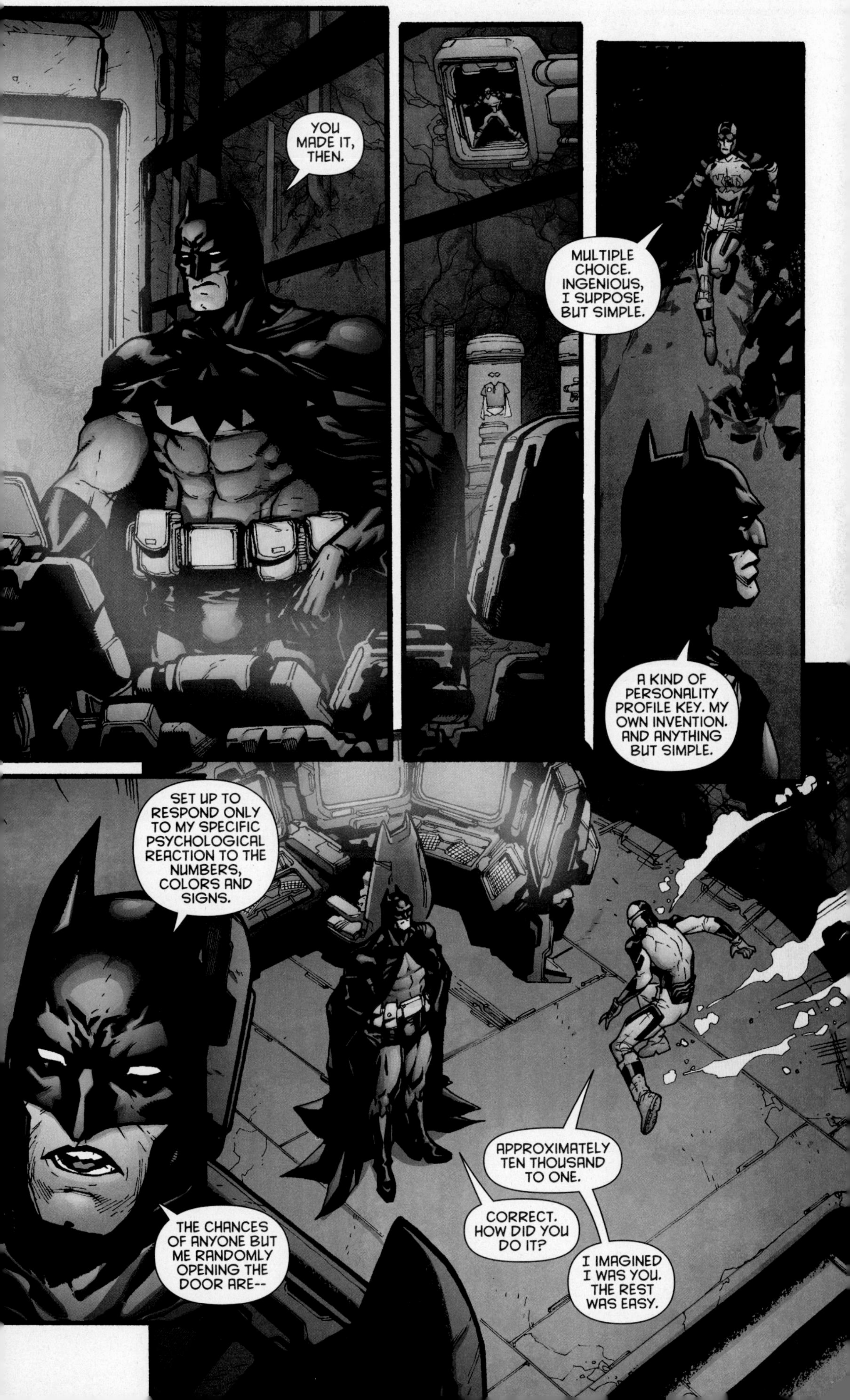
YOU MADE IT, THEN.
MULTIPLE CHOICE. INGENIOUS, I SUPPOSE. BUT SIMPLE.
A KIND OF PERSONALITY PROFILE KEY. MY OWN INVENTION. AND ANYTHING BUT SIMPLE.
SET UP TO RESPOND ONLY TO MY SPECIFIC PSYCHOLOGICAL REACTION TO THE NUMBERS, COLORS AND SIGNS.
THE CHANCES OF ANYONE BUT ME RANDOMLY OPENING THE DOOR ARE--
APPROXIMATELY TEN THOUSAND TO ONE.
CORRECT. HOW DID YOU DO IT?
I IMAGINED I WAS YOU. THE REST WAS EASY.

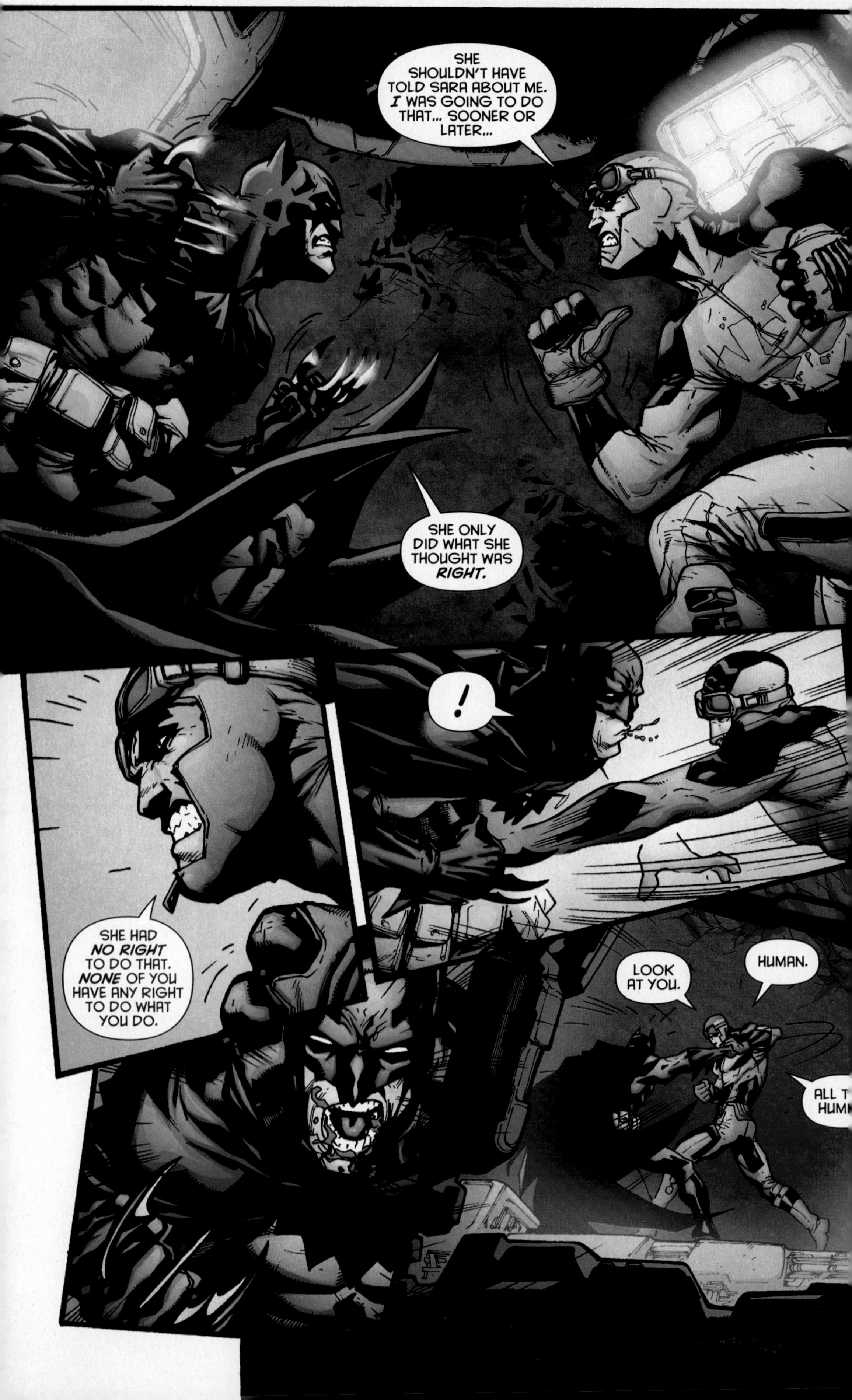
SHE SHOULDN'T HAVE TOLD SARA ABOUT ME. *I* WAS GOING TO DO THAT... SOONER OR LATER...
SHE ONLY DID WHAT SHE THOUGHT WAS ***RIGHT.***
!
SHE HAD ***NO RIGHT*** TO DO THAT. ***NONE*** OF YOU HAVE ANY RIGHT TO DO WHAT YOU DO.
LOOK AT YOU.
HUMAN.
ALL T
HUM

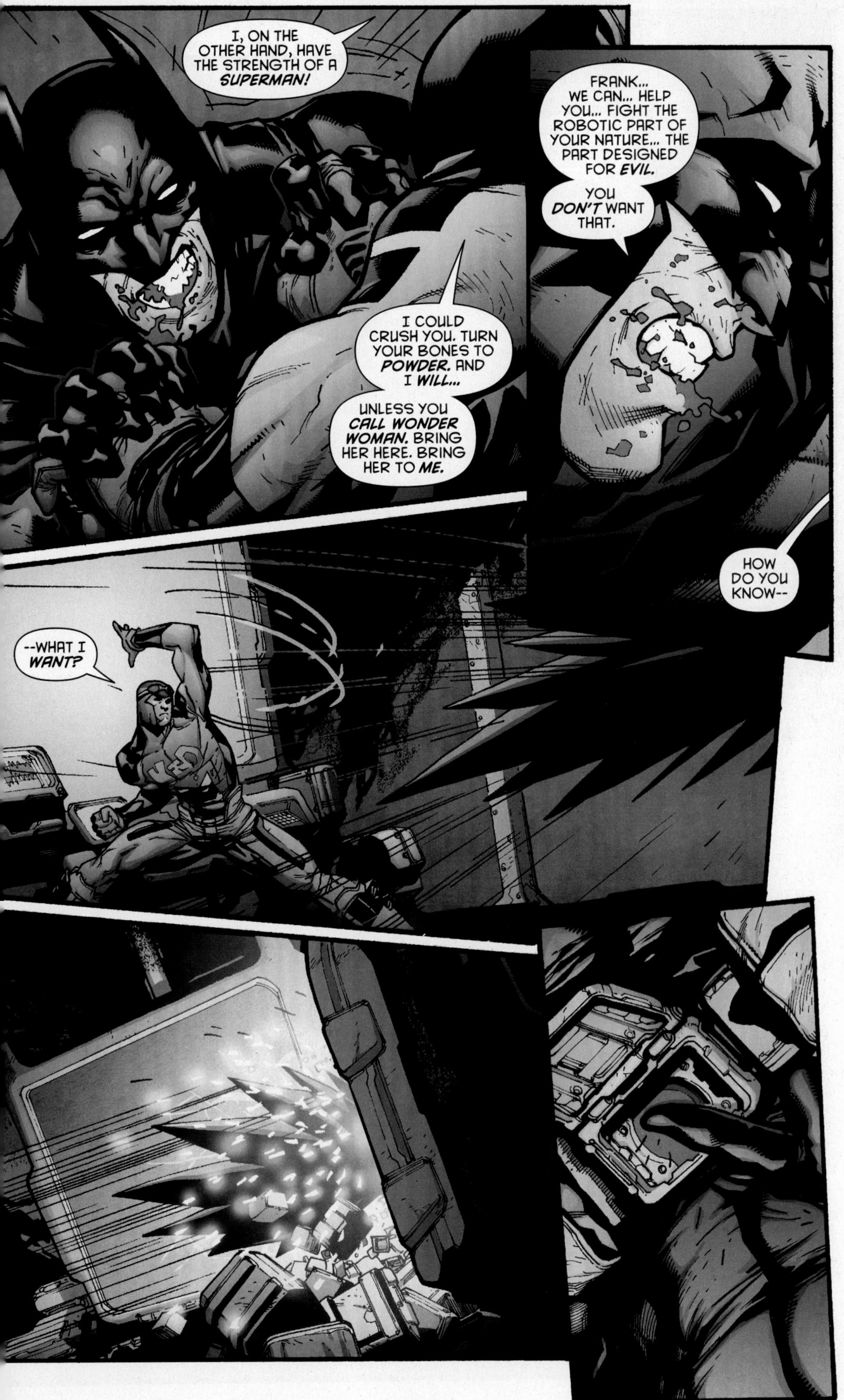

I, ON THE OTHER HAND, HAVE THE STRENGTH OF A *SUPERMAN!*
I COULD CRUSH YOU. TURN YOUR BONES TO *POWDER.* AND I *WILL...*
UNLESS YOU *CALL WONDER WOMAN.* BRING HER HERE. BRING HER TO *ME.*
FRANK... WE CAN... HELP YOU... FIGHT THE ROBOTIC PART OF YOUR NATURE... THE PART DESIGNED FOR *EVIL.*
YOU *DON'T* WANT THAT.
HOW DO YOU KNOW--
--WHAT I *WANT?*

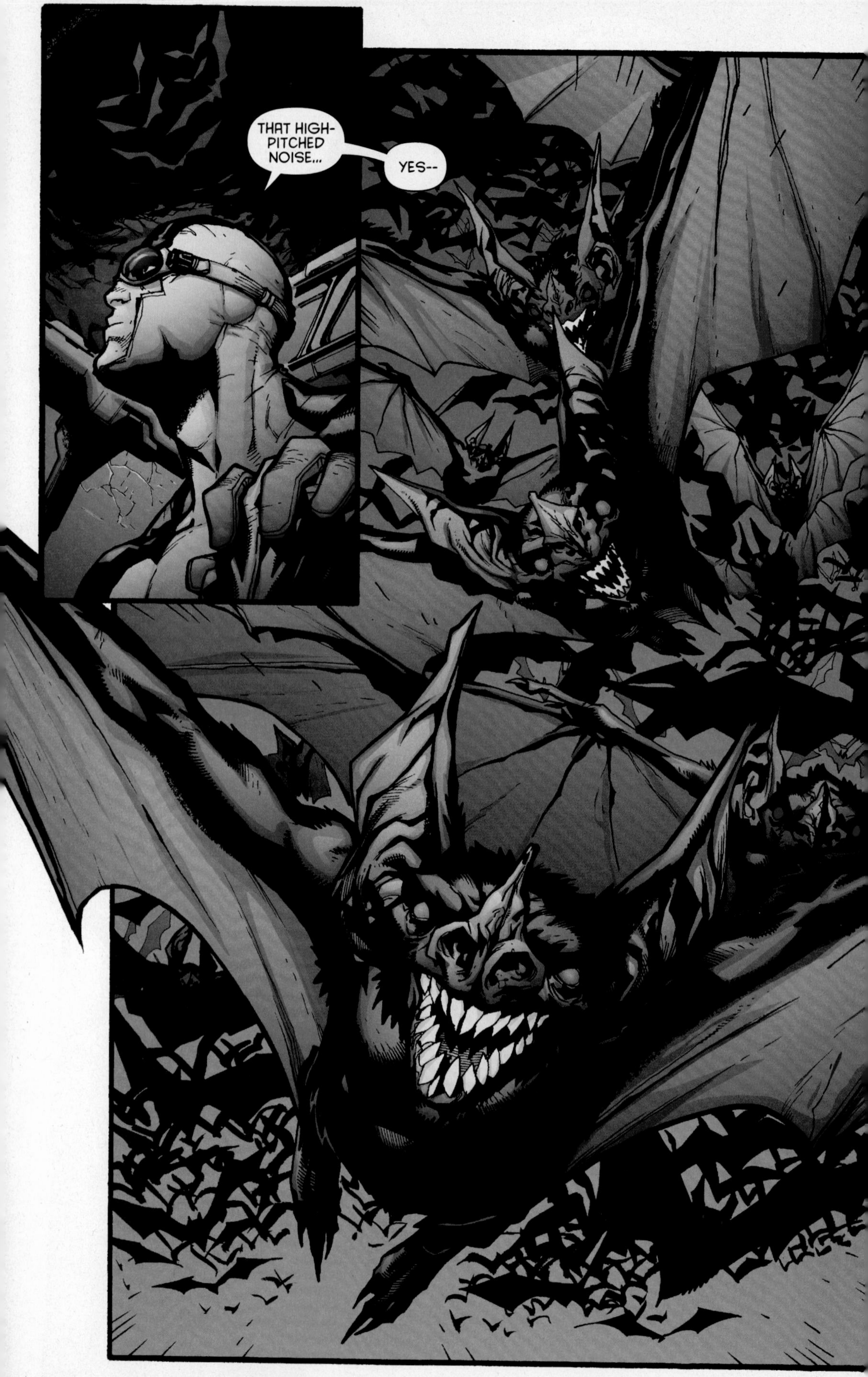
THAT HIGH-PITCHED NOISE...
YES--

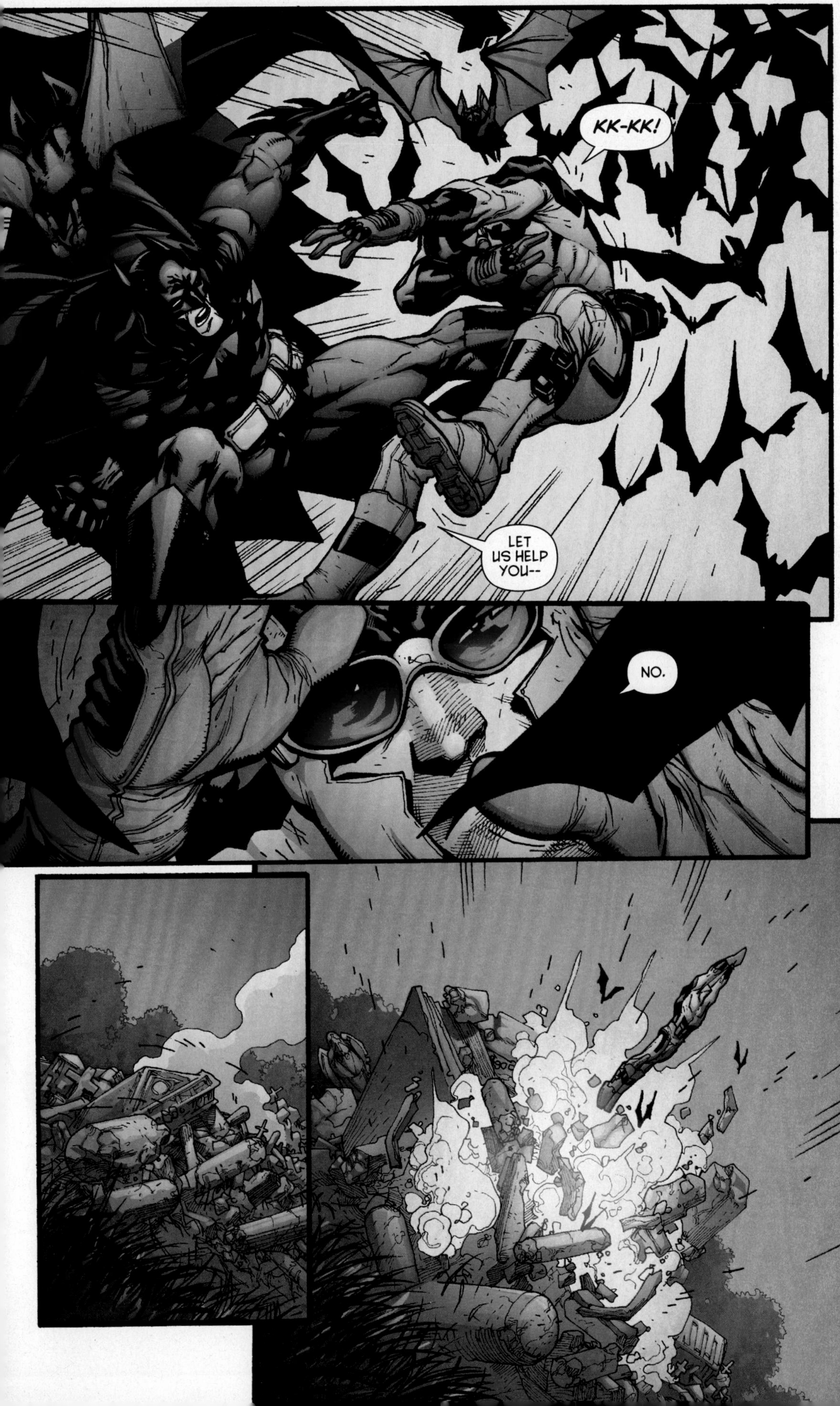
KK-KK!
LET US HELP YOU--
NO.

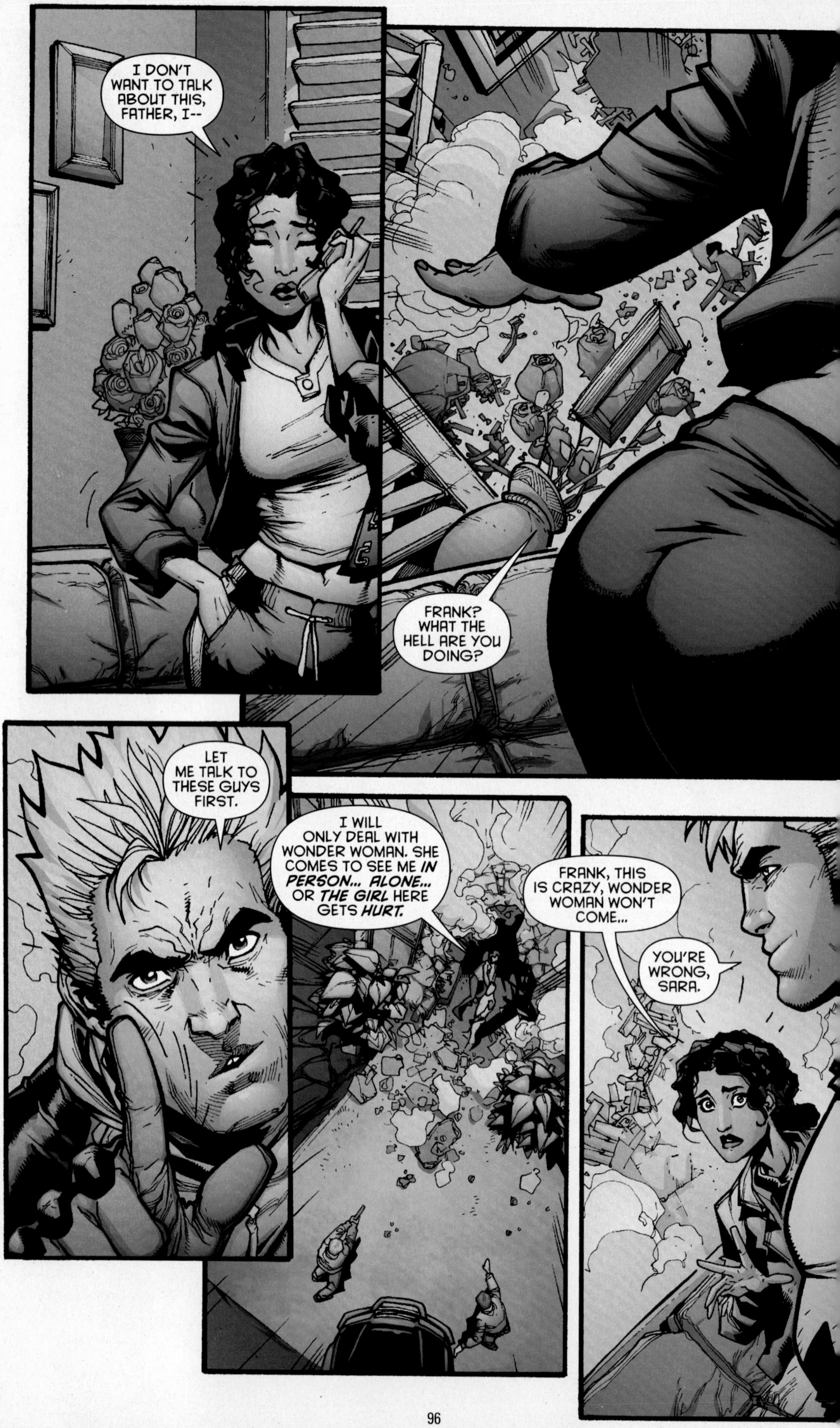
I DON'T WANT TO TALK ABOUT THIS, FATHER, I--
FRANK? WHAT THE HELL ARE YOU DOING?
LET ME TALK TO THESE GUYS FIRST.
I WILL ONLY DEAL WITH WONDER WOMAN. SHE COMES TO SEE ME *IN PERSON... ALONE...* OR *THE GIRL* HERE GETS *HURT.*
FRANK, THIS IS CRAZY, WONDER WOMAN WON'T COME...
YOU'RE WRONG, SARA.

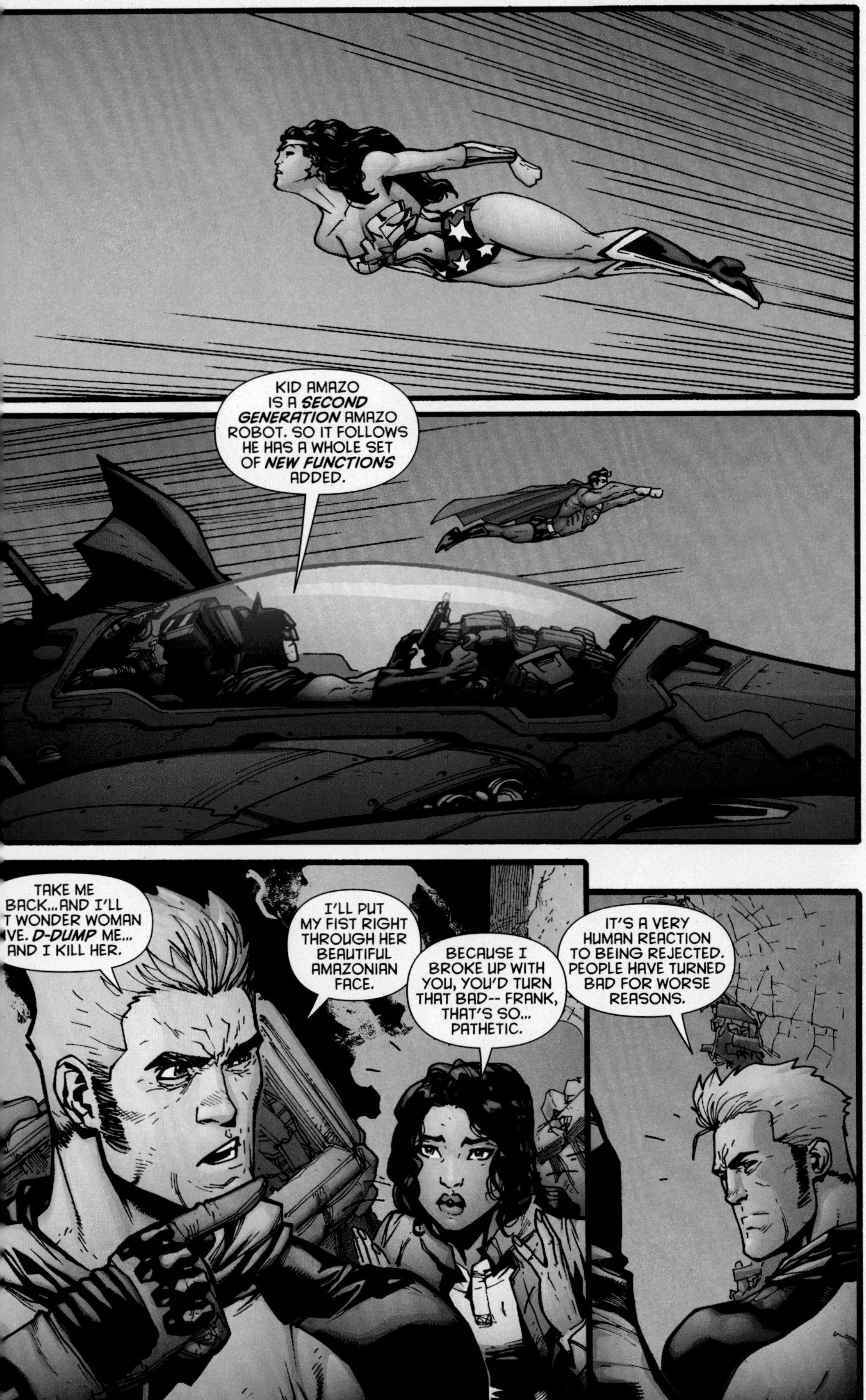
KID AMAZO IS A SECOND GENERATION AMAZO ROBOT. SO IT FOLLOWS HE HAS A WHOLE SET OF NEW FUNCTIONS ADDED.
TAKE ME BACK...AND I'LL T WONDER WOMAN VE. D-DUMP ME... AND I KILL HER.
I'LL PUT MY FIST RIGHT THROUGH HER BEAUTIFUL AMAZONIAN FACE.
BECAUSE I BROKE UP WITH YOU, YOU'D TURN THAT BAD-- FRANK, THAT'S SO... PATHETIC.
IT'S A VERY HUMAN REACTION TO BEING REJECTED. PEOPLE HAVE TURNED BAD FOR WORSE REASONS.

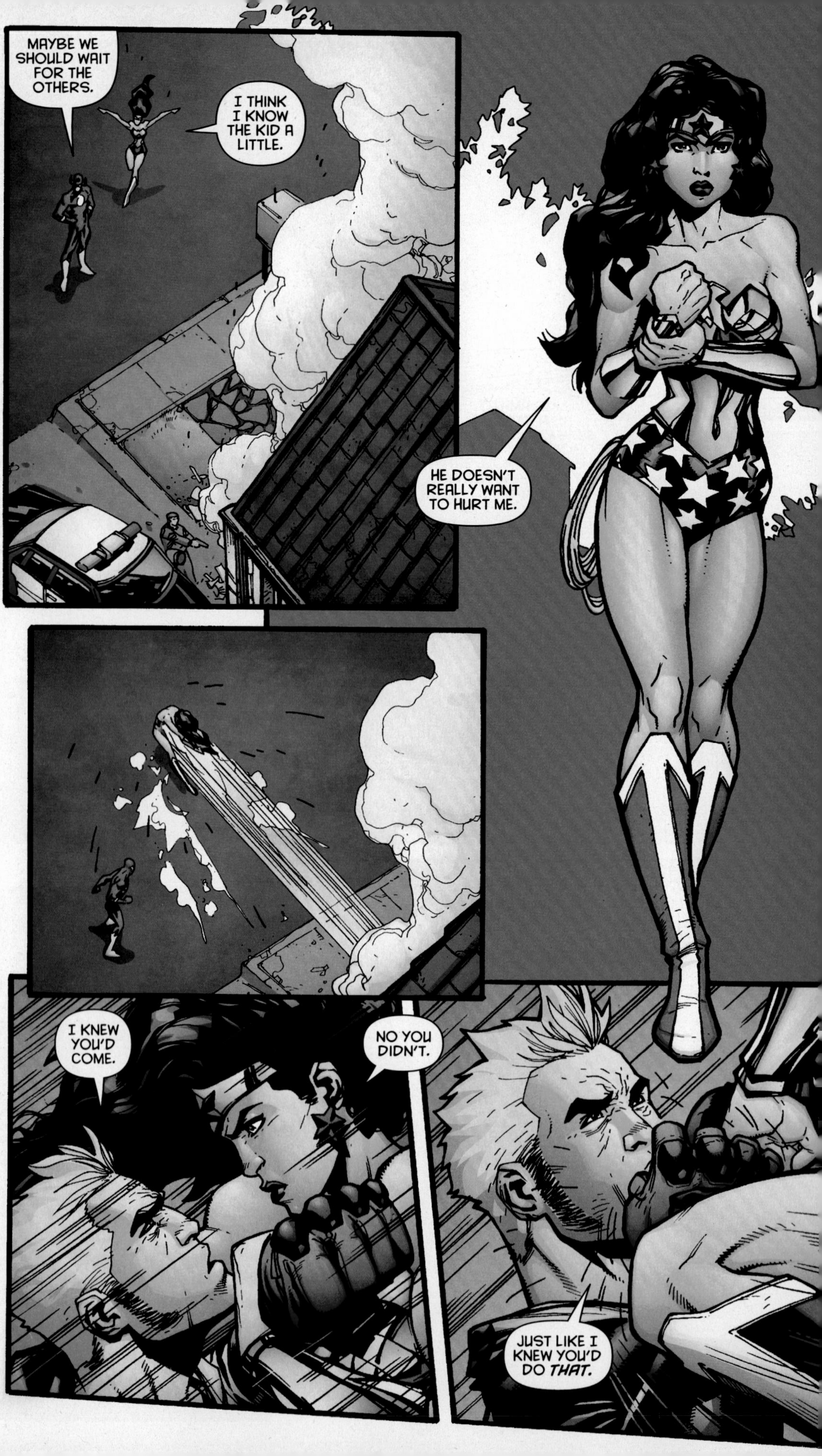
MAYBE WE SHOULD WAIT FOR THE OTHERS.
I THINK I KNOW THE KID A LITTLE.
HE DOESN'T REALLY WANT TO HURT ME.
I KNEW YOU'D COME.
NO YOU DIDN'T.
JUST LIKE I KNEW YOU'D DO *THAT*.

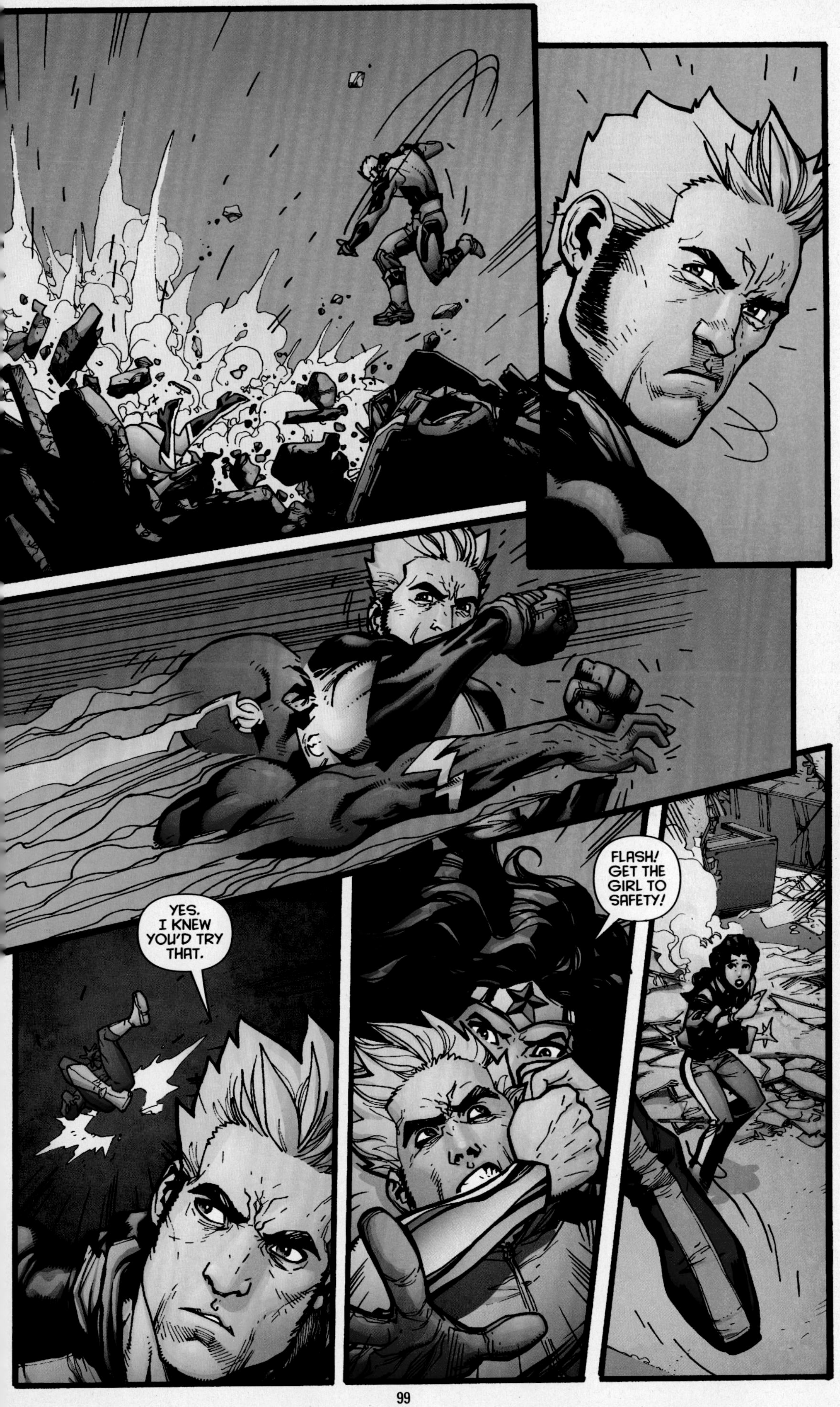
YES. I KNEW YOU'D TRY THAT.
FLASH! GET THE GIRL TO SAFETY!

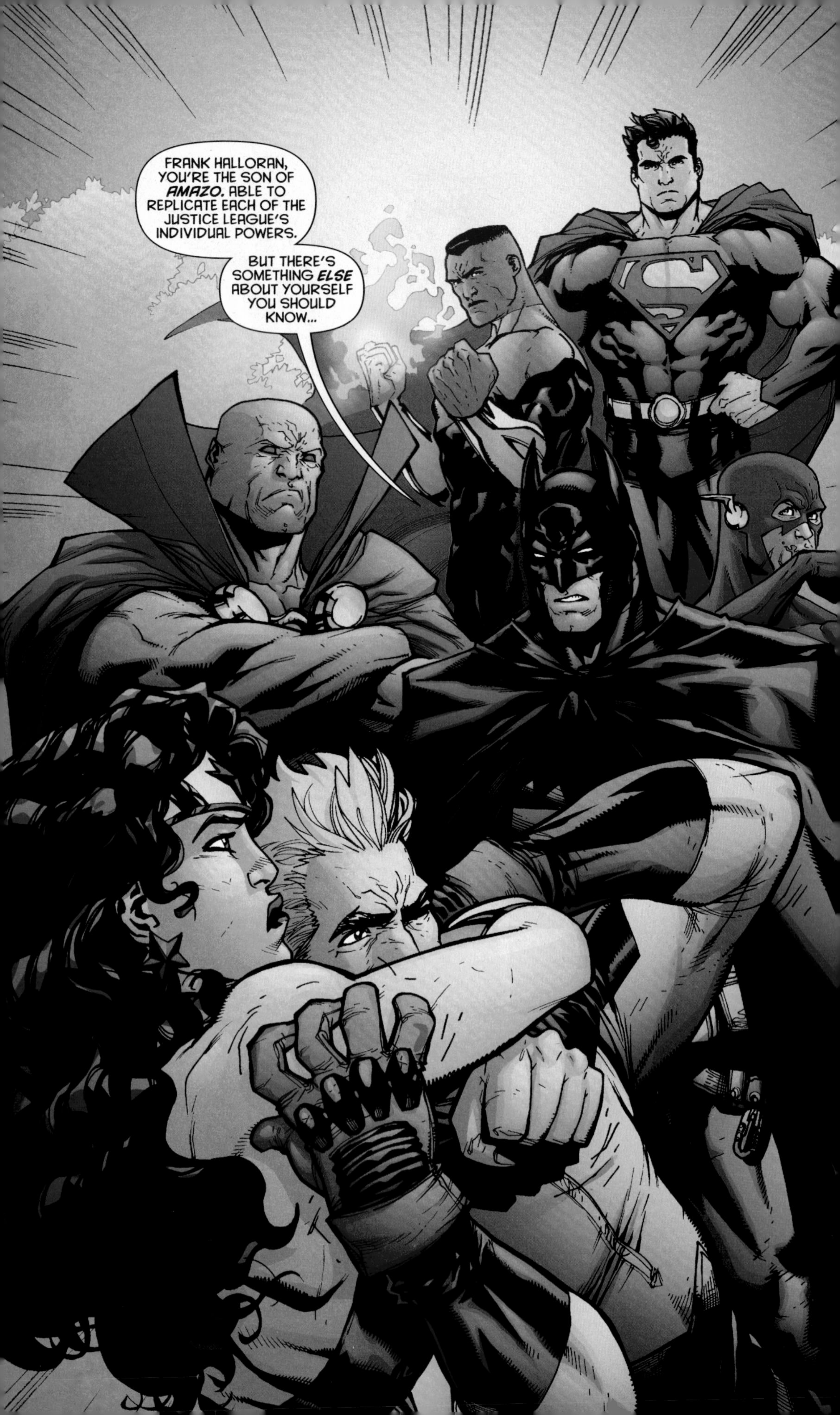
FRANK HALLORAN, YOU'RE THE SON OF AMAZO. ABLE TO REPLICATE EACH OF THE JUSTICE LEAGUE'S INDIVIDUAL POWERS.
BUT THERE'S SOMETHING ELSE ABOUT YOURSELF YOU SHOULD KNOW...

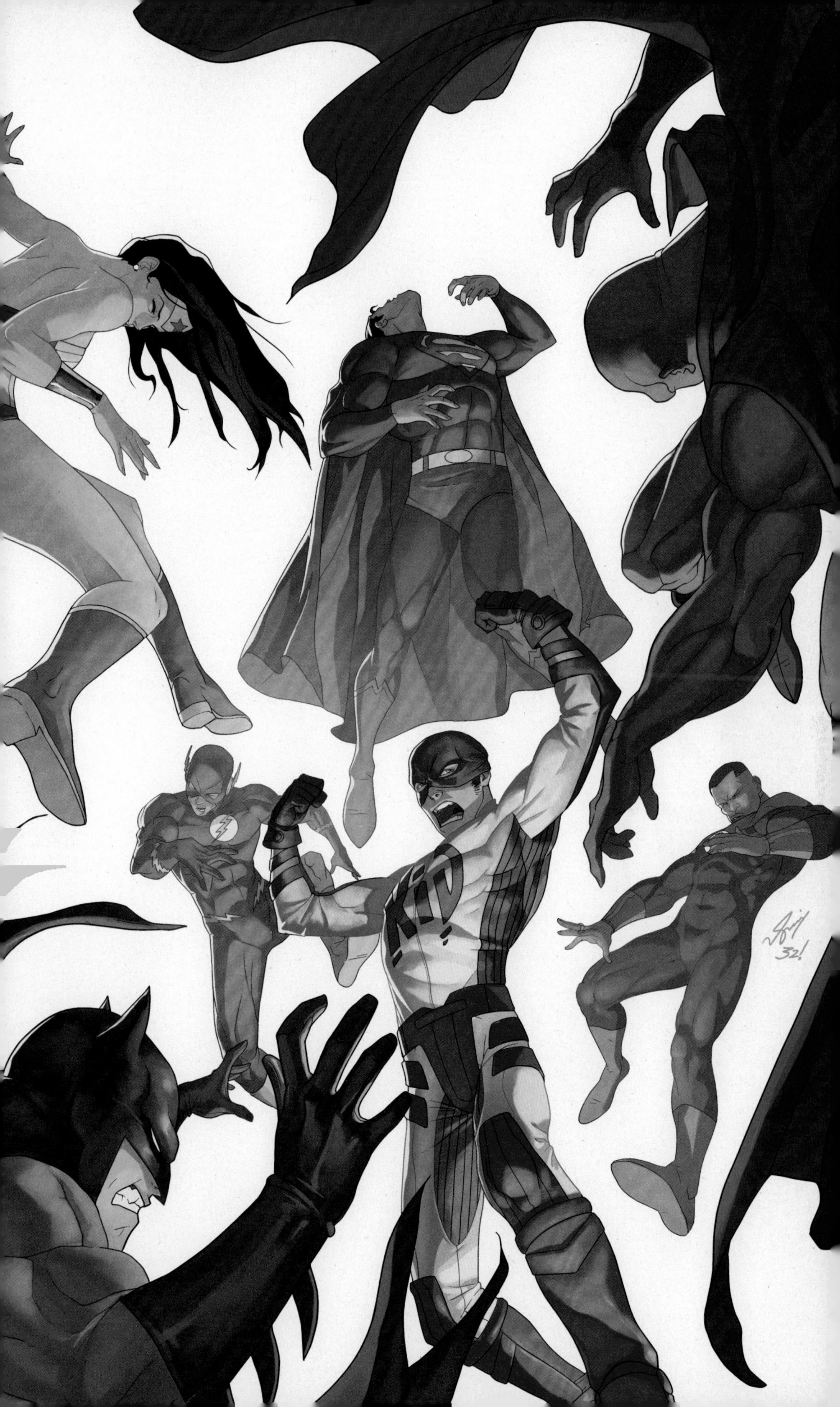

Chapter Five
TWILIGHT OF THE GODS

COVER ART BY SAMI BASRI

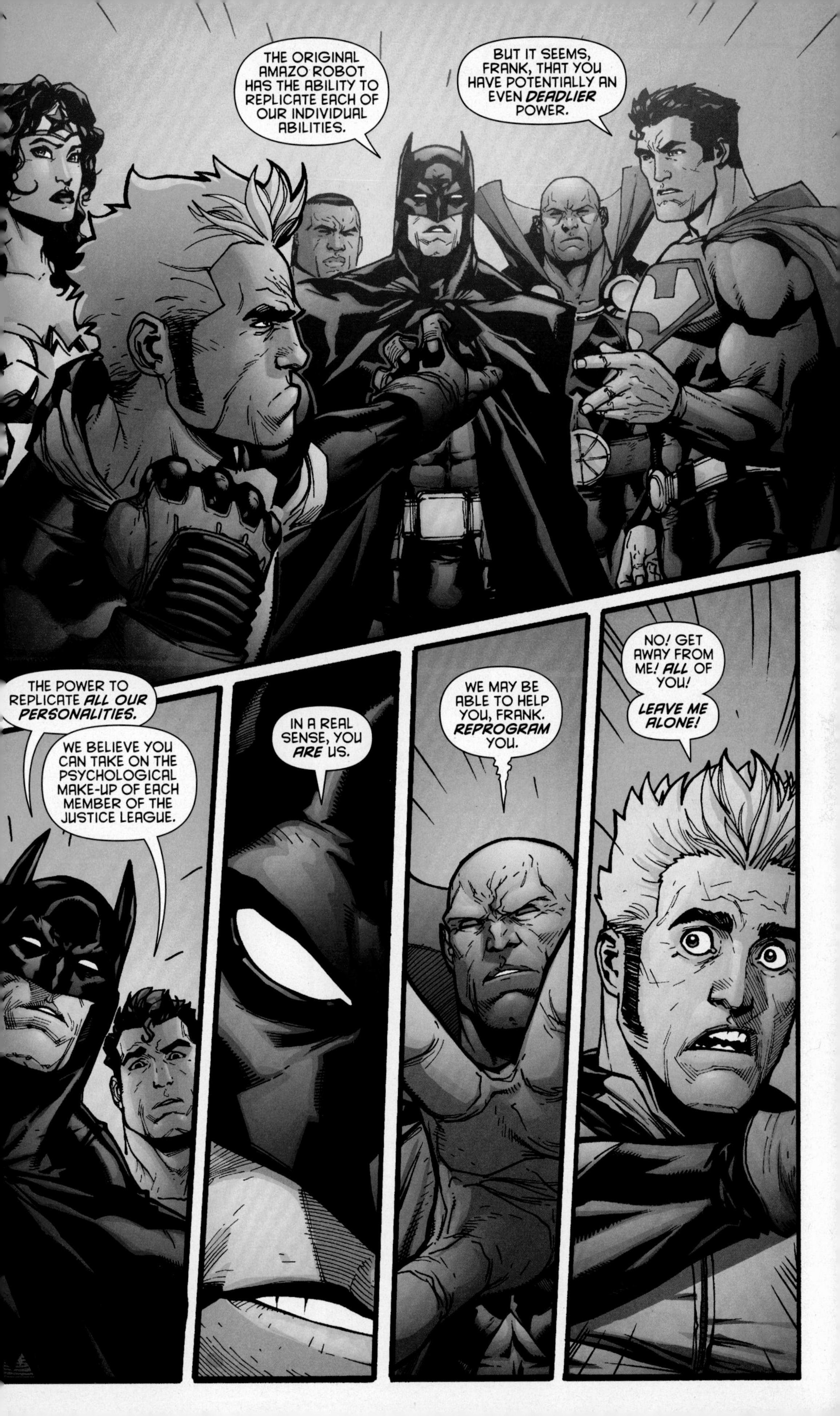
THE ORIGINAL AMAZO ROBOT HAS THE ABILITY TO REPLICATE EACH OF OUR INDIVIDUAL ABILITIES.
BUT IT SEEMS, FRANK, THAT YOU HAVE POTENTIALLY AN EVEN DEADLIER POWER.
THE POWER TO REPLICATE ALL OUR PERSONALITIES.
WE BELIEVE YOU CAN TAKE ON THE PSYCHOLOGICAL MAKE-UP OF EACH MEMBER OF THE JUSTICE LEAGUE.
IN A REAL SENSE, YOU ARE US.
WE MAY BE ABLE TO HELP YOU, FRANK. REPROGRAM YOU.
NO! GET AWAY FROM ME! ALL OF YOU!
LEAVE ME ALONE!

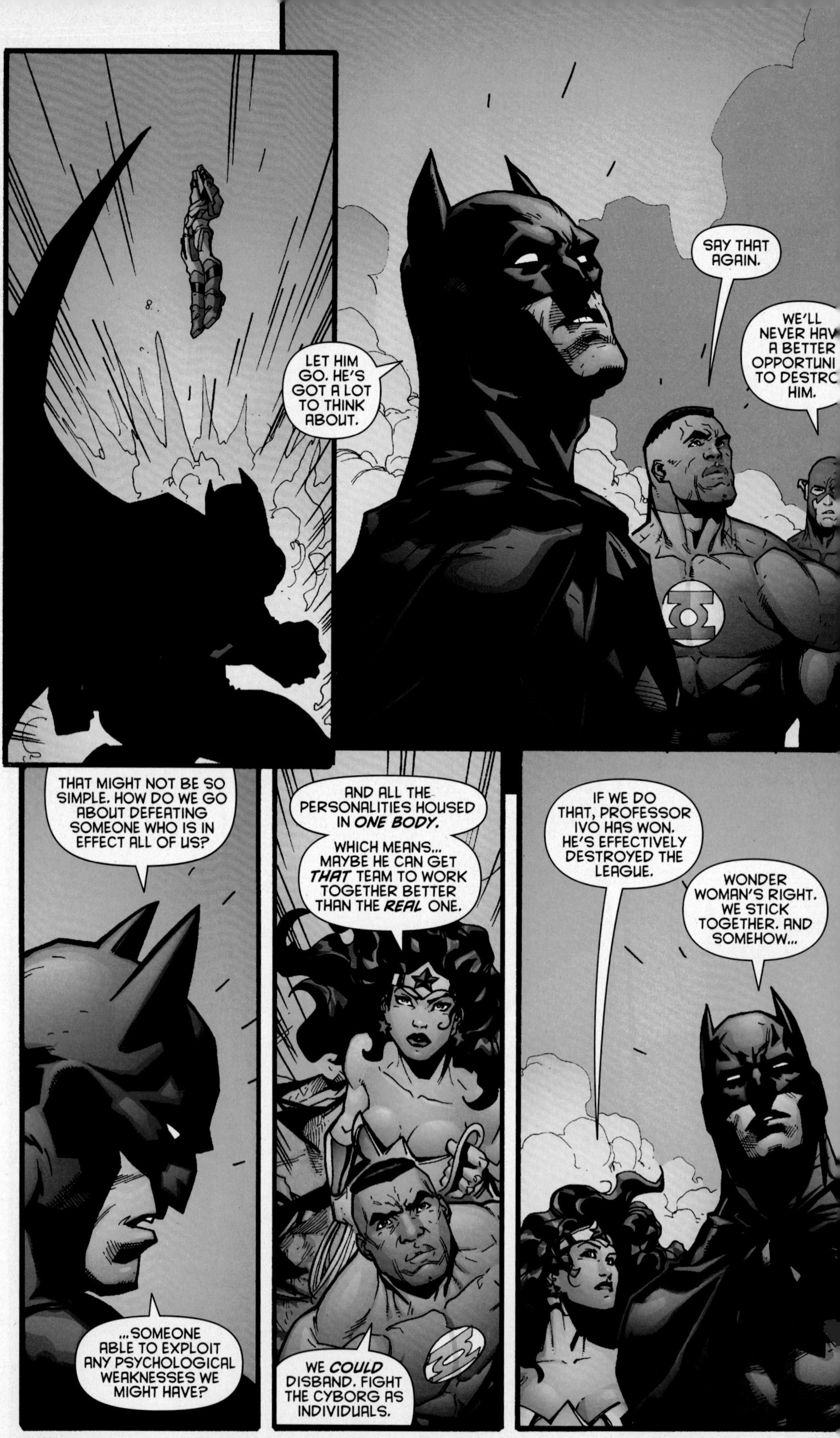
LET HIM GO. HE'S GOT A LOT TO THINK ABOUT.
SAY THAT AGAIN.
WE'LL NEVER HAV A BETTER OPPORTUNI TO DESTRC HIM.
THAT MIGHT NOT BE SO SIMPLE. HOW DO WE GO ABOUT DEFEATING SOMEONE WHO IS IN EFFECT ALL OF US?
...SOMEONE ABLE TO EXPLOIT ANY PSYCHOLOGICAL WEAKNESSES WE MIGHT HAVE?
AND ALL THE PERSONALITIES HOUSED IN *ONE BODY.*
WHICH MEANS... MAYBE HE CAN GET *THAT* TEAM TO WORK TOGETHER BETTER THAN THE *REAL* ONE.
WE *COULD* DISBAND. FIGHT THE CYBORG AS INDIVIDUALS.
IF WE DO THAT, PROFESSOR IVO HAS WON. HE'S EFFECTIVELY DESTROYED THE LEAGUE.
WONDER WOMAN'S RIGHT. WE STICK TOGETHER. AND SOMEHOW...

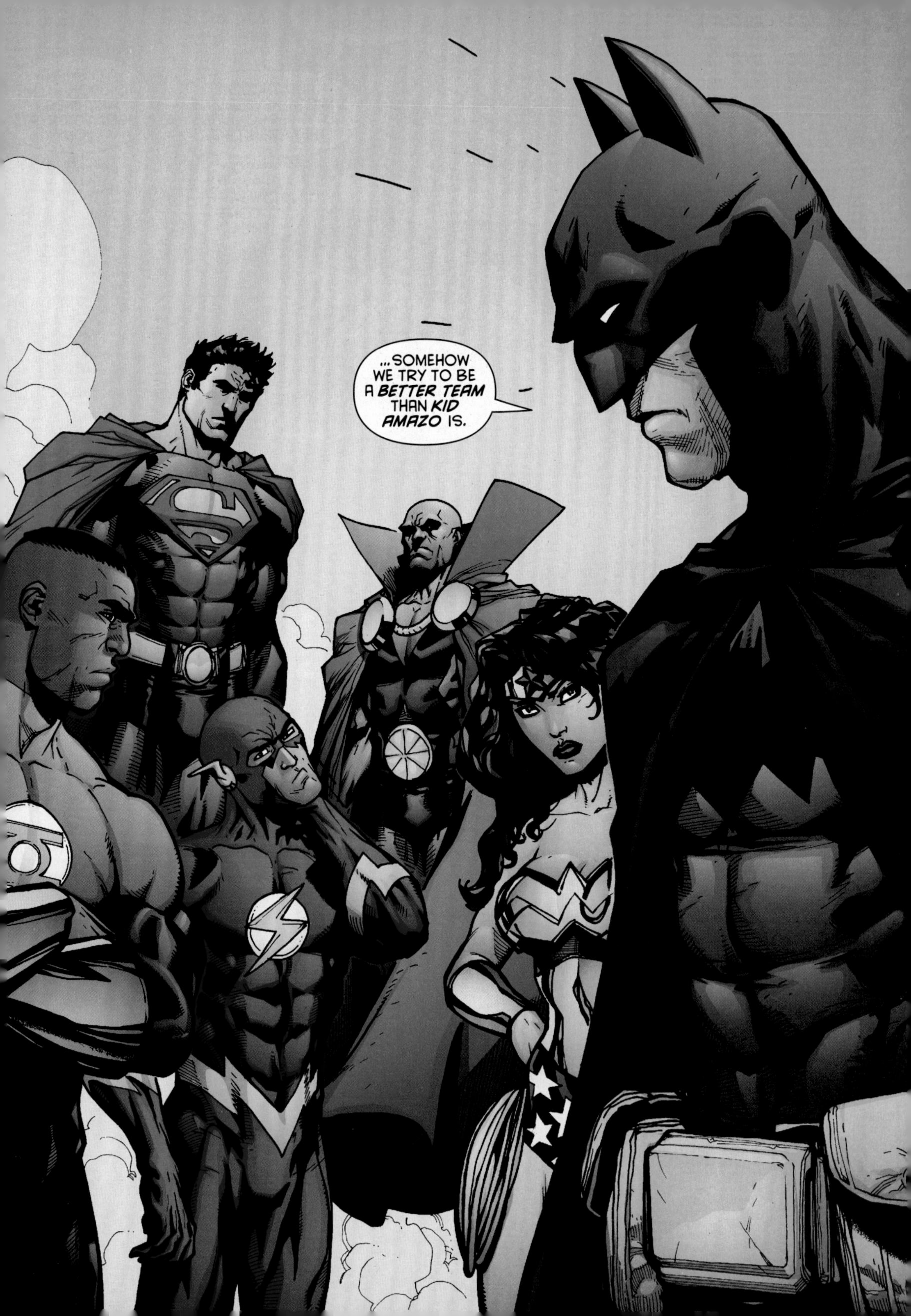
...SOMEHOW WE TRY TO BE A BETTER TEAM THAN KID AMAZO IS.

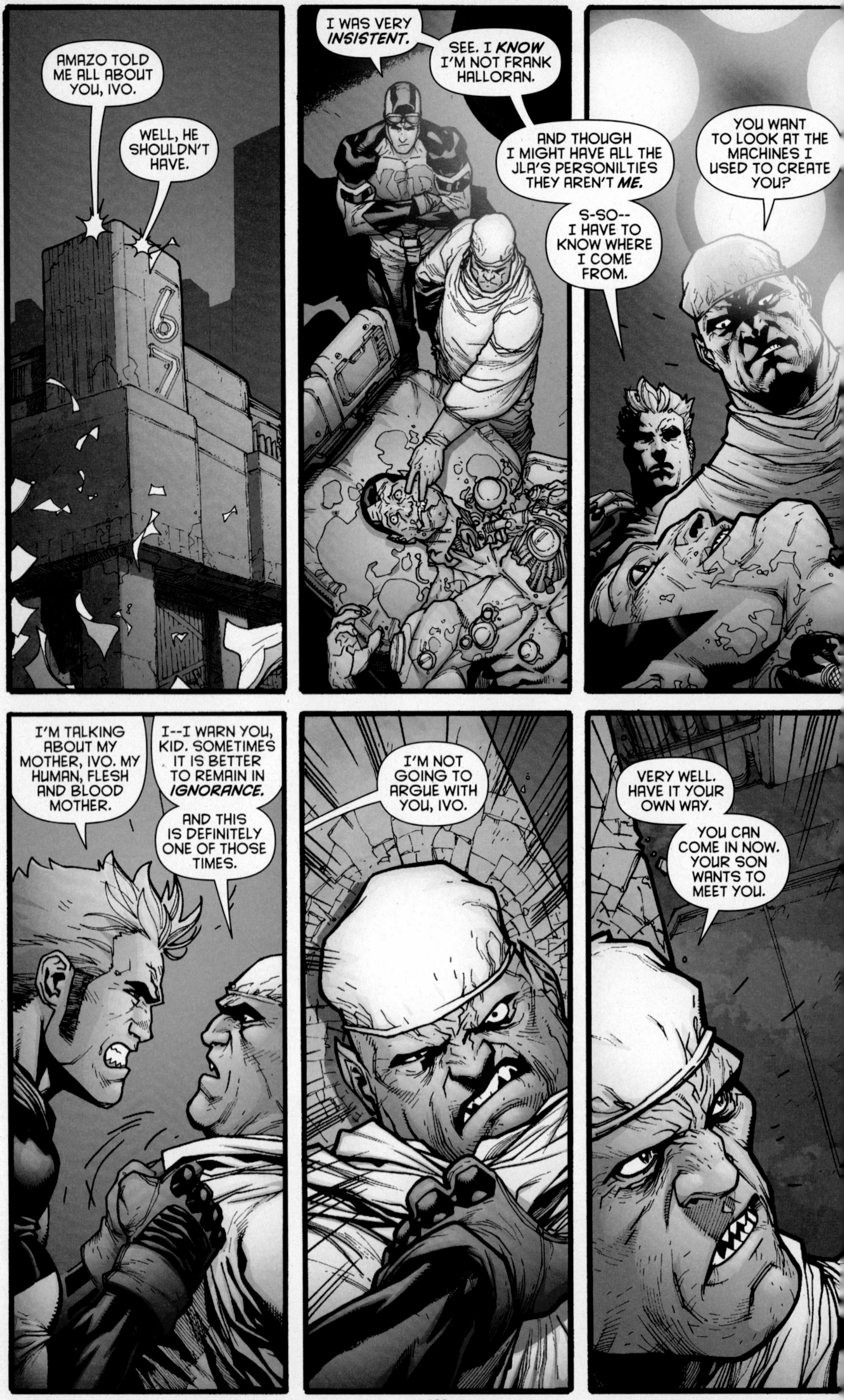
AMAZO TOLD ME ALL ABOUT YOU, IVO.
WELL, HE SHOULDN'T HAVE.
I WAS VERY INSISTENT.
SEE. I KNOW I'M NOT FRANK HALLORAN.
AND THOUGH I MIGHT HAVE ALL THE JLA'S PERSONILTIES THEY AREN'T ME.
S-SO-- I HAVE TO KNOW WHERE I COME FROM.
YOU WANT TO LOOK AT THE MACHINES I USED TO CREATE YOU?
I'M TALKING ABOUT MY MOTHER, IVO. MY HUMAN, FLESH AND BLOOD MOTHER.
I--I WARN YOU, KID. SOMETIMES IT IS BETTER TO REMAIN IN IGNORANCE.
AND THIS IS DEFINITELY ONE OF THOSE TIMES.
I'M NOT GOING TO ARGUE WITH YOU, IVO.
VERY WELL. HAVE IT YOUR OWN WAY.
YOU CAN COME IN NOW. YOUR SON WANTS TO MEET YOU.

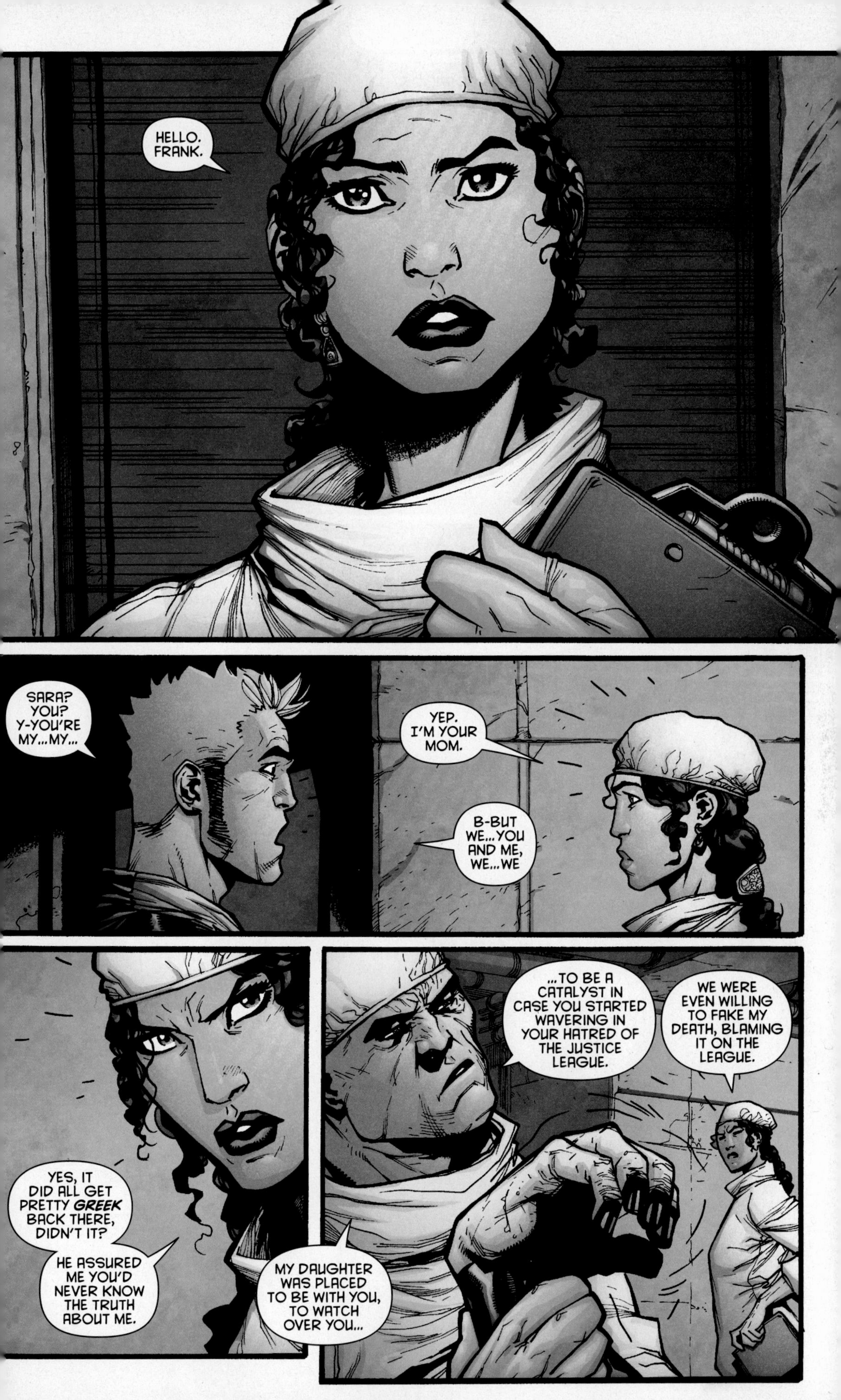
HELLO. FRANK.
SARA? YOU? Y-YOU'RE MY...MY...
YEP. I'M YOUR MOM.
B-BUT WE...YOU AND ME, WE...WE
YES, IT DID ALL GET PRETTY *GREEK* BACK THERE, DIDN'T IT?
HE ASSURED ME YOU'D NEVER KNOW THE TRUTH ABOUT ME.
MY DAUGHTER WAS PLACED TO BE WITH YOU, TO WATCH OVER YOU...
...TO BE A CATALYST IN CASE YOU STARTED WAVERING IN YOUR HATRED OF THE JUSTICE LEAGUE.
WE WERE EVEN WILLING TO FAKE MY DEATH, BLAMING IT ON THE LEAGUE.

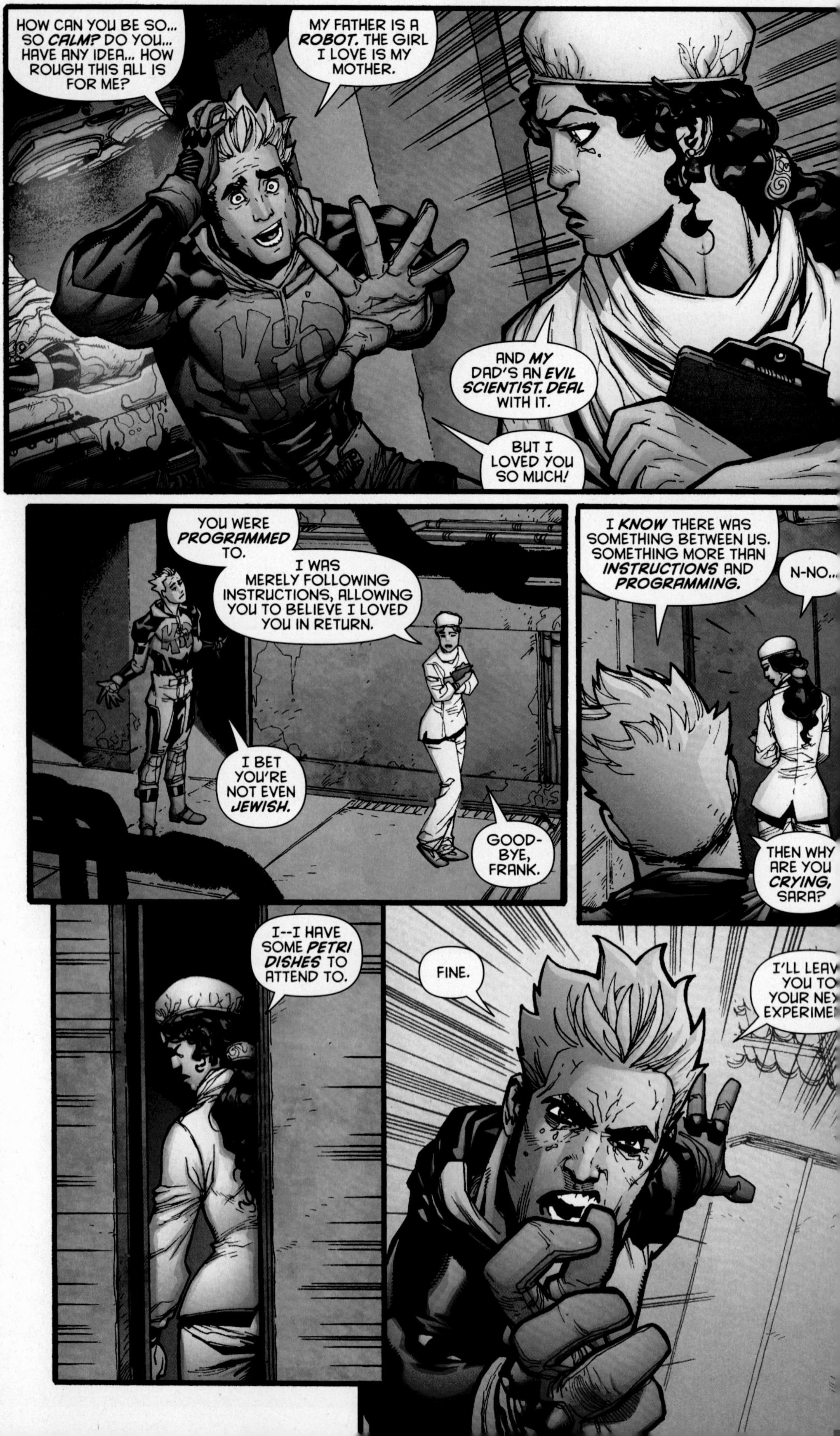
HOW CAN YOU BE SO... SO CALM? DO YOU... HAVE ANY IDEA... HOW ROUGH THIS ALL IS FOR ME?
MY FATHER IS A ROBOT. THE GIRL I LOVE IS MY MOTHER.
AND MY DAD'S AN EVIL SCIENTIST. DEAL WITH IT.
BUT I LOVED YOU SO MUCH!
YOU WERE PROGRAMMED TO.
I WAS MERELY FOLLOWING INSTRUCTIONS, ALLOWING YOU TO BELIEVE I LOVED YOU IN RETURN.
I BET YOU'RE NOT EVEN JEWISH.
GOOD-BYE, FRANK.
I KNOW THERE WAS SOMETHING BETWEEN US. SOMETHING MORE THAN INSTRUCTIONS AND PROGRAMMING.
N-NO...
THEN WHY ARE YOU CRYING, SARA?
I--I HAVE SOME PETRI DISHES TO ATTEND TO.
FINE.

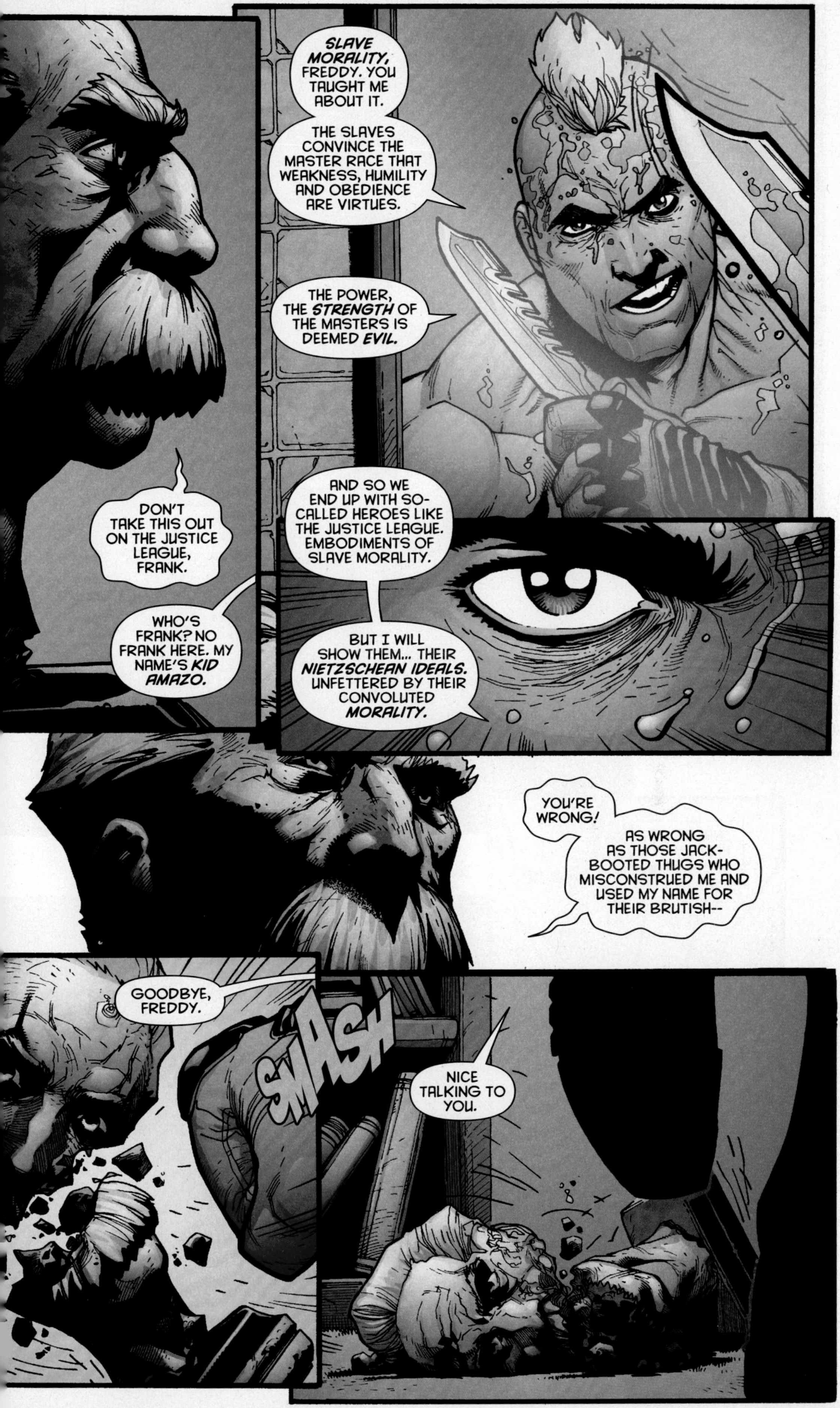
SLAVE MORALITY, FREDDY. YOU TAUGHT ME ABOUT IT.
THE SLAVES CONVINCE THE MASTER RACE THAT WEAKNESS, HUMILITY AND OBEDIENCE ARE VIRTUES.
THE POWER, THE STRENGTH OF THE MASTERS IS DEEMED EVIL.
DON'T TAKE THIS OUT ON THE JUSTICE LEAGUE, FRANK.
WHO'S FRANK? NO FRANK HERE. MY NAME'S KID AMAZO.
AND SO WE END UP WITH SO-CALLED HEROES LIKE THE JUSTICE LEAGUE. EMBODIMENTS OF SLAVE MORALITY.
BUT I WILL SHOW THEM... THEIR NIETZSCHEAN IDEALS. UNFETTERED BY THEIR CONVOLUTED MORALITY.
YOU'RE WRONG!
AS WRONG AS THOSE JACK-BOOTED THUGS WHO MISCONSTRUED ME AND USED MY NAME FOR THEIR BRUTISH--
GOODBYE, FREDDY.
SMASH
NICE TALKING TO YOU.

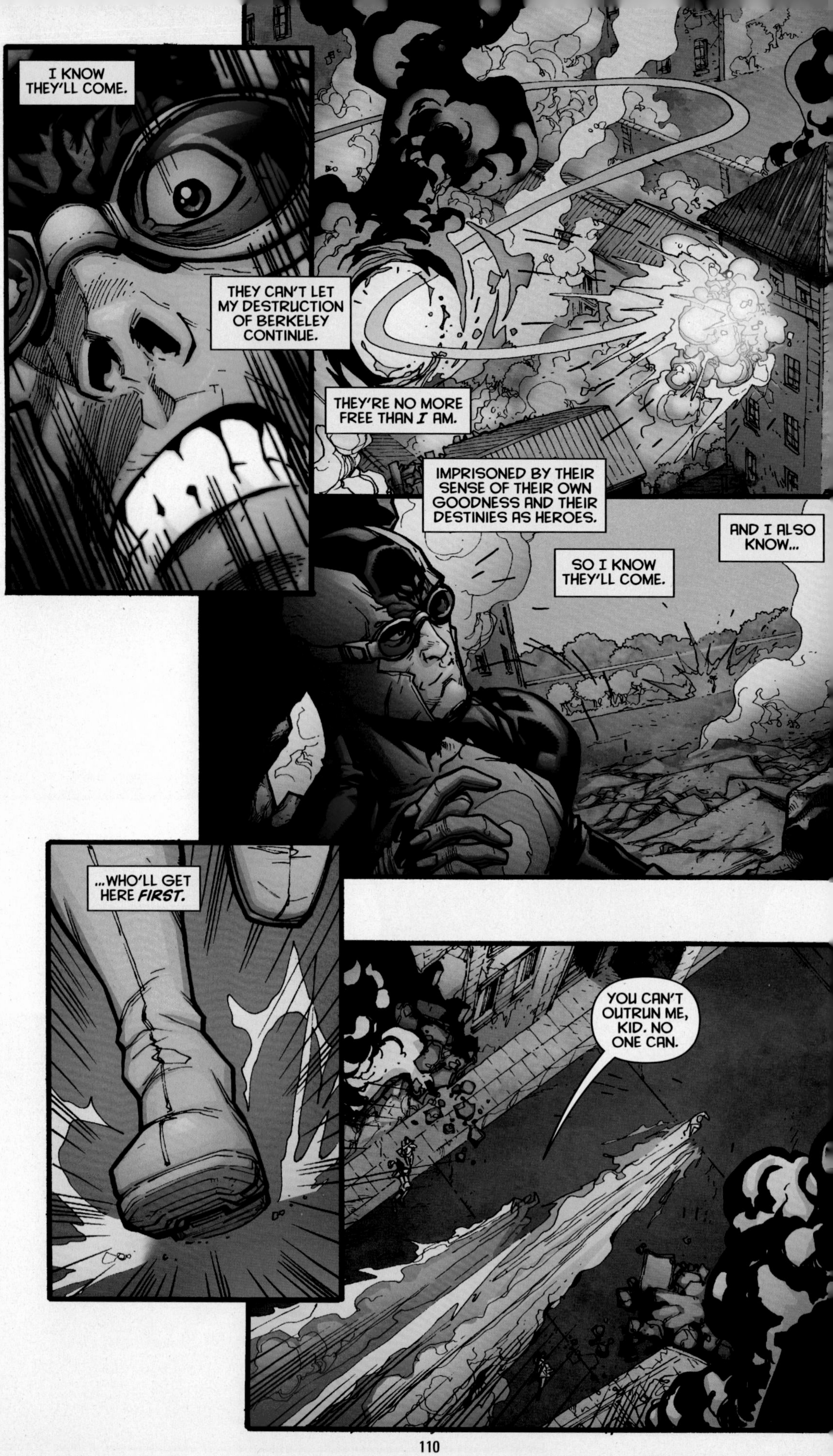
I KNOW THEY'LL COME.
THEY CAN'T LET MY DESTRUCTION OF BERKELEY CONTINUE.
THEY'RE NO MORE FREE THAN *I* AM.
IMPRISONED BY THEIR SENSE OF THEIR OWN GOODNESS AND THEIR DESTINIES AS HEROES.
SO I KNOW THEY'LL COME.
AND I ALSO KNOW...
...WHO'LL GET HERE ***FIRST.***
YOU CAN'T OUTRUN ME, KID. NO ONE CAN.

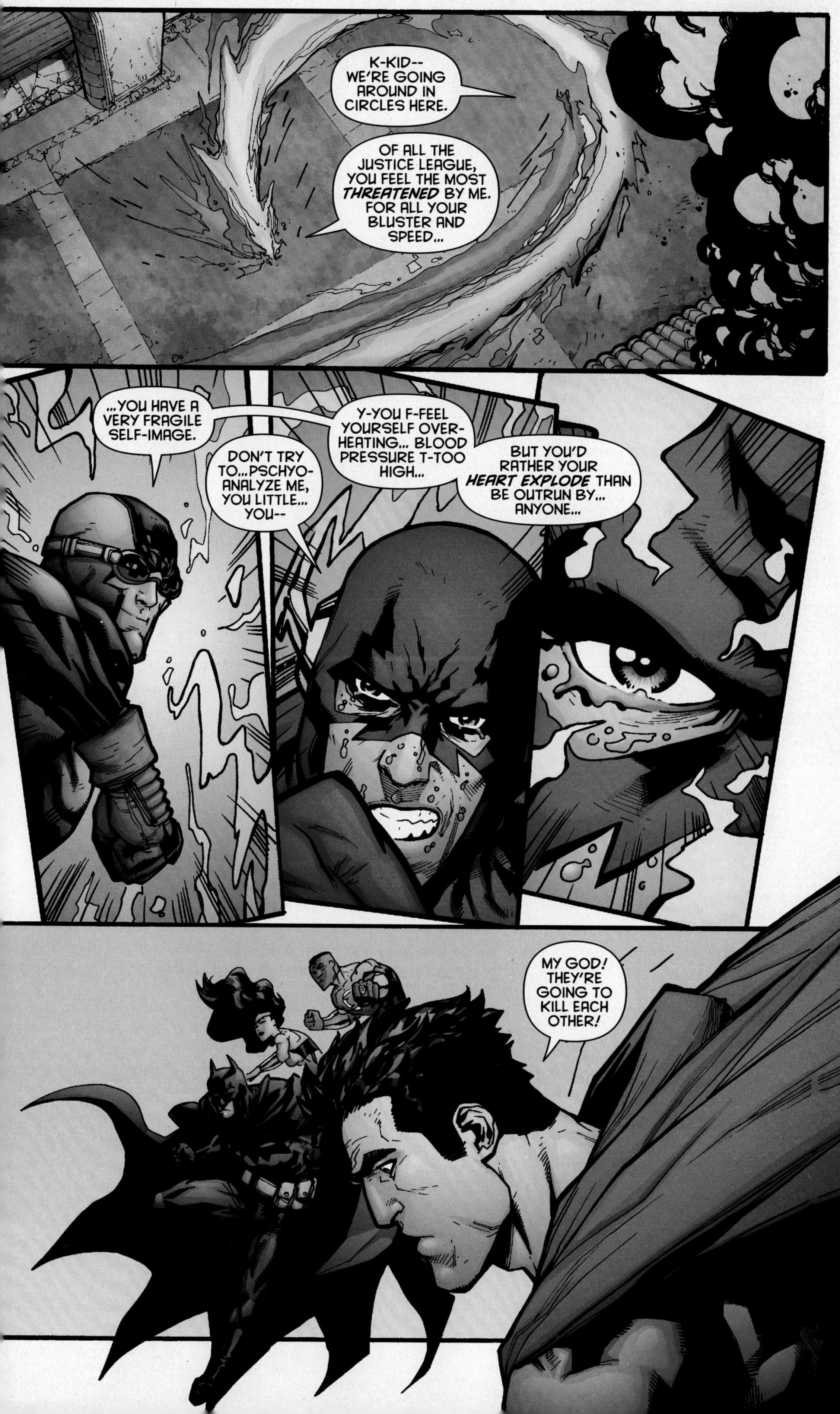
K-KID-- WE'RE GOING AROUND IN CIRCLES HERE.
OF ALL THE JUSTICE LEAGUE, YOU FEEL THE MOST *THREATENED* BY ME. FOR ALL YOUR BLUSTER AND SPEED...
...YOU HAVE A VERY FRAGILE SELF-IMAGE.
DON'T TRY TO...PSCHYO-ANALYZE ME, YOU LITTLE... YOU--
Y-YOU F-FEEL YOURSELF OVER-HEATING... BLOOD PRESSURE T-TOO HIGH...
BUT YOU'D RATHER YOUR *HEART EXPLODE* THAN BE OUTRUN BY... ANYONE...
MY GOD! THEY'RE GOING TO KILL EACH OTHER!

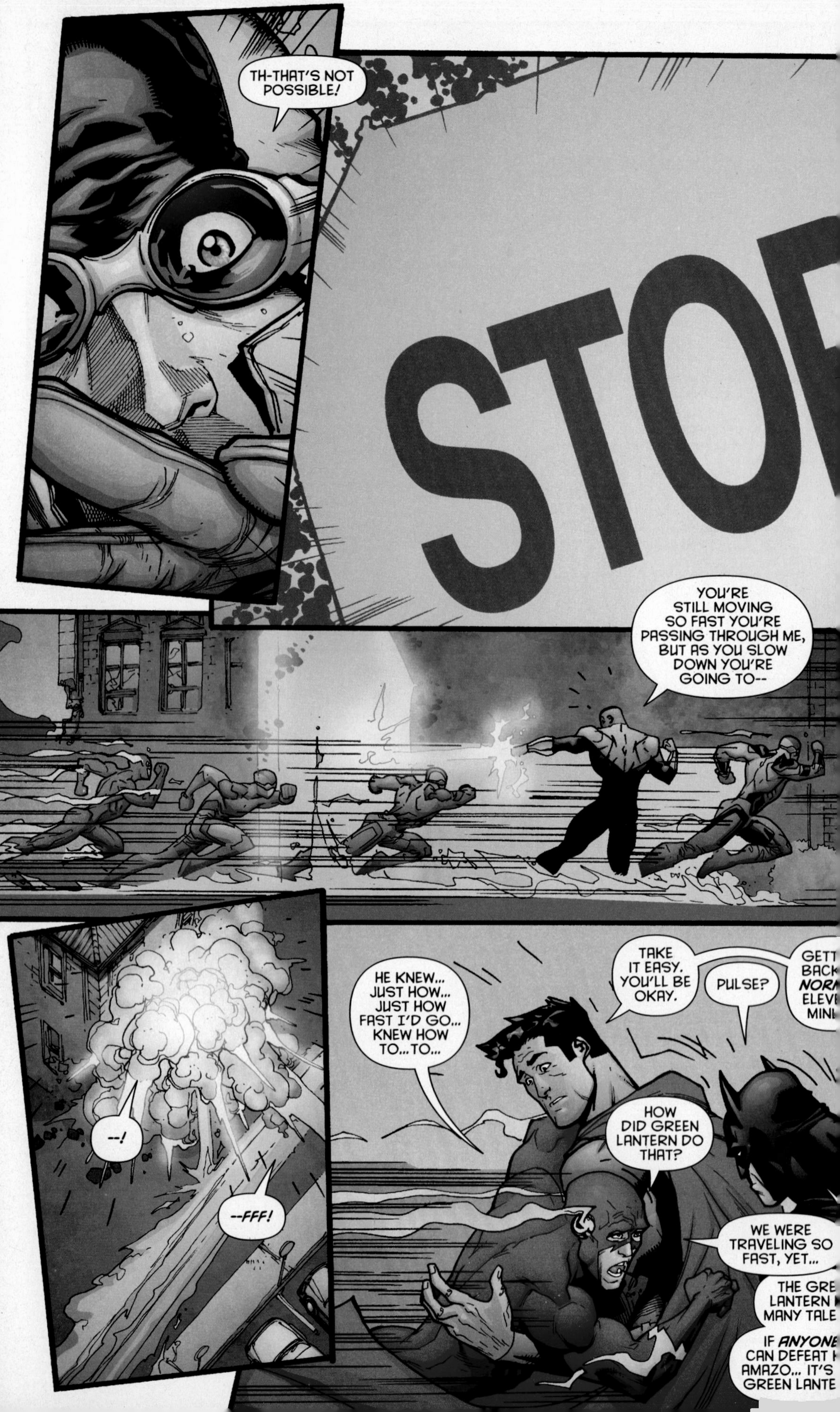

TH-THAT'S NOT POSSIBLE!
STOP
YOU'RE STILL MOVING SO FAST YOU'RE PASSING THROUGH ME, BUT AS YOU SLOW DOWN YOU'RE GOING TO--
--!
--FFF!
HE KNEW... JUST HOW... JUST HOW FAST I'D GO... KNEW HOW TO... TO...
TAKE IT EASY. YOU'LL BE OKAY.
PULSE?
HOW DID GREEN LANTERN DO THAT?
WE WERE TRAVELING SO FAST, YET...

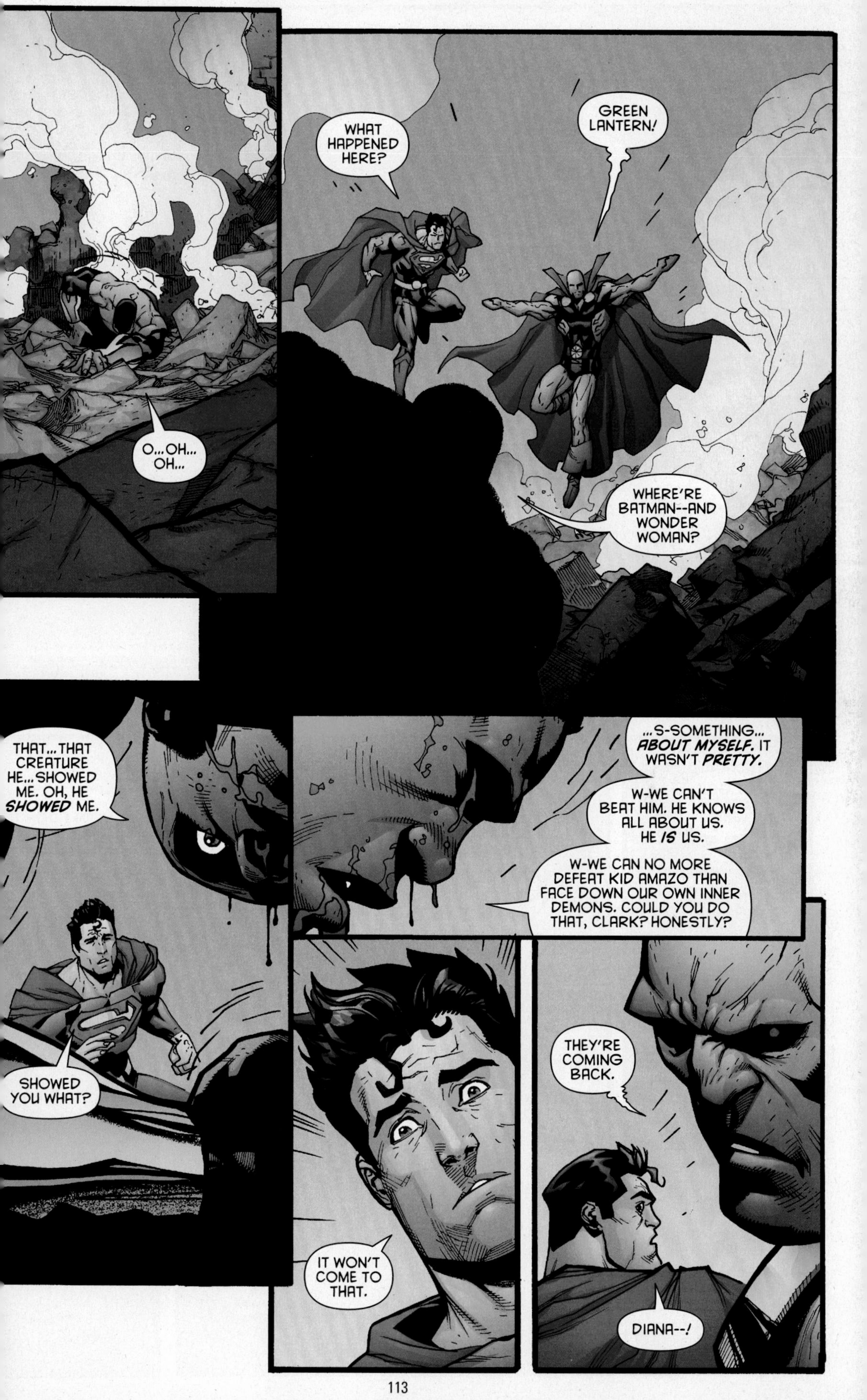
O...OH...
OH...
WHAT HAPPENED HERE?
GREEN LANTERN!
WHERE'RE BATMAN--AND WONDER WOMAN?
THAT...THAT CREATURE HE...SHOWED ME. OH, HE *SHOWED* ME.
SHOWED YOU WHAT?
...S-SOMETHING... *ABOUT MYSELF*. IT WASN'T *PRETTY*.
W-WE CAN'T BEAT HIM. HE KNOWS ALL ABOUT US. HE *IS* US.
W-WE CAN NO MORE DEFEAT KID AMAZO THAN FACE DOWN OUR OWN INNER DEMONS. COULD YOU DO THAT, CLARK? HONESTLY?
IT WON'T COME TO THAT.
THEY'RE COMING BACK.
DIANA--!

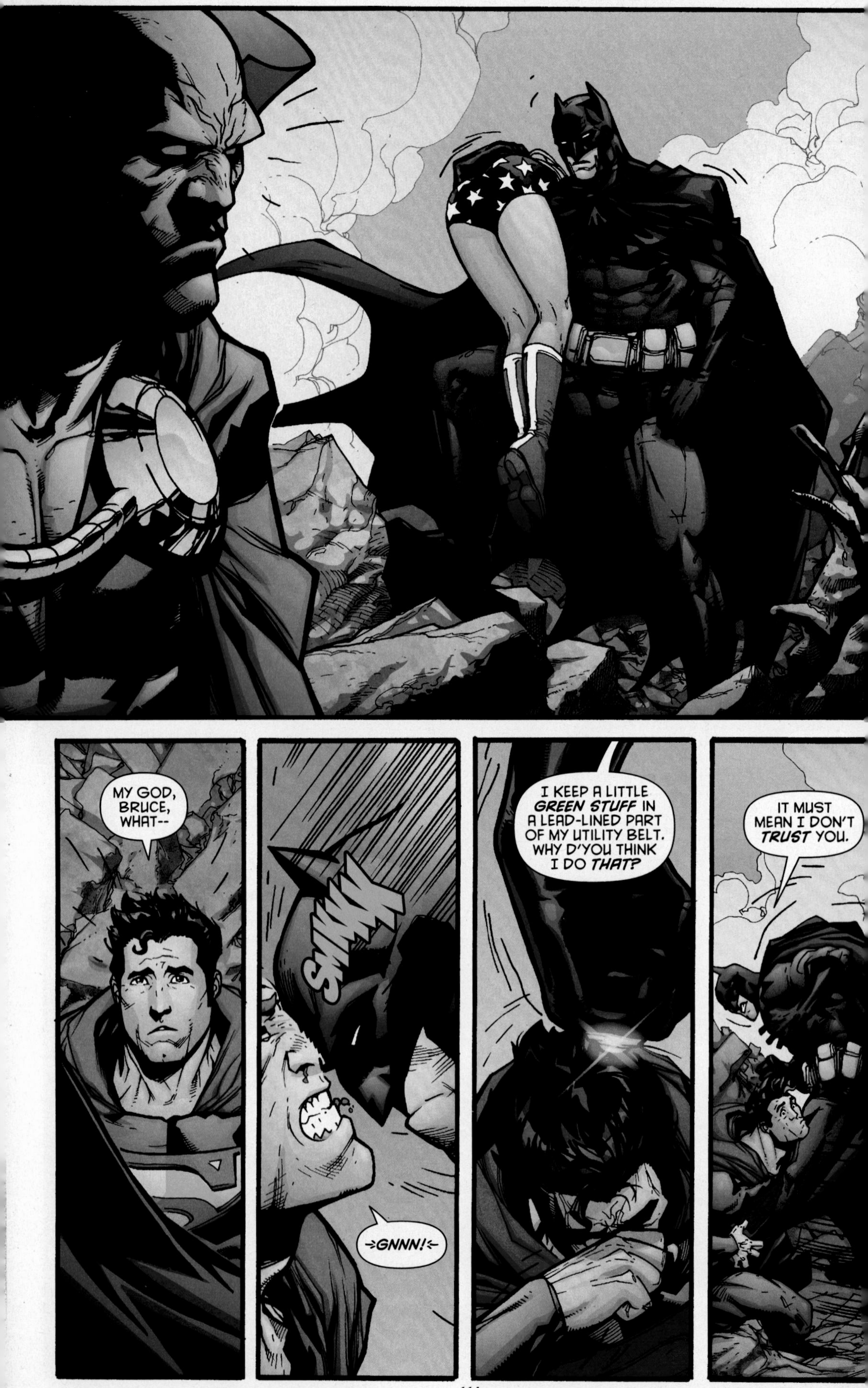
MY GOD, BRUCE, WHAT--
SHNNK
-GNNN!-
I KEEP A LITTLE GREEN STUFF IN A LEAD-LINED PART OF MY UTILITY BELT. WHY D'YOU THINK I DO THAT?
IT MUST MEAN I DON'T TRUST YOU.

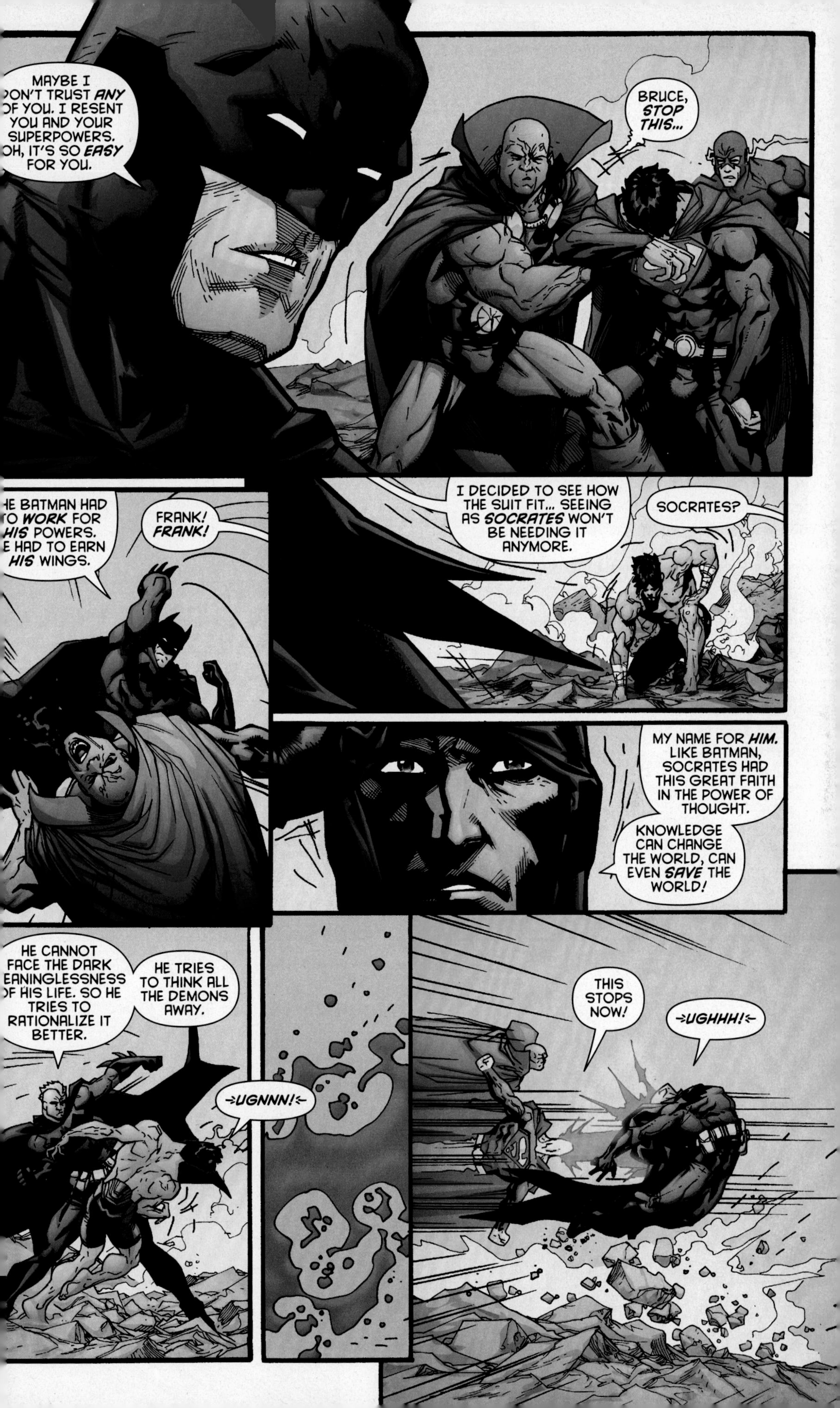

MAYBE I DON'T TRUST ANY OF YOU. I RESENT YOU AND YOUR SUPERPOWERS. OH, IT'S SO EASY FOR YOU.
BRUCE, STOP THIS...
THE BATMAN HAD TO WORK FOR HIS POWERS. HE HAD TO EARN HIS WINGS.
FRANK! FRANK!
I DECIDED TO SEE HOW THE SUIT FIT... SEEING AS SOCRATES WON'T BE NEEDING IT ANYMORE.
SOCRATES?
MY NAME FOR HIM. LIKE BATMAN, SOCRATES HAD THIS GREAT FAITH IN THE POWER OF THOUGHT.
KNOWLEDGE CAN CHANGE THE WORLD, CAN EVEN SAVE THE WORLD!
HE CANNOT FACE THE DARK MEANINGLESSNESS OF HIS LIFE. SO HE TRIES TO RATIONALIZE IT BETTER.
HE TRIES TO THINK ALL THE DEMONS AWAY.
UGNNN!
THIS STOPS NOW!
UGHHH!

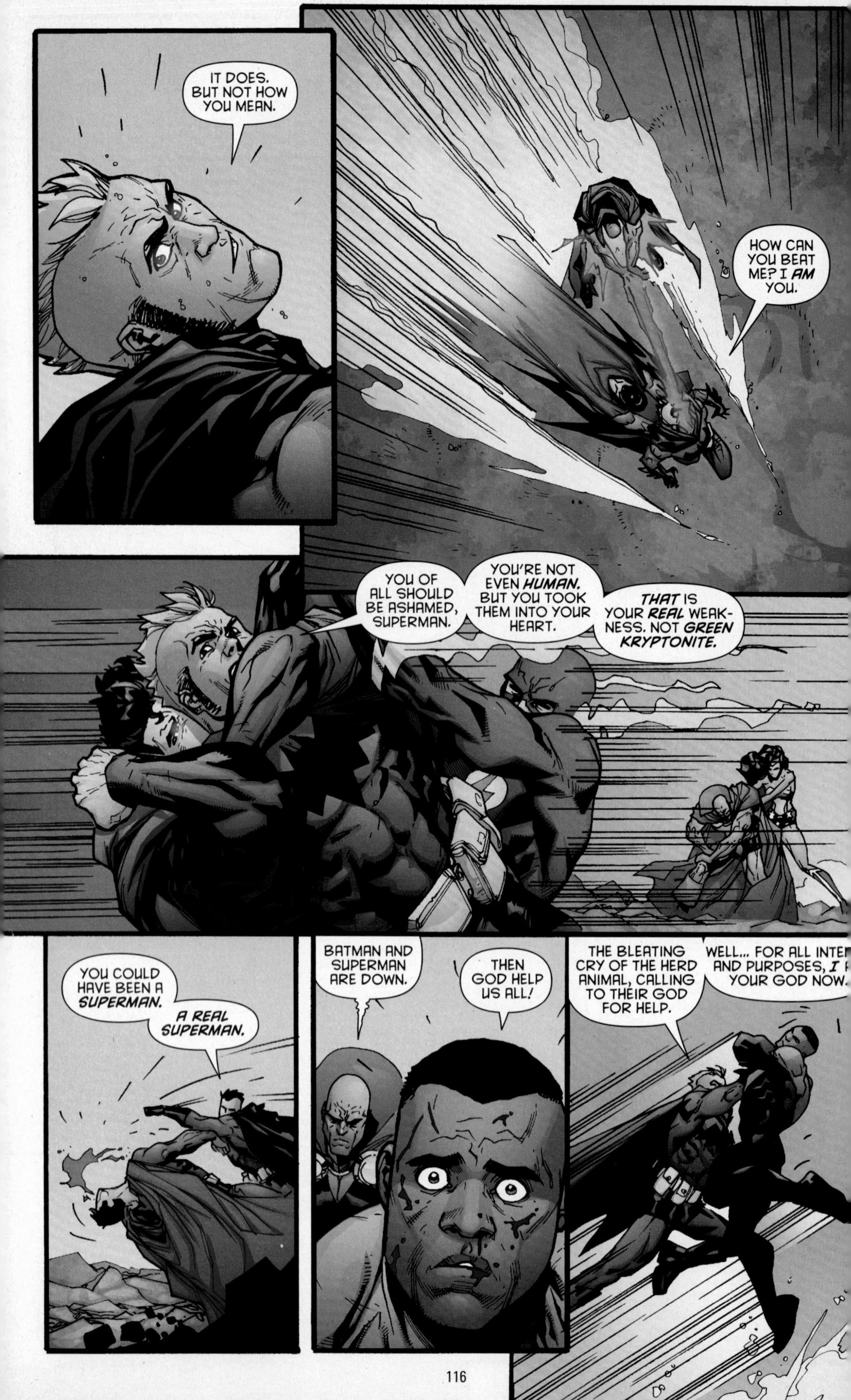
IT DOES. BUT NOT HOW YOU MEAN.
HOW CAN YOU BEAT ME? I *AM* YOU.
YOU OF ALL SHOULD BE ASHAMED, SUPERMAN.
YOU'RE NOT EVEN *HUMAN.* BUT YOU TOOK THEM INTO YOUR HEART.
THAT IS YOUR *REAL* WEAKNESS. NOT *GREEN KRYPTONITE.*
YOU COULD HAVE BEEN A *SUPERMAN.*
A REAL SUPERMAN.
BATMAN AND SUPERMAN ARE DOWN.
THEN GOD HELP US ALL!
THE BLEATING CRY OF THE HERD ANIMAL, CALLING TO THEIR GOD FOR HELP.
WELL... FOR ALL INTE AND PURPOSES, *I* YOUR GOD NOW.

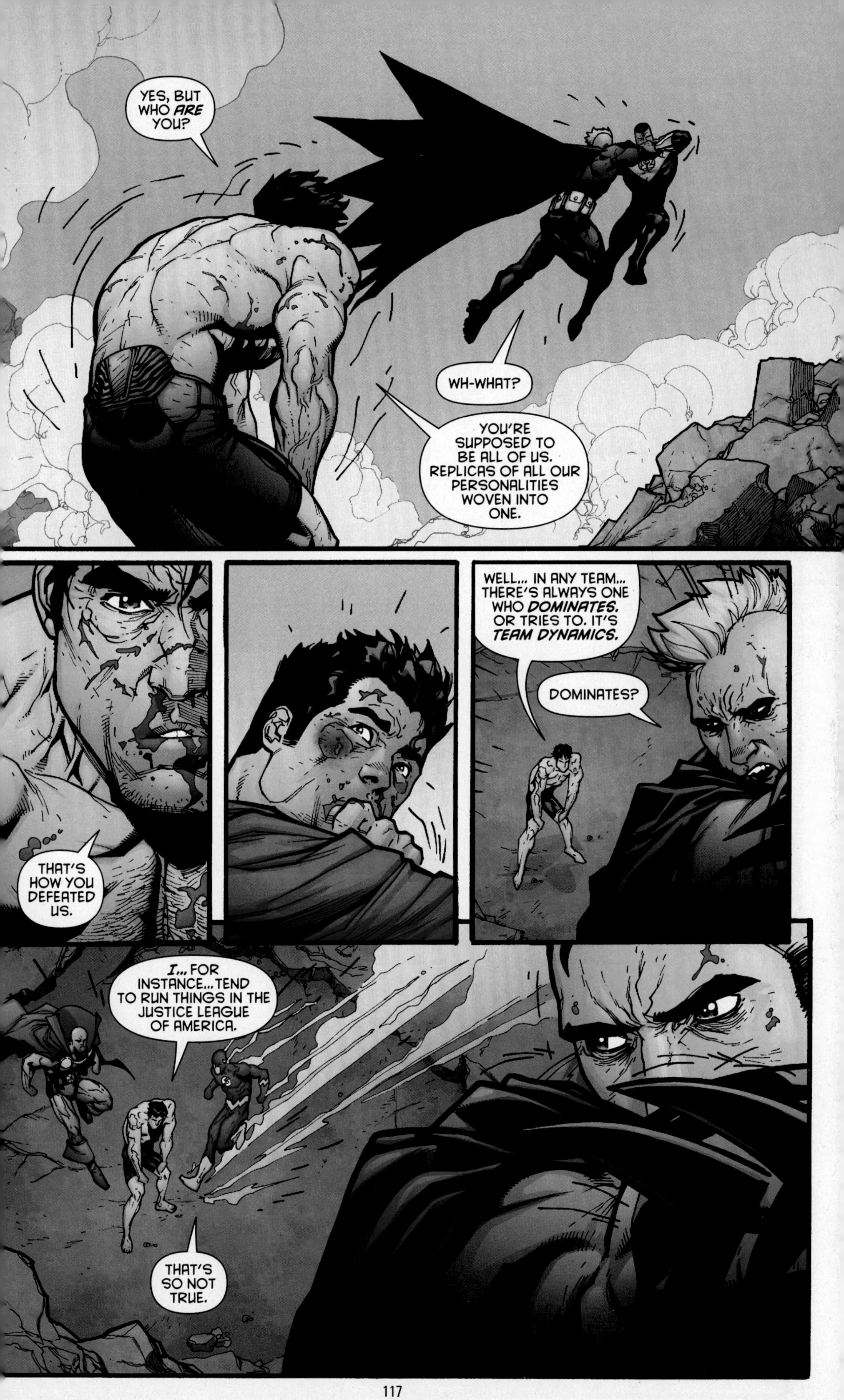
YES, BUT WHO *ARE* YOU?
WH-WHAT?
YOU'RE SUPPOSED TO BE ALL OF US. REPLICAS OF ALL OUR PERSONALITIES WOVEN INTO ONE.
THAT'S HOW YOU DEFEATED US.
WELL... IN ANY TEAM... THERE'S ALWAYS ONE WHO *DOMINATES.* OR TRIES TO. IT'S *TEAM DYNAMICS.*
DOMINATES?
I... FOR INSTANCE... TEND TO RUN THINGS IN THE JUSTICE LEAGUE OF AMERICA.
THAT'S SO NOT TRUE.

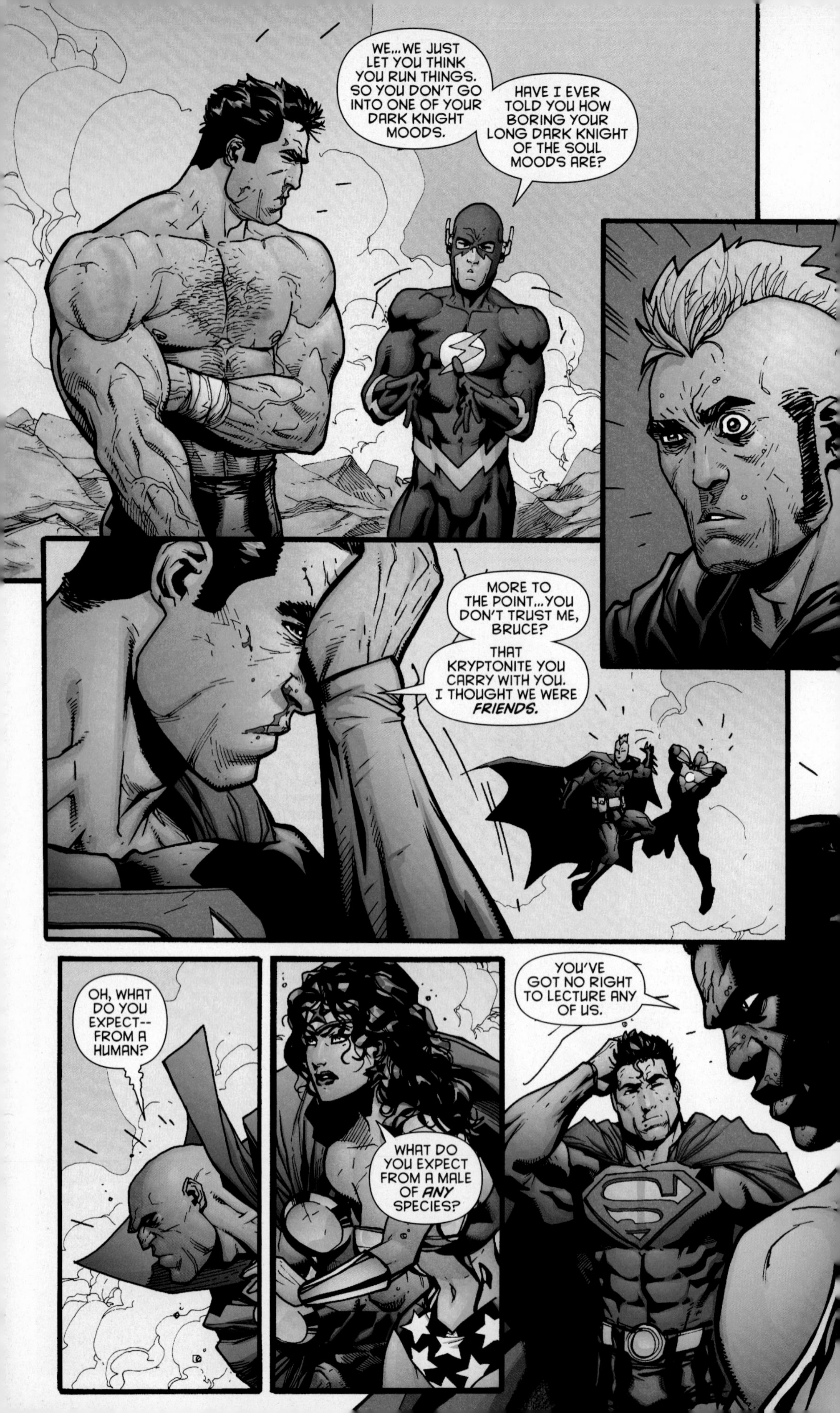

WE...WE JUST LET YOU THINK YOU RUN THINGS. SO YOU DON'T GO INTO ONE OF YOUR DARK KNIGHT MOODS.
HAVE I EVER TOLD YOU HOW BORING YOUR LONG DARK KNIGHT OF THE SOUL MOODS ARE?
MORE TO THE POINT...YOU DON'T TRUST ME, BRUCE?
THAT KRYPTONITE YOU CARRY WITH YOU. I THOUGHT WE WERE *FRIENDS.*
OH, WHAT DO YOU EXPECT-- FROM A HUMAN?
WHAT DO YOU EXPECT FROM A MALE OF *ANY* SPECIES?
YOU'VE GOT NO RIGHT TO LECTURE ANY OF US.

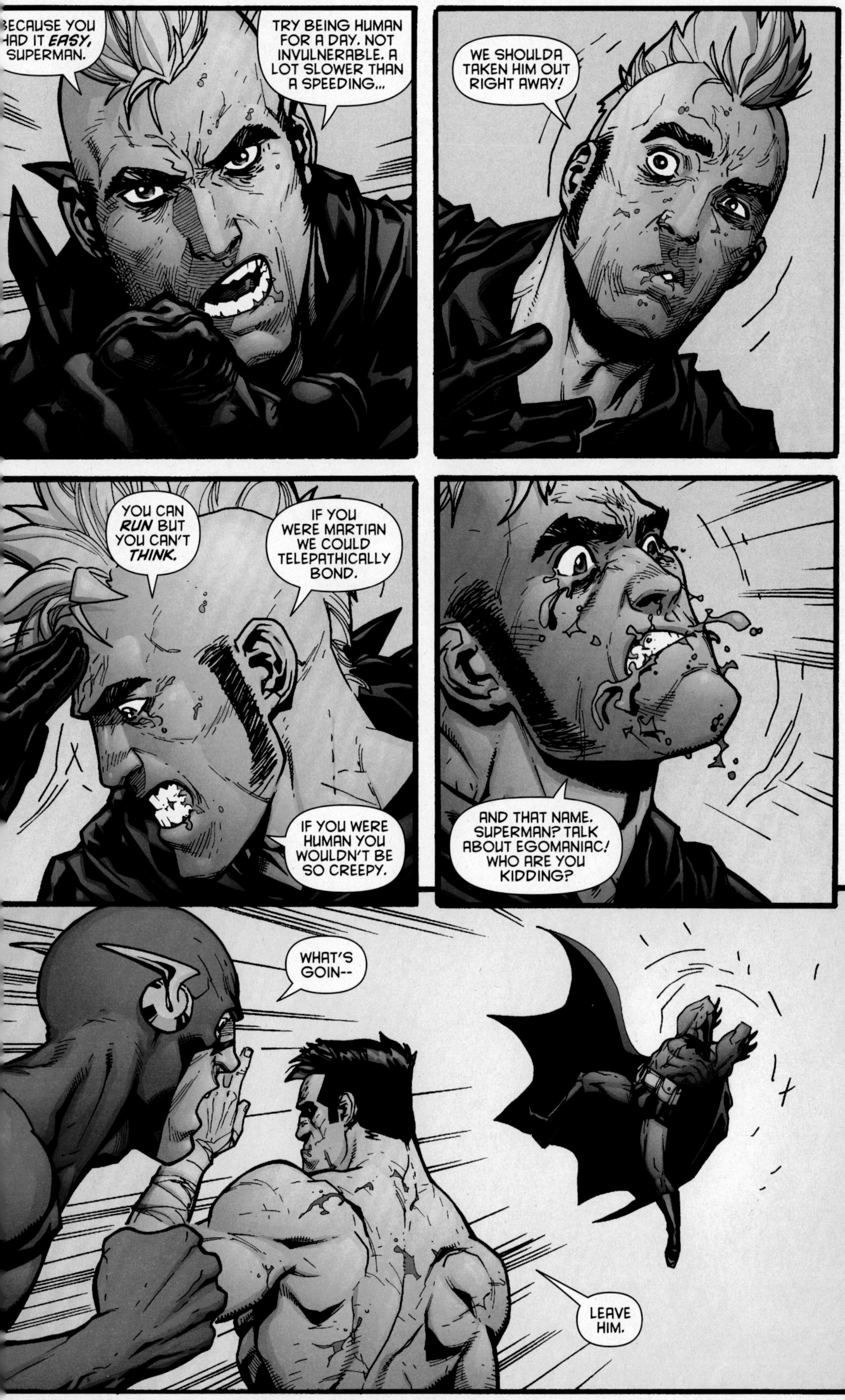
BECAUSE YOU HAD IT EASY, SUPERMAN.
TRY BEING HUMAN FOR A DAY. NOT INVULNERABLE. A LOT SLOWER THAN A SPEEDING...
WE SHOULDA TAKEN HIM OUT RIGHT AWAY!
YOU CAN RUN BUT YOU CAN'T THINK.
IF YOU WERE MARTIAN WE COULD TELEPATHICALLY BOND.
IF YOU WERE HUMAN YOU WOULDN'T BE SO CREEPY.
AND THAT NAME. SUPERMAN? TALK ABOUT EGOMANIAC! WHO ARE YOU KIDDING?
WHAT'S GOIN--
LEAVE HIM.

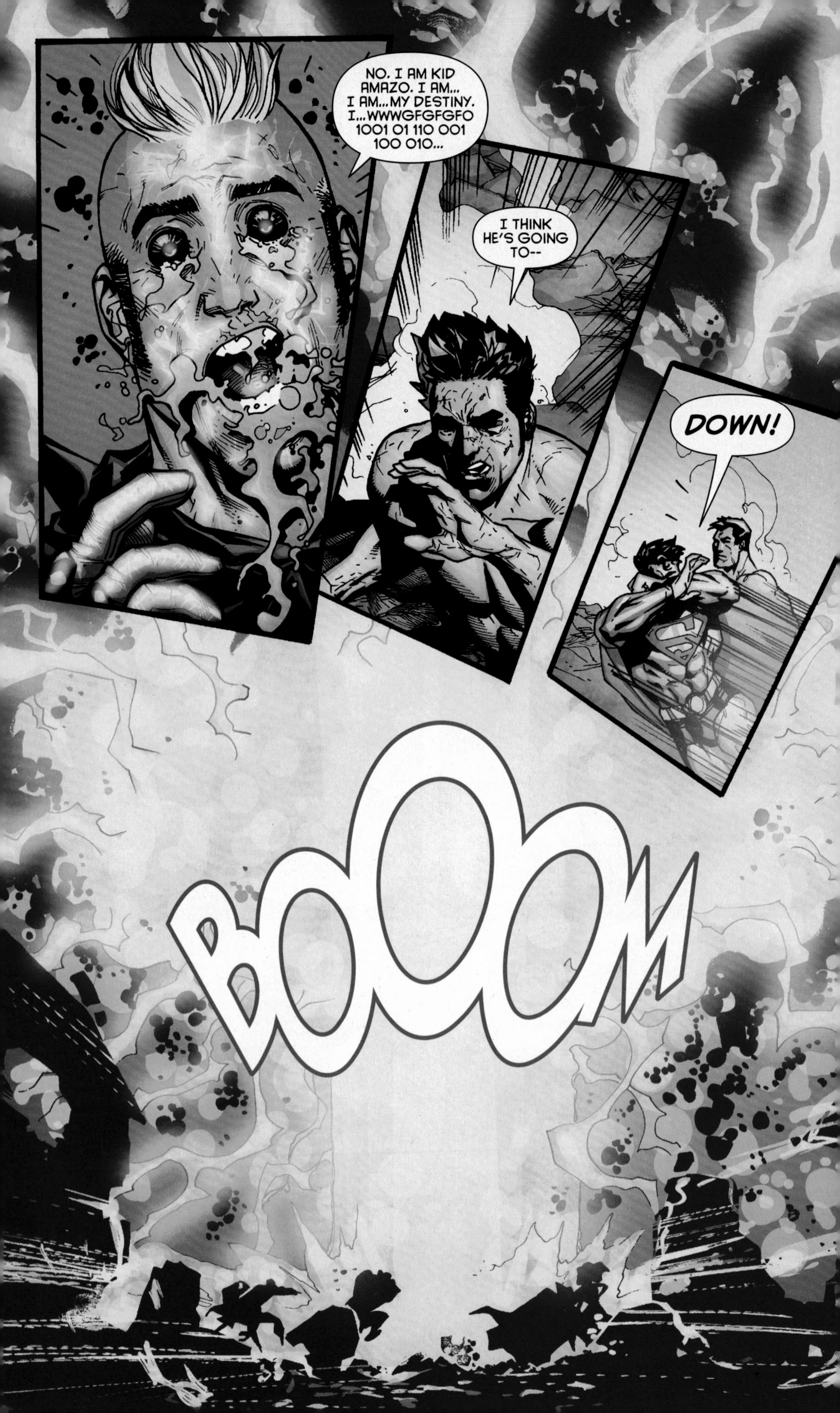
NO. I AM KID AMAZO. I AM... I AM...MY DESTINY. I...WWWGFGFGFO 1001 01 110 001 100 010...
I THINK HE'S GOING TO--
DOWN!
BOOOM

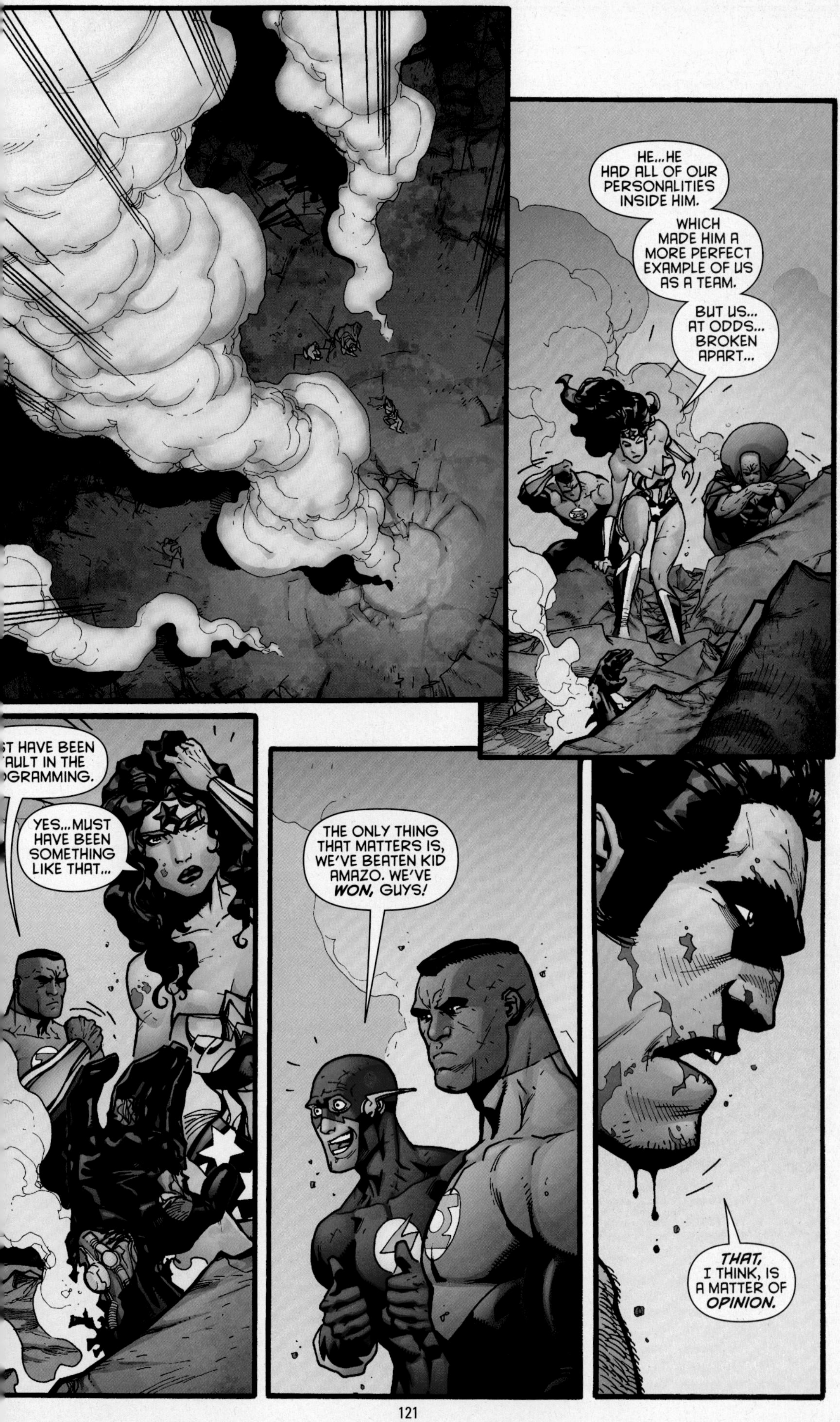
HE...HE HAD ALL OF OUR PERSONALITIES INSIDE HIM.
WHICH MADE HIM A MORE PERFECT EXAMPLE OF US AS A TEAM.
BUT US... AT ODDS... BROKEN APART...
ST HAVE BEEN AULT IN THE OGRAMMING.
YES...MUST HAVE BEEN SOMETHING LIKE THAT...
THE ONLY THING THAT MATTERS IS, WE'VE BEATEN KID AMAZO. WE'VE *WON,* GUYS!
THAT, I THINK, IS A MATTER OF *OPINION.*

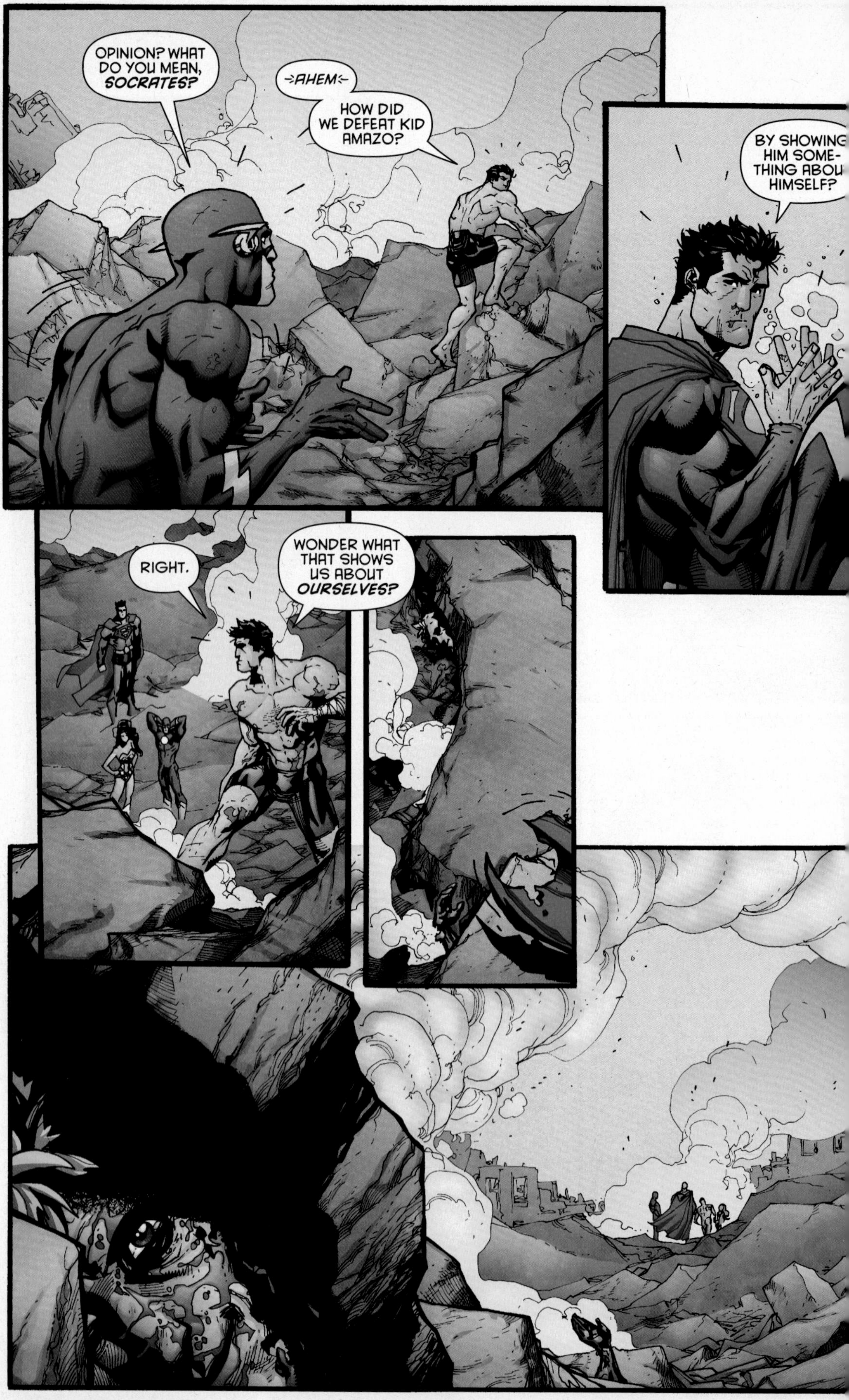

OPINION? WHAT DO YOU MEAN, SOCRATES?
AHEM
HOW DID WE DEFEAT KID AMAZO?
BY SHOWING HIM SOMETHING ABOUT HIMSELF?
RIGHT.
WONDER WHAT THAT SHOWS US ABOUT OURSELVES?

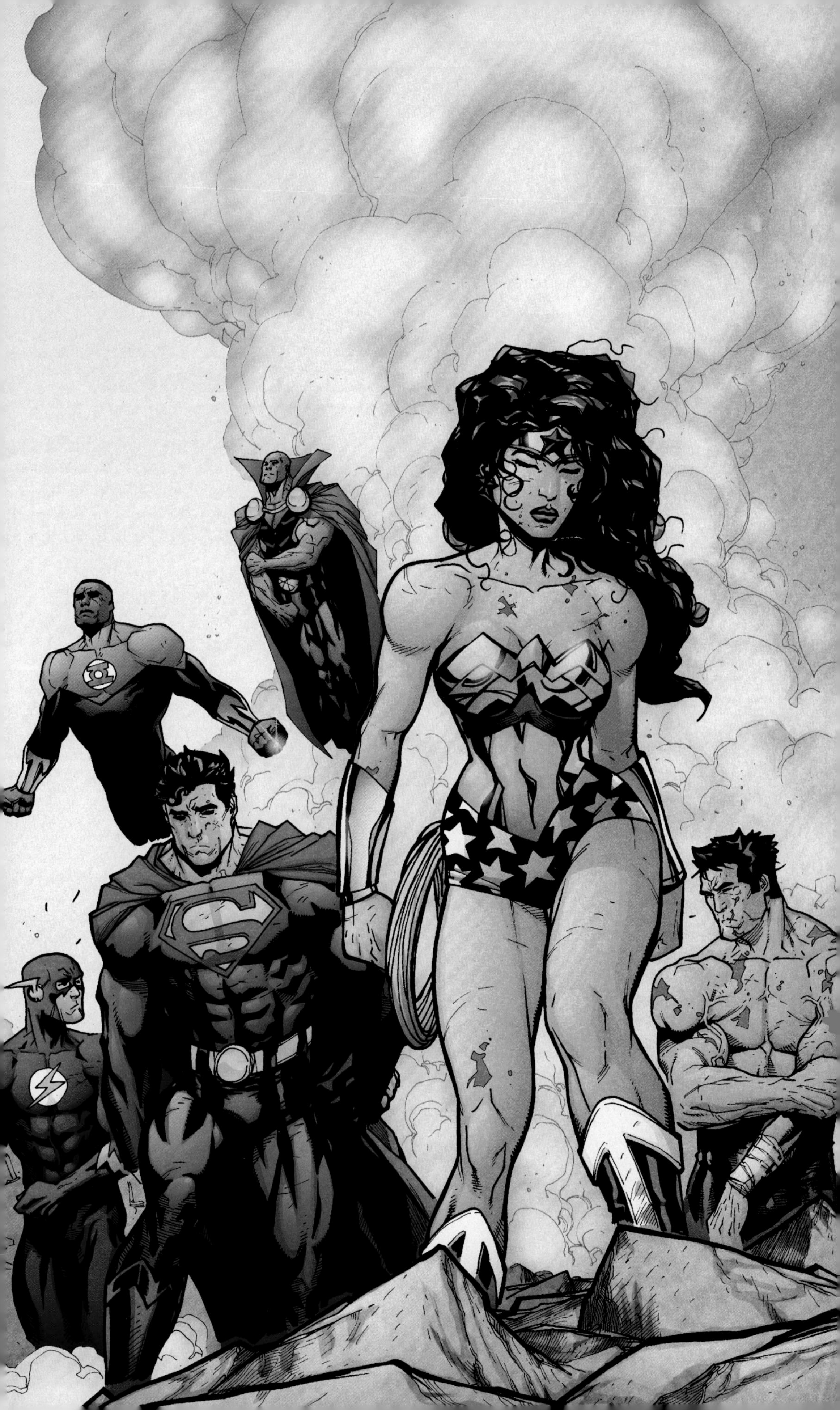

EPILOGUE.

COME ON!

I'M ALMOST FINISHED.

LEAVE IT. THOSE PETRI DISHES NEED YOUR ATTENTION.

DO I HAVE TO, FATHER?

WHAT KIND OF QUESTION IS THAT?

I'M SORRY, FATHER.

I'M COMING.

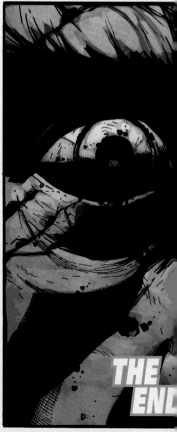

THE END

124